Victorian Homes

DAVID RUBINSTEIN

*Department of Economic and Social History,
University of Hull*

Victorian

Homes

DAVID & CHARLES

NEWTON ABBOT   LONDON

NORTH POMFRET (VT)   VANCOUVER

0 7153 6765 X

Library of Congress Catalog Card Number 74-24767

44014640 PQ

CPP
oa|oq    0016806048

Set in 11 on 13pt Baskerville and printed in
Great Britain by John Sherratt & Son Ltd
Altrincham, Cheshire WA14 5QQ
for David & Charles (Holdings) Limited
South Devon House Newton Abbot Devon

Published in the United States of America
by David & Charles Inc North Pomfret
Vermont 05053 USA

Published in Canada by Douglas David &
Charles Limited 3645 McKechnie Drive
West Vancouver BC

TO ANN

Contents

7

Introduction

Why "Victorian"?

Historians are sometimes accused of being too prone to categorise and divide, but in this case the period chosen can be defended with something stronger than convention. Before Queen Victoria's accession in 1837 there were no really large British cities outside London, which in 1831 had a population of about 1¾ million. Glasgow and Liverpool each had about 200,000 inhabitants, and five other cities had populations in excess of 100,000. The growth of the British city had already begun, but in 1901, when Victoria died, thirty-three cities, their boundaries often enlarged, had populations of over 100,000; London now had 4½ million and four others exceeded half a million. The industrial processes which were to create the modern city began well back in the eighteenth century, but at the beginning of the Victorian period the enormous growth of cities was still new enough to be a thing of wonder and constant discussion. As British people became urban and suburban in overwhelming numbers, their homes changed too. An urban society meant a different kind of home for the large majority of the population. The urban slum, the semi-detached suburban house, and new forms of heating, lighting and sanitation were among the principal features of the period after 1837, though all had their origins earlier, in some cases much earlier.

As to the end of the story, the temptation was strong to carry it to the more obvious stopping point of 1914. But, quite apart from considerations of length, 1901 also makes a convenient ending. By that date important new developments had begun, but they had not yet achieved dominance. Baths, water closets and electric light were all accepted features of upper-class and middle-class homes by 1901. Likewise, council housing, town planning and the building of new communities had begun to affect the working-class homes. But by 1914 all had become far more solidly entrenched.

Admittedly, drawing hard and fast lines is never easy. Some working-class homes enjoyed baths and water closets before 1901 and many middle-class homes did not. It took the havoc and social change of a Great War to begin the really rapid growth of council housing which now provides nearly a third of all British homes. Garden Cities and New Towns, bravely begun at Letchworth in 1903, needed not one but two wars and over 40 years before they finally became firmly established. Nonetheless, by 1914 some of the principal trends in twentieth-century housing were clearly established; 1901, by contrast, looked both backwards and forwards.

Social Class

There was no such thing as "the Victorian home". It hardly needs to be said that in Victorian Britain there were many graduations of rank, station and degree, within as well as between social classes. There was, as Documents 90–5 show, a prosperous working class, some members of which owned their own homes; these often had solid, well built furniture and a piano in the sitting room. There was no single yardstick to divide all working-class homes from those of other Victorians.

Yet the divisions were abundant and clear. The middle and upper classes did not live in urban or rural slums. For all the jerry-building, for all the shoddiness and inadequate plumbing which marred their homes, they were more likely to be concerned with the servant than the housing problem. They looked upwards, they followed fashion or tried to, they read the numerous journals and books which attempted to guide their taste, and, if they were wealthy, they hired people to tell them how to build or decorate their homes. Even if they were not wealthy, which was usually the case, the people who spent between £100 and £1,000 a year for whom J. H. Walsh wrote his *Manual* (Documents 17 and 33) in the 1850s (not to mention those who spent much more) did not include the large majority of the British population.

The working classes were very differently placed. Even by the standards of the day the majority lived below, at or near the poverty line. They could seldom afford to be concerned with changes in fashion. Although working-class homes tended to vary in quality within a given area or even the same street, they tended also to be distinct from the homes of the middle classes. Transport changes as well as mere growth in numbers created concentric rings in cities, so that most wealthier people had no need to know how the poorer classes lived, as Friedrich Engels among others repeatedly observed (eg 64). In general, to be a member of the working classes in Victorian Britain meant to lead either a poor or a precarious existence or both. This was more true of housing than of any other facet of life, and, therefore, with all the immense differences within and between the middle and upper classes, working-class housing must be treated as a subject quite distinct from the housing of superior social classes.

Middle- and Upper-class Homes

Many changes took place, inside and out, in the two generations of Queen Victoria's reign. Architectural style changed, as did styles of decoration and furniture. All of this is perfectly explicable, if complex, and an attempt is made below (17–31) to unravel the pattern. The unsolved mystery is the lack of technical progress. During the Victorian period technical and engineering developments took place at a rate which dwarfed the whole of past history. Yet the heating, lighting and sanitation of the homes of the better-off classes lagged far behind what could have been achieved.

The easy availability of domestic servants, to householders
down to the lowest ranks of the middle classes, to do the dirty
and smelly work for their social betters is only part of the
answer to the delay in technical progress. For surely it was
more comfortable, more hygienic and even more aesthetically
pleasing to have electric light than gas or oil lamps, baths with
constant hot water than jugs and basins and tubs, and efficient
water closets than their inefficient or non-existent predecessors.
J. C. Loudon discussed baths and central heating in 1838 (32,
40) and J. H. Walsh thought constant hot water "almost a
necessary" in 1857 (33); yet at the end of the century none of
these amenities was universal in a fully practicable form even
in the wealthiest homes. Less prosperous members of the upper
social classes were in most cases much worse off. (As late as
1920 only 730,000 of the approximately 10 million British
households were consumers of electricity.)

Thus the homes of the Victorian middle and upper classes
were as beautiful as they could be made, and modern changes
of taste and fashion have emphasised their many attractions.
(Even some Victorian working-class homes seem relatively
spacious by today's standards.) But they were in most cases
neither utilitarian, comfortable, labour-saving nor wholesome.

Working-class Homes

The problem in the case of working-class homes is quite
different. It is to discover what proportion lived comfortably
and what proportion were badly housed. A major difficulty lies
in the fact that it was not until nearly the end of the nineteenth
century that modern social surveys and statistical reports
became common: Charles Booth's work began in 1886,
Seebohm Rowntree's in 1899, and the first Government census
of overcrowding took place in 1891. For earlier periods the
material is abundant but difficult to quantify. There is plenty
of evidence to show how slum dwellers lived; it would have been
easy to fill a book several times as long as this one with descriptions of slum conditions or "low life", especially in London.

Descriptions of the prosperous working classes, while less numerous, are also quite easy to find. It is much less easy to find evidence about those who lived between the extremes, and the greatest difficulty lies in assessing the proportion belonging to each group. Nor is it always easy to interpret such statistical data as exist. For example, Seebohm Rowntree found that "many" of the 26 per cent of the working classes who lived in the poorest districts of York inhabited slums. On the other hand he decided that only about 12 per cent of the working classes lived in "comfortable and sanitary" homes. "The housing conditions of many of the remaining 88 per cent leave much to be desired." (See *Poverty*, 1901, 147, 179.) Thus the proportion of badly housed working-class people in York may be regarded as quite small, very large or somewhere in between.

Such cautious use of statistics is not very helpful. But if some kind of generalisation is to be attempted, it will run along the following lines. Throughout the Victorian period there was a slow improvement in urban housing conditions, following rises in wages, more advanced technical standards, new legislation and more adequate municipal services. Slums became less vile and less numerous, and overcrowding declined. Even so, standards improved far more slowly than growing wealth and technical knowledge would have made possible; descriptions of urban slum housing in 1840 could be applied with little change to some homes in 1900. In rural areas progress was even slower. Perhaps 10–15 per cent of the Victorian working classes lived comfortably according to the standards of the time.

It was a dismal situation. Two principal reforms had to come about before the housing problem could begin to be solved, and it is worth pointing out that with vastly superior resources and knowledge the 1970s have still to find their own solution. The first reform was higher wages. "When people are very poor, you *cannot* help them", said Bernard Shaw's Sartorius (81), and between the wars, when better housing at higher rents preceded adequate regular wages, the result was likely to be dietary deficiencies which produced a significantly higher death rate. (See G. C. M. M'Gonigle and J. Kirby. *Poverty and Public Health*, 1936, Chs VII and XII.) The second step was council housing, hardly out of infancy at the turn of the century but a factor of major importance in later years.

It would not be true to say that all urban working-class Victorians were poorly housed, but it would be better than a half truth. Their homes, and even more those of rural labourers, demonstrate the failure of British industrial society to spread prosperity to all sections of the community. The best that can be said for Victorian society perhaps is that it also created the social conscience and the working-class movements which began to attack its inadequacies and its inequalities.

The book is as comprehensive as possible, given limitations of space and availability of sources. An attempt has been made to give each aspect its due weight, avoiding, for example, undue emphasis on the homes of the very poor. Special attention has been given to relatively neglected aspects, such as sanitation, heat and light.

The spell of London has been resisted so far as possible. But London was the capital, the source of the scholarly journals and other national publications, the home of the arbiters of fashion and taste and many of the authorities on working-class housing. London was the place where debates about social conditions were fiercest. Moreover, London was by far the largest city, twice as large in 1881, for example, as Glasgow, Liverpool, Birmingham and Manchester, the four next largest, put together. Accordingly, some emphasis on London is inevitable.

The dates of publication given for documents are of the earliest versions in the present form which have been traceable. Extracts have normally been taken from books rather than from earlier newspaper or journal publication. Passages have not normally been used if they have already been published in other books of extracts, but this rule has been broken in particularly useful and relevant cases. Finally, in a book of this kind the available sources have had to be ruthlessly pruned to arrive at a book of no more than reasonable length. Where the choice has had to be made between material well known to scholars and lesser known sources, the former has usually been preferred, on the assumption that the book is more likely to be useful to students or to interested lay readers than to scholars working in the field.

PART ONE

The Homes of the Middle and Upper Classes

THE GROWTH OF TOWNS AND MIDDLE-CLASS HOUSING PROBLEMS

The Fact of Expansion

To contemporary observers the expansion of towns was one of the leading phenomena of the time, causing dismay and alarm to those fortunate enough to have homes in more settled areas. Writer after writer comments on the growth of towns since his childhood and the disappearance of once cherished countryside. These feelings are well summarised by prophets like Ruskin (1819–1900) and novelists like Wells (1866–1946). Although it was London (2) which grew most strikingly, other towns also expanded; this is seen in an early comment on Glasgow (1) by the distinguished German scientist and writer Carl Gustav Carus (1789–1869), who travelled as physician to the King of Saxony. The population of Glasgow, 275,000 in 1841, reached 420,000 in 1861, and 522,000 in 1871. A favourite pastime of the upper middle class, sneering at the less well off in their own class, is evident in the extract from Ruskin (3). Note also his reference to the development of the semi-detached house. Wells's "Bromstead" is Bromley, Kent, where he was born in 1866, and which was then rapidly becoming part of Greater London (4).

1 C. G. Carus The King of Saxony's Journey through England and Scotland in the Year 1844
(1845; English translation 1846), 283

The part of the town in which the Exchange is situated, lies higher, and is much more airy than that through which we had driven. The streets are better built, kept clean, and almost free from that smoke, which enwraps every thing in these manufacturing towns. Still better, however, is the situation of the new town, as it is called, which lies much higher; it is built quite in the same style as the West-End of London, and well laid out in squares, which are so favourable to health. In this quarter we saw whole streets with several churches, some of them just completed—and some recently occupied—with others still in course of erection. The town, in this manner, appears to be in a course of rapid increase in various directions. Mr. Brown conducted us to a place, still free from buildings, on the declivity of the hill, from whence we had an excellent view of the town, stretching far below us, and up the hill towards the place on which we stood. The beautiful summer evening shed an enchanting air over the masses of houses and churches which lay beneath, and the distant hills. The city, partially veiled in dark smoky clouds, still presented all the appearance of a manufacturing town; but the pure crescent moon rose beautifully in the clear, slightly reddened horizon, above the cloudy atmosphere beneath. Thus it is that the lofty poetical feeling of the human mind rises placid and clear above the active but grovelling occupations of every-day life.

In such a general view one would almost believe it possible to see with the eye the rapid growth and increase of the city! In the eighth decennium of the last century the inhabitants of Glasgow amounted to little more than 60,000, at present the number is greater than 200,000, and in a few decennia it will probably double that amount.

2 Morning Herald   Leading Article
(20 September 1848), 4; reprinted as "The Building Mania", *The Builder* (14 October 1848), 500–1

No one, who has recently travelled with his eyes open, in

search of a home, a friend, or a little fresh air, in the environs
of this over-grown metropolis, can have failed to observe,
whatever directions his peregrinations may have taken, that
houses are springing up in all quarters, for the reception of the
ever-increasing population of densely-populated London. In
the vicinity of other large cities, especially if they boast the
advantage of a railway the same observation will have been
made. There is no lack of brick and mortar, east, west, north,
and south; our cities and towns are extending themselves into
the country. Money is scarce. The whole nation is in difficulties. But houses spring up everywhere, as though capital
were abundant, as though one-half the world were on the
look-out for investments, and the other half continually in
search of eligible family residences, desirable villas, and aristocratic cottages, which have nothing in the world of the cottage
about them except the name.

Houses, we say, spring up everywhere in the outskirts of our
great towns. A suburb, in these days, is one congeries of crude
brick and mortar. It is the most melancholy thing in existence.
There is no getting rid of the reflection that a number of very
worthy people must be ruining themselves outright. Streets,
squares, crescents, terraces, Albert villas, Victoria villas, and
things of the same inviting character, stand up everywhere
against the horizon, and mutely beseech us to take them. You
may get a new house, of almost every conceivable pattern, and
at any conceivable price, down to £60 per annum. You may
take your choice, according to the length of your purse, of
"noble reception rooms" and "neat parlours". But your purse
must have some length to accomplish even the latter. There is
a leaven of aristocracy in the parlour with folding doors. We
only build now-a-days for the gentry. If a man has a little land,
or a little money, or a little speculativeness, or a little unemployed timber, or a number of idle workmen, he straightway
buildeth a villa. The villa mania is everywhere most obtrusive.
You would smile, perhaps, at the vulgarity of the thing if it
were not for the certainty that the enterprising villa-builder

must be building his fortune to death. Fortunes must grow upwards, even more rapidly than they are growing downwards in these days, before all these splendid visions of wealthy tenants can be realised. Indeed, when we come to consider the number of pursy citizens that it will take to populate these snug suburbs, we are absolutely lost in wonder to determine where they can all come from.

We may talk about "signs of the times"—but there is not one more surprising than this. As it was asked with reference to the astounding array of good husbands, fathers, citizens, &c., whom we meet, in monumental existence, in our churchyards, where all the bad ones were buried, so we are disposed to ask in these days, when we contemplate the number of houses in course of erection for the rich, where the poor are to be housed? One would think that there was no increase of population lower down than the classes which rejoice in five hundred a year, or that there was something of so cumulative a character in the times that every man must needs be on the look-out for the means of expending a larger income that he has heretofore had facilities of scattering abroad.

3 John Ruskin Fors Clavigera
Letter 29, "La Douce Amie" (1873), *Library Edition of the Works of John Ruskin*, Vol XXVII (1907), 528–30

What a pestilence of [houses] and unseemly plague of builders' work—as if the bricks of Egypt had multiplied like its lice, and alighted like its locusts—has fallen on the suburbs of loathsome London?

The road from the village of Shirley, near Addington, where my father and mother are buried, to the house they lived in when I was four years old, lay, at that time, through a quite secluded district of field and wood, traversed here and there by winding lanes, and by one or two smooth mail-coach roads, beside which, at intervals of a mile or two, stood some gentleman's house, with its lawn, gardens, offices, and attached fields, indicating a country life of long continuance and quiet respectability. Except such an one here and there, one saw no dwellings above the size of cottages or small farmsteads; these, wood-built usually, and thatched, their porches embroidered with honeysuckle, and their gardens with daisies, their doors mostly ajar, or with a half one shut to keep in the children, and a bricked or tiled footway from it to the wicket gate,—all neatly kept, and vivid with a sense of the quiet energies of their contented tenants,—made the lane-turnings cheerful, and gleamed in half-hidden clusters beneath the slopes of the woodlands at Sydenham and Penge. There were no signs of distress, of effort, or of change; many of enjoyment, and not a few of wealth beyond the daily needs of life. That same district is now covered by, literally, many thousands of houses built within the last ten years, of rotten brick, with various iron devices to hold it together. They, every one, have a drawing-room and dining-room, transparent from back to front, so that from the road one sees the people's heads inside, clear against the light. They have a second story of bedrooms, and an underground one of kitchen. They are fastened in a Siamese-twin manner together by their sides, and each couple has a Greek or Gothic portico shared between them, with magnificent steps, and highly ornamented capitals. Attached to every double block are exactly similar double parallelograms of garden, laid out in new gravel and scanty turf, on the model of the pleasure grounds in the Crystal Palace, and enclosed by high, thin, and pale brick walls. The gardens in front are fenced from the road with an immense weight of cast iron, and entered between two square gate-posts, with projecting stucco cornices, bearing the information that the eligible residence within is Mortimer House or Montague Villa. On the other side of the road, which is laid freshly down with large flints, and is deep at the sides in ruts of yellow mud, one sees Burleigh House, or Devonshire Villa, still to let, and getting leprous in patches all over the fronts. . . .

That is the typical condition of five-sixths, at least, of the "rising" middle classes about London—the lodgers in those damp shells of brick, which one cannot say they inhabit, nor call their "houses"; nor "their's" indeed, in any sense; but packing-cases in which they are temporarily stored, for bad use.

4 H. G. Wells The New Machiavelli
(1911), Book I, Chapter 2, Section 5

Roofs of slate and tile appeared amidst and presently prevailed over the original Bromstead thatch, the huge space of Common to the south was extensively enclosed, and what had been an ill-defined horse-track to Dover, only passable by adventurous coaches in dry weather, became the Dover Road, and was presently the route first of one and then of several daily coaches. The High Street was discovered to be too tortuous for these awakening energies, and a new road cut off its worst contortions. Residential villas appeared occupied by retired tradesmen and widows, who esteemed the place healthy, and by others of a strange new unoccupied class of people who had money invested in joint-stock enterprises. . . .

. . . Bromstead had almost doubled in size again long before the railway came; there was hardly any thatch left in the High Street, but instead were houses with handsome brass-knockered front doors and several windows, and shops with shop-fronts all of square glass panes, and the place was lighted publicly now by oil lamps. . . .

. . . Hard on the gasworks had come the railway and cheap coal; there was a wild outbreak of brickfields upon the clay-lands to the east, and the Great Growth had begun in earnest. . . .

This enterprising person and then that began to "run up" houses, irrespective of every other enterprising person who was doing the same thing. A Local Board came into existence, and with much hesitation and penny-wise economy inaugurated drainage works. Rates became a common topic, a fact of accumulating importance. Several chapels of zinc and iron appeared, and also a white new church in commercial Gothic upon the common, and another of red brick in the residential district out beyond the brickfields towards Chessington.

The population doubled again and doubled again, and became particularly teeming in the prolific "working-class" district about the deep-rutted, muddy, coal-blackened roads between the gasworks, Blodgett's laundries, and the railway goods-yard. Weekly properties, that is to say small houses built by small property owners and let by the week, sprang up also in the Cage Fields, and presently extended right up the London Road. . . . The whole of Bromstead as I remember it, and as I saw it last—it is a year ago now—is a dull useless boiling-up of human activities, an immense clustering of futilities. It is as unfinished as ever; the builders' roads still run out and end in mid-field in their old fashion; the various enterprises jumble in the same hopeless contradiction, if anything intensified. Pretentious villas jostle slums, and public-house and tin tabernacle glower at one another across the cat-haunted lot that intervenes.

Town or Suburb?

The question whether to live in a city or its suburbs is a very old one. It was being discussed at least as early as the very beginning of the Victorian period, and reached a crescendo during the first decade of this century, when Mrs Peel's snobbish tones were widely echoed. The Webster-Parkes book (5) was one of the many guides for the Victorian middle class about the house and housekeeping, the best known of which was Isabella Beeton's *Book of Household Management* (1861). Mrs Peel (?1872–1934), was an interesting and prolific writer, an early woman journalist and a perceptive historian (6).

5 Thomas Webster and Frances Parkes   An Encyclopaedia of Domestic Economy (1844), 1–2

One of the first objects which usually engage the attention of those who are just setting out in life, and on the eve of forming a domestic establishment, is the acquisition of a dwelling. In England it is generally the desire of every one whose finances can afford it, to have a house of his own. In other countries, even wealthy families are often contented to occupy a part of a large mansion, but this practice is inconsistent with those views of domestic comfort which an Englishman looks forward to at his own fireside, where he may plan his arrangements of a permanent nature without molestation. This feeling is peculiarly characteristic of England; and the anticipation of these domestic pleasures is perhaps one of the strongest inducements to those exertions of industry which are not surpassed in any other part of the world. The great improvements which have been made of late in the interior of our houses are in a great measure the results of this national taste.

1. *The primary consideration in the choice of a residence is generally the situation;* and the next is the suitableness of the building to the wants of the family that is to inhabit it. It is not always the good fortune of those who are desirous of possessing a house of their own to meet with one that will suit them in every respect, and more particularly when they have limited themselves to a particular locality. A house already built may stand in need of some repair—perhaps to be modernised, or to have additions made to it; and where considerable alterations are required, it may be a question, which is too seldom asked, whether it would not be better to build a new one: for it happens not unfrequently that from one alteration giving rise to another, the expense of these at last exceeds the cost of a new house. To make a judicious choice of a residence, it is therefore necessary that the intended occupier should not only well consider his principal wants, but understand all the essential points to be attended to in supplying them. An improper choice is often very difficult to remedy, and may destroy much of the comfort that was anticipated. To supply the requisite information on this subject will therefore be our first endeavour.

2. *The situation of a domestic residence* may be conveniently reduced to three classes—that of a town, suburban, and a country house; each of which has its peculiar advantages.

3. *A residence in town* is superior to any other for social intercourse and varied enjoyment by means of public and private parties, theatres, concerts, balls, public libraries, museums, exhibitions of works of art, with numerous opportunities of acquiring general knowledge. In the choice of a town residence, one must be guided not only by peculiar views, but by the comparative healthiness of the street—its aspect, neighbourhood, and many other local circumstances, which are, in general, pretty well understood. Not only the width of the street, but its direction, is important: one running east and west must have one front of the houses looking to the north, and deprived of the sun almost the whole of the day, while the other is exposed to its full radiance.

4. *A suburban residence*, or one in the environs of a city or town, offers some advantages that cannot be obtained by living in town. The situation is, in general, more healthy, the air not being so much contaminated by the thousands of chimneys that are perpetually throwing out smoke and deleterious gases. Ground not being so valuable as in town, many more conveniences can be acquired, such as a garden, and perhaps a field or two, attached to the house; and this additional space may be built upon, according to any proposed plan. Thus this kind of residence, while it possesses many of the advantages of the country, such as good air and plenty of room, may at the same time enable the occupier to enjoy occasionally the conveniences of a town life. The pleasure to be derived from a garden, and from the cheerful and enlivening effect of trees and vegetation in general, together with quiet and absence of smoke, and innumerable disagreeable objects constantly presented in cities, are circumstances worthy of consideration. It should be mentioned, however, that in the immediate vicinity of towns the atmosphere is still in some degree charged with noxious matters, particularly when the

wind blows in certain directions; and therefore, in order to enjoy the full benefit of pure air, it is necessary to remove to a sufficient distance beyond their influence.

6 Dorothy Peel   The New Home
(1898), 14–16

Let us now consider the relative advantages of residing in town and suburb. I must confess honestly that the suburbs of any large town appear to me detestable, but to be strictly just, suburban life has perhaps some decided advantages over town life. Rents as a rule are lower in the suburbs, and although houses are if anything worse built, they are planned with some consideration for the needs of a family. When young children have to be thought of, good rooms must be provided for them. While it may not be easy to secure these at a moderate rent in London, there will be little difficulty in selecting a roomy residence in a suburb. When the income is limited, a small garden is a convenience, as the older children can be sent out to play by themselves. So far as the actual expenses of living go, the prices of food and household necessaries and the amount of the rates and taxes are much the same in the suburbs as in any large town. It must further be borne in mind that when the master of the house is obliged to go into the city every day the amount of his railway or omnibus fares must be added to the rent. Nor must the house mistress who exiles herself in the suburbs lose sight of the fact that she will find it difficult, and as regards fares etc. expensive, to keep in touch with London society and amusements. Those people who yearn for the pleasures of the country and who find their diversion in golf, tennis, bicycling, boating, or gardening, and whom cruel fate prevents from living in the real country, might find suburban life preferable to town life. But before making a decision it is wise to take lodgings for a month or two in the neighbourhood selected, and thereby gain an insight into its advantages and disadvantages.

And lastly with regard to living in London or some other large town. Putting aside the requirements of the lover of the country and of young children, I am inclined to think the advantages of town life very much outweigh those of suburban life. In a large town we can pick and choose our friends and acquaintance, and only affect the society which pleases us most. We can have the best of music and of theatres, good libraries and lectures, and the highest educational advantages, all at a moderate price, while by the help of omnibus and underground railway and occasional hansom cabs, our bill for conveyances need not be a large one.

In the Hands of the Jerry-builder

Remaining Victorian middle-class houses may appear to be solidly built and sturdy. As these extracts show, the reverse was often the case. We shall see again later that building laws and bylaws were inadequate and frequently flouted, so that builders of poor quality had often a virtually free hand. Henry Burdett (1847–1920) looks at the matter from the point of view of the medical and sanitary writer (7) and H. G. Wells from that of the successful novelist who, just before the turn of the century, faced similar housing difficulties to his fictional Kipps a few years later (8). Both Wells and Kipps rose suddenly from the lower middle class and neither forgot his origins. Whether the arrival of 1975 has justified Wells's hopes or not the reader may judge, but the decline of living-in domestic servants and the reduced size of middle-class houses will be quickly brought to mind in reading the passage from *Kipps*.

7 Henry C. Burdett   The Dwellings of the Middle Classes

Transactions of the Sanitary Institute of Great Britain (1883–4), 237–41

There is much that demands attention in the dwellings of

the middle class, and especially in those of the lower middle
classes. The wealthier classes are able to take care of themselves
by the employment of such able architects as they may like to
select, and the poorer classes—artizans and the like—have
thousands of well-arranged and carefully-constructed dwellings
erected for them from the designs and under the superintendence
of the same class of architects. But the poorer middle classes
have no such power or means of securing healthy dwellings for
their own occupation. To prove this and to realize the crying
nature of the evils attaching to the dwellings of the middle
classes, it is necessary to pay a visit to a suburban district under
the control of a Local Board, and to make an inspection of
several houses in various stages of erection. These houses will
be to let at from £35 to £50 to £75 a-year, and possibly at a
higher rate still. They will be occupied by that hard-working
class, bank clerks, commercial clerks, civil service clerks, and
others, who have to present a decent appearance and to keep
and bring up a young family on an income little, if at all, in
excess of that earned by a skilled artizan or mechanic—say £3
to £5 per week. The occupier of these houses will often have a
lodger or a parent to share the house and lessen the expenses,
so that the four or five bed rooms are always fully occupied.

   Such houses are erected by speculating builders, known as
"jerry" builders, are usually mortgaged as the work proceeds,
and have no one to look after their construction except the
surveyor to the Local Board. He, poor man, often without an
apology for assistance, cannot be in every part of his scattered
district at the same time, even if he wished to supervise all this
class of work efficiently. Besides, it too frequently happens that
the jerry builder is a member of the Local Board himself, or
has powerful friends there; and in such cases the surveyor finds
it inexpedient to interfere with certain houses which are
consequently the worst of their class. In the model buildings'
bye-laws, published under the authority of the Local Government Board, nearly every essential for a healthy properly
constructed dwelling is provided for, but in many districts,

even where the bye-laws are in use, they are practically a dead letter, owing to the unwillingness of the Sanitary authority to enforce them with uniform energy. Yet the power taken in such bye-laws, and which might be brought to bear upon the builders, would render jerry buildings an impossibility, if the Local Boards were determined to enforce such bye-laws without fear or favour. Every Local Board, that is, the large majority, does not so enforce the bye-laws, and is consequently in league with the jerry builder.

... Here is a house, empty, which was completed and occupied two years ago. Notice how the inside is finished, to take the eye: good mantel-pieces, showy grates, and attractive papers. Now look at the floors. Not one of them is level; they are at all sorts of angles, owing to the sinking of the walls. You have to walk up and down hill, as it were, to cross each room in the house. Notice how the damp has risen, even to the second-floor rooms, and in all the water has come through the roof, not in one, but in many places. The bath room, &c., is conspicuous, but only to the practised eye, by reason of the scamped plumbing and forbidden fittings used. Look at the exterior. The footings of the chimneys are above the ground level, the garden walls are all bulging out, the piers cracking and coming to pieces; and, if left to themselves much longer, they will fall down. Observe how the roof sags, owing to the scantlings of the rafters being insufficient; and in case of fire, though a detached house, it is so close to the next, that the fire must spread because the usual protection against fires spreading from one house to the next is absent—no parapet being carried up on the external side walls. Built on clay, containing, practically, no cellars and no damp course, it is literally placed flat on the ground. Notice that the floor level of the house is now below the level of the garden: and on this fine summer's day the dampness is shown many feet up the walls of the house.

... Observe what the bye-laws of the Willesden Local Board, with respect to new streets and buildings passed in

1881, provide. The whole ground surface or site of a house must be properly asphalted and covered with a layer of good cement concrete, rammed solid at least six inches thick. The building must be solidly put together (1) with good mortar, compounded of one part of good lime, and of three parts of clean sand or other suitable material, or (2) with good cement, or (3) with good cement mixed with clean sharp sand. Every wall shall have a proper damp course of sheet lead, asphalte or slates laid in cement, or other durable material impervious to moisture, beneath the level of the lowest timbers, and at a height of not less than six inches above the surface of the ground adjoining such wall. All footings shall rest upon some solid and sufficient substructure as a foundation, or not less than nine inches of good concrete. Every party wall shall be carried up at least nine inches in thickness, for a height of at least fifteen inches above the roof, flat, or gutter of the highest adjoining building. Every soil pipe shall be at least four inches in diameter, shall be outside the building, and be continued up without diminution of its diameter, and without any needless bend or angle being formed in such soil pipe. Every cesspool shall be at least fifty feet from a dwelling house, the brickwork shall be imbedded in cement, and shall be made watertight, with a backing of at least nine inches of well puddled clay around and beneath such brickwork.

Many other provisions might be quoted, but enough has been said to prove that in some cases, at any rate, if not throughout the district of Willesden, the builders set these regulations at defiance, and wholly and openly disregard them. This curious state of affairs is often due to the astuteness of the builder in becoming a member of the Local Board. In one suburb one of the most notorious offenders was, I am informed, once turned off the Board by the indignant ratepayers, but when a vacancy occurred soon afterwards the Local Board sent a deputation to the builder in question and invited him to fill the vacancy thus caused, which he accordingly did. He secured the Board's approval of certain plans for the erection of a number of houses, before the model bye-laws were passed in 1881, and because of this he claims to be able and is still allowed to build without check or hindrance the class of houses we have inspected and examined together.

It must not be supposed, however, that in naming Willesden I do so because it is especially bad. Far from this being the case, I wish it to be understood that in some respects Willesden is far better managed than certain other localities.

8 H. G. Wells Kipps
(1905), Book III, Chapter 1, Sections 2-3

They did not clearly know what they wanted, but whatever it was they saw, they knew they did not want that. Always they found a confusing multitude of houses they could not take, and none they could. Their dreams began to turn mainly on empty, abandoned-looking rooms, with unfaded patches of paper to mark the place of vanished pictures, and doors that had lost their keys. They saw rooms floored with boards that yawned apart and were splintered, skirtings eloquent of the industrious mouse, kitchens with a dead black-beetle in the empty cupboard, and a hideous variety of coal-holes and dark cupboards under the stairs. They stuck their little heads through roof trap-doors, and gazed at disorganised ball-traps, at the black filthiness of unstopped roofs. There were occasions when it seemed to them that they must be the victims of an elaborate conspiracy of house agents, so bleak and cheerless is a second-hand empty house in comparison with the humblest of inhabited dwellings.

Commonly the houses were too big. They had huge windows that demanded vast curtains in mitigation, countless bedrooms, acreage of stone steps to be cleaned, kitchens that made Ann protest. She had come so far towards a proper conception of Kipps' social position as to admit the prospect of one servant. "But lor!" she would say, "you want a man-servant in this house." When the houses were not too big, then they were

V.H.—B

almost always the product of speculative building, of that multitudinous, hasty building for the extravagant swarm of new births that was the essential disaster of the nineteenth century. The new houses Ann refused as damp, and even the youngest of those that had been in use showed remarkable signs of a sickly constitution—the plaster flaked away, the floors gaped, the paper moulded and peeled, the doors dropped, the bricks were scaled, and the railings rusted; Nature, in the form of spiders, earwigs, cockroaches, mice, rats, fungi, and remarkable smells, was already fighting her way back. . . .

And the plan was invariably inconvenient, invariably. All the houses they saw had a common quality for which she could find no word, but for which the proper word is "incivility". "They build these 'ouses," she said, "as though girls wasn't 'uman beings." Sid's social democracy had got into her blood, perhaps, and, anyhow, they went about discovering the most remarkable inconsiderateness in the contemporary house.

"There's kitching stairs to go up, Artie!" Ann would say. "Some poor girl's got to go up and down, up and down, and be tired out, jest because they haven't the sense to leave enough space to give their steps a proper rise—and no water anywhere —every drop got to be carried! It's 'ouses like this wear girls out.

"It's 'aving 'ouses built by men, I believe, makes all the work and trouble," said Ann. . . .

The Kippses, you see, thought they were looking for a reasonably simple little contemporary house; but indeed they were looking either for dreamland or A.D. 1975, or thereabouts, and it hadn't come.

[They took] a house for a year, with a basement, no service lift, blackleading to do everywhere, no water upstairs, no bathroom, vast sash windows to be cleaned from the sill, stone steps with a twist and open to the rain into the coal-cellar, insufficient cupboards, unpaved path to the dustbin, no fire-place to the servant's bedroom, no end of splintery wood to scrub—in fact, a very typical English middle-class house.

Flats

Living in flats is much older than may be supposed, though English cities lagged behind Continental and Scottish ones. The first English flats for families seem to have been working-class "model dwellings" in Birkenhead in 1845. They were soon followed, on a much larger scale, by developments in London. The middle class took the idea up, their earliest flats probably being those in Ashley Place, Victoria, London, completed about 1854. It was some time before flat dwelling spread widely, but by the mid-1870s, as the following passages show, the movement had become highly successful, though restricted to London. Henry Hankey's Queen Anne's Mansions (9), Queen Anne's Gate, now destroyed, was the first high block of flats, the highest elevation being fourteen storeys. It was built between 1873 and 1889, and Hankey, a developer, designed the early stages of the building himself. Later stages were designed by E. R. Robson (1835–1917), best known for his London School Board buildings. In 1890 legislation limited London building heights (other than churches and chapels) to 90 ft, with some modifications for storeys in the roof and ornamental towers. The height was reduced to 80 ft in 1894, but though no other Victorian flats were so high, more and more blocks were built, despite the reservations of some architects and critics. T. H. S. Escott (1844–1924) was a prominent journalist and writer (10), editor of the *Fortnightly Review* from 1883 to 1886.

9 Queen Anne's Mansions and Milton's Gardens
The Builder (2 June 1877), 556

Some time since we gave a notice in the *Builder* of the monster blocks of dwellings,—more appropriately speaking, perhaps, residential towers,—which Mr. Hankey has for some time past been engaged in erecting at Queen Anne's-gate, St. James's Park, for that portion of the community who prefer living in "houses in flats" rather than in separate and detached mansions. The demand for the blocks already completed, which are 116 ft. in height, and contain ten stories, has been so great as to have induced Mr. Hankey to erect still more blocks, and the fact that with the assistance of the lift instead of the ordinary staircase the upper floors are easily reached, has caused these upper floors to be to a great extent preferred, notwithstanding their unusually lofty altitude. This is attributed in a great degree to the fine panoramic view of the country for miles around which they command, the Crystal Palace and the Surrey hills being prominent objects to the south-east, whilst there is an equally interesting prospect in a north-westerly direction, extending to Highgate, Hampstead, Edgware, and the surrounding districts. This circumstance appears to have led to the erection of still loftier buildings than those already finished and now fully occupied, for the blocks at present in progress contain eleven stories, and are 130 ft. high, an altitude loftier than the average church tower and spire. The rents which these buildings command may perhaps be regarded as another inducement to continue Babel-like structures. When a floor containing six rooms, without any grounds, commands 300*l.* per annum, and two rooms 60*l.* per annum, there is a strong encouragement to continue the erection of such a class of structures. These are the rents which Mr. Hankey is receiving from tenants who, with few exceptions, are persons of position.

. . . With regard to the buildings themselves it is sufficient to state that in their general construction and appearance they in nearly every respect resemble the completed blocks, the difference consisting in the increased height of those in progress, and the additional thickness of the main walls owing to the higher altitude. These walls are 4 ft. 6 in. in thickness at the base, gradually reduced until they come to 14 in. at the top story. They also differ internally from the finished block, so far as regards the floors, all of which are said to be strictly fireproof, constructed with iron girders, and filled in with concrete. There are likewise ventilating valves in the walls, both at the floor and ceiling line of each story. As a precaution against fire there will be tanks at the top of the buildings with a capacity for containing 40,000 gallons of water, the tanks being connected with hydrants, jets, and hose to every floor.

10 T. H. S. Escott   England: Its People, Polity and Pursuits
Vol II (nd; 1879) 3–5

The "flat" system, borrowed from France, has now existed on a considerable scale in London some fifteen years, and at the present time is in great and growing favour. In the course of five years the rents of flats have doubled; Victoria Street, Westminster, is about equally divided into the offices of parliamentary lawyers, colonial agents, engineers, and into domestic dwellings. These last consist in every case of flats. The sum paid annually for a suite of eight rooms on the ground floor is not less than £250. The drawing-room floor commands a still larger sum; and unless the tenant chooses to ascend to the lofty level of the garrets, no set of apartments can be procured in this quarter of the town for less than £150. At Queen Anne's Gate there has sprung up a colossal block wherein resides an immense aggregate of families. Here attendance and cookery are forthcoming as well as house-room, with, of course, a proportionate charge for both. Dinners and other meals may be taken in the private apartments of the occupiers, or in the public saloon. The rents paid are fixed at figures which might be thought prohibitory, yet few sets of rooms ever remain long vacant. No arrangement can be imagined more diametrically antagonistic to the tastes with which Englishmen are generally credited. A flat, it may be said, is merely a house, with this difference, that the rooms are arranged, not on the perpendicular plan, but on the horizontal. It also possesses what may well seem a great advantage to busy men or women who are anxious to purchase the seclusion of domestic life at the cost of as little inconvenience as possible.

The tenant of a flat is able to compound for all the various petty charges incidental to the householder by payment of a lump sum. The flats belong to a company; the company has a secretary, and it is the business of that officer to see that the fabric of the apartments of each tenant is kept in proper order, and that no just complaint remains without attention. There are other advantages connected with the flat system of which the English paterfamilias is fully as conscious as the Continental. He can leave London at a moment's notice with his wife, children, and servants; or he can take his children and wife with him, sending the servants on a holiday, secure in the knowledge that his abode is hermetically sealed behind him; that there is danger neither from the street burglar nor from the charwoman—the traditional custodian of the London house when the family are out of town—and the strange relatives and unsavoury friends whom that person may invite into the drawing-room during the period of her occupancy.

GREAT HOUSES

The Cult of the Picturesque
    The picturesque, romantic style favoured by many early Victorian architects of country houses (though opposed by others) is well caught in this passage (11) by Disraeli (1804–81), the greatest of romantics. His fictional St Geneviève, here described, was in reality Garendon Hall, Leicestershire. It was an early eighteenth-century Palladian house, but plans for its remodelling on gothic lines had been drawn up by A. W. N. Pugin (see 26) in 1841. However, alterations were not carried out at Garendon until 1866, when the architect was Pugin's son, Edward Welby Pugin (1834–75).

11 Benjamin Disraeli   Coningsby
(1844), Book III, Chapter IV

In a valley, not far from the margin of a beautiful river,

raised on a lofty and artificial terrace at the base of a range of wooded heights, was a pile of modern building in the finest style of Christian architecture. It was of great extent and richly decorated. Built of a white and glittering stone, it sparkled with its pinnacles in the sunshine as it rose in strong relief against its verdant background.

. . . The first glance at the building, its striking situation, its beautiful form, its brilliant colour, its great extent, a gathering as it seemed of galleries, halls, and chapels, mullioned windows, portals of clustered columns and groups of airy pinnacles and fretwork spires, called forth a general cry of wonder and of praise . . .

Far as the eye could reach there spread before them a savage sylvan scene. It wanted, perhaps, undulation of surface, but that deficiency was greatly compensated for by the multitude and prodigious size of the trees; they were the largest, indeed, that could well be met with in England; and there is no part of Europe where the timber is so huge. The broad interminable glades, the vast avenues, the quantity of deer browsing or bounding in all directions, the thickets of yellow gorse and green fern, and the breeze that even in the stillness of summer was ever playing over this table-land, all produced an animated and renovating scene. It was like suddenly visiting another country, living among other manners, and breathing another air. They stopped for a few minutes at a pavilion built for the purposes of the chase, and then returned, all gratified by this visit to what appeared to be the higher regions of the earth.

Descriptions

The genealogist Burke (1814–92) here describes Bayons Manor, Lincolnshire (12), rebuilt between 1836 and 1842 by William Nicholson (1803–53) and the owner, Charles Tennyson d'Eyncourt (1784–1861), with assistance from Anthony Salvin (1799–1881). Eaton Hall (13), near Chester, was the seat of the first Duke of Westminster (1825–99) and one of the best known of Victorian country houses. The Duke spent £600,000 on reconstructing the house between 1870 and 1882, the architect being the prominent Alfred Waterhouse (1830–1905). Grandeur, expense and opulence are the most striking features of this late flowering of the English country house.

12 John Bernard Burke A Visitation of the Seats and Arms of the Noblemen and Gentlemen of Great Britain
Vol 1 (1852), 236–7, describing Bayons Manor

A lake, peopled by curious aquatic birds, and studded with islands, one of which forms a pleasaunce, spreads itself at the foot of the eminence on which the manor house is placed. The park, abounding with deer, is broken by every variety of hill, dale, wood, and water, and through it passes a rushing stream, which, rising in the hills to the east in the d'Eyncourt property, forms the source of the river Ancholme, and turns several mills in its progress through the country.

The interior comprises a long range of noble apartments. The stately and spacious hall is entered through a Gothic oak screen, above which is a minstrel's gallery; its height rises to the exterior roof of the building, which is loftily pitched, and gracefully framed in the style of Westminster Hall, with open arched trusses of massive timber, resting on stone corbels, carved into heraldic lions and eagles, bearing shields of arms. The walls are adorned by numerous suits of armour, crossbows, and other ancient weapons of war and chace; also with various banners, tilting lances, portraits, armorial escutcheons in genealogical series, and other characteristic accessories. Among the portraits are two very fine pictures of Edward III., and his Queen Philippa, in their royal robes. The high and painted windows, with a deep Oriel in the western gable, shed a mellow light through coats of arms and other heraldic devices, and in this hall are suspended the brazen chandeliers which illuminated the late House of Commons.

The library, which is well stored in every department of elegant literature, constitutional history, topography, and antiquities, contains some curious MSS. Here also is an open and ponderous timber roof, resting on massive stone corbels, and, like the hall, this apartment equally occupies the whole height of the house. Its general construction, elevated and painted Gothic windows, hanging gallery, and dark panelling, bring the mind back to the monastic ages, and are strikingly picturesque. . . .

. . . The principal withdrawing-room is cruciform, 54 feet in length and 36 feet in the transept, with an oak ceiling thrown into Gothic arches, resting on highly decorated corbels; the windows rich both in architecture and blazonry, illustrate the pedigree and quarterings of the family, and all the adornments maintain the combined dignity and elegance of this beautiful saloon. Three or four other rooms on the principal floor deserve notice, especially the Gallery, which is remarkable for its antique tone and character; but the Tapestry, or state bed chamber, on the first floor, has perhaps the most quaint and mediæval effect. It has, like the other apartments above mentioned, an open wooden roof with interior arches above the cross-beams. Fine tapestry on classical subjects decorate the walls. A magnificent Gothic window with ancient stained glass fills the west end, and imparts a warm and subdued colouring to the interior. . . .

. . . The floors are of fine oak. Some of the stone chimney-pieces are remarkably handsome, and elaborately sculptured with appropriate devices and mottos.

13 Eaton Hall
The Builder (11 December 1880), 694

The grand corridor, which passes between the eastern end of the hall and the saloon, leads towards the south to the great drawing-room and the library, and northward stretches right away, though diminished in width, throughout the whole length of the building to the cross corridor, connecting the chapel with the bridge which leads to the Grosvenor wing. The northern portion has a groined ceiling.

The library occupies nearly the whole of the south front, and is 90 ft. by 30 ft. It has a deep bay in the ground-story of the tower . . . and two large bay-windows. . . . Two angle bays at the west end further diversify the plan. It is fitted with walnut. At the east end stands the organ, in a richly-carved case, and the bookcases extend round the walls of the room. The various panels, friezes, and cornices are brilliant with inlay of mother-of-pearl and boxwood. The chimneypieces are on the north side, and are of walnut, and they are enriched with carving and the inlay of pearl and box. The upper portions of them project, and are supported by caryatides representing the relation of all ranks to a library,—royalty, the church, chivalry, minstrelsy, husbandry, &c., being represented. The hexagonal panel in the centre contains in the one a clock and in the other an anemometer. The ceiling consists of walnut-cased beams and plaster panels, highly enriched with foliage, &c. The windows will be filled with heraldic stained glass. Over the entrance to the library is the "Caxton Memorial" which was illustrated in our volume for 1877, p. 687. The floor is to be of oak parquet.

The great drawing-room, 45 ft. by 36 ft., communicates with the grand corridor on the west, the garden, porch, lobby, and library on the south, and ante-room on the north. At the east, it has one large recess, in which we understand, will be placed Mr. Thornycroft's "Artemis", exhibited this year in the Royal Academy. The old plaster groined ceiling is retained, with certain modifications, and has been re-decorated. The chimney-piece is one of various marbles, purchased by the Duke while in Italy.

The ante-drawing-room adjoining has also its old ceiling, which has been decorated afresh. This room will be celebrated for its twelve panels of birds painted by Mr. H. S. Marks, R.A. The saloon has a high wainscot dado, and the walls above are painted also by Marks, illustrating the "Canterbury Pilgrims". The chimneypiece is of alabaster, and the central panel contains a procession of world-famous lovers, from Antony and Cleopatra to Raffaelle and the Fornarina. The smaller panels in this and the other chimneypieces before described contain allegorical figures, which have all some reference to the principal subjects, e.g., Truth, Valour, Constancy, Love &c. The ceiling is groined, and of wainscot. It is of very elaborate design, and is to be decorated with colours and gilding.

We now come to the ante-dining-room, with its walnut dado, in the panels of which family portraits by Gainsborough, Millais, &c., are framed. As in the drawing-room, the old plaster ceiling is retained, and has been re-decorated.

The great dining-room is of the same shape and size as the drawing-room. It is being fitted up with all-becoming magnificence in walnut. At the north end is the sideboard recess, which has a groined walnut ceiling, and a serving-room adjoins. To the west of the dining-room and on either side of the corridor, are the billiard and smoking rooms. They are treated similarly, and have wainscoted dados, with dark oak panels. The ceilings are also of wainscot, and the walls are hung with stamped leather. The floors are of parquet.

The grand staircase is enclosed in walls of Grinshill stone, with bands of Robin Hood and Forest of Dean. The steps are of Portland, and the balustrade of alabaster, carried on small shafts of various granites, in pairs. The ceiling is of oak, and is supported by massively-framed principals, filled in with tracery. At the second-floor level a bridge is thrown across for the use of the servants. The corridors in the east side are glazed with tinted quarry glass, and those on the west side with clear plate, so as to command a view of the park and the Welsh mountains. This staircase leads to the state apartments, which are on the first floor.

We have now described the principal apartments in the main building, and proceed to the north wing, the Grosvenor wing, the stables, &c.

In the north wing is the magnificent kitchen, lined with terra cotta, and a groined ceiling filled in with the same material. The Grosvenor wing is in itself a large house, and much space might be occupied with a description of it. It has a central hall, round which the principal apartments are ranged, and which is lighted by a centre light. From this hall, the principal staircase rises, and at the first-floor level a gallery is carried round it which gives access to the various rooms. The floor is of coloured mosaic, and the ceiling is decorated with heraldry. The apartments on the ground-floor generally have parquet floors and wainscot fittings and dados, and ceilings of plaster panelling in geometric patterns, enriched with colours. The duchess's room is panelled with views of Cliveden, Trentham, and Dunrobin, by O'Connor.

Plan

Document 14 is a plan for a relatively modest country house. It was designed by C. H. B. Quennell (1872–1935), who with his wife was later to be the author of children's social histories of outstanding quality. As late as the turn of the century (and, indeed, later) it was rightly assumed that a significant number of readers would be interested in building a house with ten bedrooms ("besides servants' rooms") costing £3,000. C. J. Cornish (1858–1906) was a naturalist and journalist.

14 C. J. Cornish   A River-side Mansion
Country Life (15 April 1899), 471

For the benefit of those of our readers who intend to build for themselves, we give some designs and elevations for a good house suited for any flat site, but more particularly meant to stand on those level meads which border the Thames, the Avon, or the other "full-fed rivers" of the South. Light and space are the two main features of the interior. There are five bedrooms and two nurseries on the first floor, and five bed-

rooms on the second, besides servants' rooms. Outside, the
gardens, terraces, and very large verandah are meant to make
the outdoor life around the house especially enjoyable. Boat-
houses have been omitted from the designs, because they can
be fitted in according to taste, and must be constructed with
reference to the amount of "shipping" the owner may wish to
keep.

The designs and plans in great part explain themselves. The
dwelling-rooms and reception-rooms, for instance, all look
towards the river. The verandah, a feature most appreciated
by the elder members of the family, is so spacious (18 ft. by
34 ft.) as to make a kind of winter garden if removable glass
screens are fitted into it, as they might be. Both drawing-room
and dining-room are directly connected with this verandah by
doors, and a third door leads into it from the corridor between
the two. But the feature of the interior is the billiard-hall and
conservatory.

The entrance is from a forecourt on the side furthest from
the river. From this a lobby leads to a broad flight of steps, at
the top of which is the billiard-hall, the largest and most
attractive room in the house. It makes a kind of general room,
in which all members of a large house-party can sit, chat,
read, play billiards, or do nothing, as suits them. In the ingle-
nook are two good oak settles on either side of the fire-place,
while above, on the same front as the mantel, are shelves to
hold such a stock of thoroughly sound books on sport, natural
history, and outdoor life as the proprietor may like to accumulate in this attractive room. The corridor flanking this holds
the stair-foot at one end and leads to the dining and drawing
rooms at the other.

On the opposite side from the corridor the hall gives into a
fine lofty bow-fronted conservatory, which extends not only
along the whole front of the hall, but also across the end of
the drawing-room, and makes not only a lounge, but a means
of communication between the two. Steps lead down from this
into the formal garden, beyond and behind which is the rose

garden. There is immense bedroom space above, two stories of large and well-lighted rooms. The gables are large and white, the roofs deep and substantial. Along the whole river front run two very long terraced walks, the lower one gravelled, the upper of turf. It is on this that the tennis-courts will be made, so as to run parallel with the river, and avoid the losing of balls, and of temper. The bay-window of the dining-room is carried up into the bedroom above, and rises from a small separate raised court, intended for outdoor breakfast in summer. The material of the house depends on local conditions, as it always should; but if in the Thames Valley, we may safely set it down as red brick and white plaster. The mouldings, window-frames, and mullions are all of solid and good design, without any "artists' fancies" or finicking ornament. The estimated cost of such a house is £3,000; and provision is made in the plan for extending it, if wanted, by building round the square at the back, and making a stable-yard and a curtilage.

Comfort

The French writer Hippolyte Taine (1828–93) wrote one of the best accounts of English life in the nineteenth century. His material was gathered mostly in the 1860s and revised in 1871. The country house (15), which he describes as within "forty or fifty miles from London", was clearly regarded as lavishly appointed, but it is without a bathroom; nor, obviously, did Taine expect one.

15 Hippolyte Taine   Notes on England
(1872; English translation 1872), 179–83

Their dwellings [are] huge machines, partly Italian or partly Gothic, without distinctive character. One sees that they are spacious, comfortable, well-kept—nothing more. These are the houses of the rich, who understand comforts, and who some-times rather unfortunately, have had architectural fancies; many elegant cottages, covered and encumbered with turrets, seem playthings in glazed pasteboard. All their imagination, all their national and personal invention, have been expended upon their parks. . . .

The house is a large mansion, rather commonplace, solid in appearance, arranged in modern style; the furniture of the ground floor and of the first floor, recently renewed, cost four thousand pounds. Three rooms or drawing-rooms, sixty feet long, twenty high, are furnished with large mirrors, good pictures, excellent engravings, with bookcases. In front is a glazed conservatory, where one passes the afternoon when the weather is bad, and where, even in winter, one can fancy that it is spring. Bedrooms for the young ladies who come as visitors; fresh, clear, virginal, papered in blue and white, with an assortment of pretty feminine objects and fine engravings, they are well fitted for their amiable occupants. As for the rest, the picturesque sentiment of decoration and of the arrangement of the whole is less keen than among us; for example, the objects and the tones are rather placed in juxtaposition than in accord. But there is grandiosity and simplicity; no fondness for crowding and for old curiosities. They readily submit to large bare plane surfaces, empty spaces; the eye is at ease, one breathes freely, one can walk about, one has no fear of knocking against the furniture. Attention is given to comfort, notably to what relates to the details of sleeping and dressing. In my bedroom, the entire floor is carpeted, a strip of oilcloth is in front of the washing-stand, matting along the walls. There are two dressing-tables, each having two drawers, the first is provided with a swing looking-glass, the second is furnished with one large jug, one small one, a medium one for hot water, two porcelain basins, a dish for toothbrushes, two soap-dishes, a water-bottle with its tumbler, a finger-glass with its glass. Underneath is a very low table, a sponge, another basin, a large shallow zinc bath for morning bathing. In a cupboard is a towel-horse with four towels of different kinds, one of them thick and rough. Another indispensable cabinet in the room is a marvel. Napkins are under all the vessels and utensils; to provide for such a service, when the house is occupied, it is necessary that washing should be always going on. Three pairs of candles, one of them fixed in a small portable table. Wax-matches, paper spills in pretty little holders, pin-cushions, porcelain extinguishers, metal extinguishers. Whiteness, perfection, softest tissues in every part of the bed. The servant comes four times a day into the room; in the morning to draw the blinds and the curtains, open the inner blinds, carry off the boots and clothes, bring a large can of hot water with a fluffy towel on which to place the feet; at midday, and at seven in the evening, to bring water and the rest, in order that the visitor may wash before luncheon and dinner; at night to shut the window, arrange the bed, get the bath ready, renew the linen; all this with silence, gravity, and respect. Pardon these trifling details; but they must be handled in order to figure to oneself the wants of an Englishman in the direction of his luxury; what he expends in being waited upon and comfort is enormous, and one may laughingly say that he spends the fifth of his life in his tub.

Discomfort

Lady Diana Cooper (b 1892), daughter of the eighth Duke of Rutland, is here describing (16) the rigours of life in Belvoir Castle, Rutland, before the death of the seventh Duke at the age of 88 in 1906. For a picture of warmer great houses which enjoyed a measure of central heating see F. M. L. Thompson. *English Landed Society in the Nineteenth Century* (1963), 92–3.

16 Diana Cooper   The Rainbow Comes and Goes
(1958), 27, 35–7

These passages in winter were arctic—no stoves, no hot pipes, no heating at all.

. . . There were the lamp-and-candle men, at least three of them, for there was no other form of lighting. Gas was despised, I forget why—vulgar, I think. They polished and scraped the wax off the candelabra, cut wicks, poured paraffin oil and unblackened glass chimneys all day long. After dark they were busy turning wicks up or down, snuffing candles, and de-waxing extinguishers. It was not a department we liked much to visit. It smelt disgusting and the lamp-men were too busy. . . .

The water-men are difficult to believe in today. They seemed to me to belong to another clay. They were the biggest people I had ever seen, much bigger than any of the men of the family, who were remarkable for their height. They had stubbly beards and a general Bill Sikes appearance. They wore brown clothes, no collars and thick green baize aprons from chin to knee. On their shoulders they carried a wooden yoke from which hung two gigantic cans of water. They moved on a perpetual round. Above the ground floor there was not a drop of hot water and not one bath, so their job was to keep all jugs, cans and kettles full in the bedrooms, and morning or evening to bring the hot water for the hip-baths. We were always a little frightened of the water-men. They seemed of another element and never spoke but one word, "Water-man," to account for themselves.

If anyone had the nerve to lie abed until eleven o'clock, which can seldom have happened, there were many strange callers at the door. First the housemaid, scouring the steel grate and encouraging the fire of the night before, which always burned until morning, and refilling the kettle on the hob until it sang again. Next the unearthly water-giants. Then a muffled knock given by a knee, for the coal-man's hands were too dirty and too full. He was a sinister man, much like his brothers of the water, but blacker far and generally more mineral. He growled the single word "Coal-man" and refilled one's bin with pieces the size of ice-blocks. . . .

Lastly there were the watchmen, who frightened many a newcomer to death. There was a little of the water-men about them, but they were dreadfully silent and they padded. All night they walked the passages, terraces and battlements, yet no one really saw them. One would leave a paper with a request (as one put a letter to Father Christmas in the grate) on the floor of the passage. The paper would disappear and the request would be granted by this remote, unseen power. Always if one woke in the night, as the fire flickered to its death, one would hear a padded foot on the gravel outside and a voice, not loud enough to waken but strong enough to reassure, saying "Past twelve o'clock. All's well."

Nothing changed until my grandfather died. . . .

As soon as the Castle became my father's property the old order began to change. Bathrooms were carved out of the deep walls, rooms and passages were warm without the coalman's knock, the water-men faded away into the elements. Forty strong horses turned to the power of one motor-car. Only the kettles remained, singing night and day on the hobs.

ARCHITECTURE, DESIGN AND ORNAMENT

House Size and Income

Manuals like Walsh's (17), aimed at the aspiring middle class, were in abundant supply (see also 5). The common Victorian dedication to an ordered class structure is here reflected in fitting the house to the income. It is significant how cursorily Walsh (1810–88), a writer on sporting and household subjects, dismisses the four- and six-roomed houses.

17 J. H. Walsh   A Manual of Domestic Economy Suited to Families Spending from £100 to £1000 a Year (2nd ed, 1857), 96, 99–100

Sect. 4. Plans of Houses Suited to Towns
SUB-SECT. A.—THE SIXTEEN-ROOMED HOUSE
. . . By carrying story over story a large and roomy house may be constructed, composed of sixteen rooms, besides dressing-rooms, and quite sufficient for any ordinary family. In it are good-sized dining and drawing-rooms, with a corres-

ponding family and eight bedrooms, in addition to two servants'
rooms in the roof. . . . The kitchens are underground, which is
universally the custom in London; but this will make little
difference, as, in case of there being room for them, they may
be easily added at the back under a separate roof. In a house
of this description the front and back walls require to be of a
solid construction.

. . . The whole of the work . . . can be executed at prices
varying from £1200 to £1800. This range provides for fluctua-
tions in the prices of materials, such as bricks, lime, &c., &c.,
which make a great difference in the outlay; and also for the
difference in the cost of chimney-pieces, grates, bath, &c., in
which items alone £100 or £150 may easily be added to the
lower sum mentioned. I am, however, inclined to think that
no one could build such a house without having had considerable experience in all the mysteries connected with
joiners, and other journeymen, at a less cost than £1500.

SUB-SECT. B.—THE TEN-ROOMED HOUSE

In this house, which is intended to afford a much more
limited accommodation than that last described, much is
sacrificed to economy; but still, for a small family, it may be
made very comfortable. The small size of the rooms precludes
all large social meetings, though not such as are perhaps most
conducive to comfort. The principle of the arrangements is
much the same as that already described, the variation being
chiefly in point of the number and sizes of rooms. This is the
ordinary style of London houses in inferior streets, which let at
an average of about £55 a-year, the rent rising and falling
according to the situation. Such a house, built pretty substantially with neat internal fittings, will cost in London from
£800 to £1000; but in many cases where an inferior class of
material is allowed to be used, £600 have covered the cost.
Here, however, the staircase must be of common description,
narrow and dog-legged.

SUB-SECT. C.—THE FOUR AND SIX-ROOMED HOUSES

These houses are calculated for persons having an income of

from £100 to £200 a-year, and they are composed simply of a basement-ground and first-floor, in each of which there are two rooms, or sometimes as follows,—namely—of a basement consisting of a kitchen and scullery, while the other floors are entirely occupied by one or two rooms and the staircase. They are seldom ornamented in any way externally, though in some few cases, of late years, such an attempt has been made by means of stucco and cement, covering very inferior brickwork, and only resulting in premature decay. It is seldom, however, that a plot of ground can be obtained to build one of these houses by itself, and therefore, it is quite useless to attempt any description of them. Indeed, as I have before remarked, it is very seldom the case in towns, that a house can be built with advantage to the occupier; and when such is the case, it is only in a superior style, when a plot of ground sometimes presents itself. In smaller houses, the ground which can be afforded is so limited, that it must in all probability be part of an estate; still this does sometimes offer itself at a fair price, and then it may be advantageously seized upon, and a house put up for about £50 per room, more or less according to circumstances. In this estimate the rooms are calculated at about 14 feet by 12, and 9 feet high, and the stairs of the commonest dog-legged construction. Supposing this to be the case, and the ground rent or interest of money sunk in the ground to be £2 to £5, then a house with six rooms ought to be obtained in this way for a rental of from £15 to £20, which is very little below the current rate, and therefore scarcely worth the investment.

New Materials

This description of the construction of the Crystal Palace (18) by the architect Matthew Digby Wyatt (1820–77), one of the moving spirits behind the Great Exhibition, reflects both the pride in Britain's industrial achievements typical of the period, and also faith in the new materials, glass and iron. Although many architects were prepared to extend a

cautious welcome (at least in principle) to the use of these
new materials, John Ruskin's opposition to "the ferruginous
temper which . . . has changed our merry England into the
Man in the Iron Mask" (footnote dated 1880 to *The Seven
Lamps of Architecture*, first published 1849), was the more
influential view in practice. The Crystal Palace was sneered
at as an enormous greenhouse, and not without some reason,
as its architect, Joseph Paxton (1801–65), was gardener and
architect to the sixth Duke of Devonshire, and had built a
huge conservatory at Chatsworth which served in part as a
model for the Palace. Plate glass, increasingly popular from
the 1850s, and iron were used more and more widely, as
Ruskin's comment suggests, but as primary architectural
materials they were not to come into their own until the
twentieth century.

18 Matthew Digby Wyatt   The Construction of the Building

In Robert Ellis (ed). *Official Descriptive and Illustrated Catalogue
of the Great Exhibition*, Vol I (1851), 49, 56, 80

That it should have been possible in any country to have so
speedily collected such a vast quantity of materials, without
previously sounding the note of preparation, would have
furnished strong evidence of the abundance of its native
resources, and conveyed some faint idea of the extent of the
stores of raw material kept ever ready to supply the exigencies
of sudden demand. That that raw material should have been
moulded into forms so various, so complex, and so original, in
so short a time, would argue that such a result could alone
have been effected by the natives of a country in which a
knowledge of the principles and practice of mechanics and
machinery had been long deeply studied and widely diffused.
The facility with which the machinery employed must have
been brought to bear upon the masses of raw material supplied,
would have evidenced a power to produce, and to elaborate

matter into manufacture, of the very highest order; while the grace with which the charm of decoration has been superadded, to so utilitarian a structure, would have served to show, that mindful as the English habitually are, of the practical and economical, they are by no means indifferent to the beautiful in the Fine Arts. . . .

In thus estimating the sufficiency of the girders, the load they might possibly be called on to support has been considered only as what is called "dead weight," or load to which no momentum of any kind had been imparted. In order, then, to test them under the action of a moving weight as well, a series of experiments was instituted. A perfect bay of gallery, 24 feet square, was constructed, with connecting pieces, girders, flooring, &c., complete. Its surface was first crowded with the contractors' workmen, as tight as they could be packed. The men were then set to walk over it, run over it, and, finally, to jump upon it with all their force.

In order further to observe the effects which would be produced by a load to which a uniform, instead of an irregular motion, had been conveyed, a number of soldiers of the corps of Royal Sappers and Miners were ordered to march over it, to run over it, and, finally, to mark time upon it in the most trying manner. The result of these experiments developed the correctness of the theory upon which the dimensions of the girders had been based, since not the slightest damage was done to the bay of gallery; and the fact was fully evidenced, that the quality of elasticity or springiness in the floor served to protect the girders from the effect of sudden shocks, and prevented the danger of the communication to them of the accumulating momentum, generated by the possible isochronous movements of a crowd.

Emboldened by the satisfactory result of these experiments, a yet more conclusive series was instituted. An apparatus was contrived by Mr. FIELD, the late President of the Institution of Civil Engineers, by means of which it was possible to draw, at a quick walking pace, over the whole of the galleries on which the public would have to tread, a number of 68-pounder shot, collected together so as to produce a uniform load of 100 lbs. per foot superficial. No damage whatever was produced by these rude tests, and they may be considered to have conclusively set at rest any doubts as to the sufficiency, in point of strength, of the gallery-floor, or of the girders which support it. . . .

The glazing of the nave roof presented formidable difficulties, from the great extent of work to be got through, in so short a space of time. The ingenuity of the contractors was, however, brought to bear upon the subject, and provisions were made by them for the simultaneous glazing of large areas, entirely independent of variations of weather. 76 machines were constructed, each capable of accommodating two glaziers; these machines consisted of a stage of deal about 8 feet square, with an opening in its centre sufficiently large to admit of boxes of glass, and supplies of sash-bars, putty, &c., being hoisted through it. The stage rested on four small wheels, travelling in the Paxton gutters, and spanned a width consisting of one ridge and two sloping sides. In bad weather the workmen were covered by an awning of canvas, stretched over hoops for their protection.

In working, the men sat at the end of the platform next to whatever work had been last done; from which they pushed the stage backward sufficiently far to allow them to insert a pane of glass, and as soon as that was completed they moved again far enough to allow of the insertion of another. In this manner each stage travelled uninterruptedly from the transept to the east and west ends of the building. The dexterity acquired by the men in working the machines was very remarkable. By means of them 80 men in one week put in upwards of 18,000 panes of glass, being not less than 62,600 feet superficial. The greatest number of panes inserted by a man in one day was 108, being 367 feet 6 inches of glazing. A somewhat similar machine has been constructed for the purpose of effecting any repairs that may be necessary in the finished roof, with the difference that its wheels travel upon the ridges instead of in the gutters, and that of course there is no aperture for the purpose of hoisting.

Gothic Style

Although the "battle of the styles" between classical and gothic architecture endured until at least 1870, the gothic cause had abler propagandists and, for a time, seemed to have the best of the argument. The later revival of "Queen Anne" and Georgian styles were still in the future. Here is Ruskin, one of the most determined exponents of the gothic style and most influential of Victorian writers, preaching the faith (19). What may bemuse a much later generation is the quality of Christian morality which the "Goths" felt characterised their chosen style of architecture.

19 John Ruskin Lectures on Architecture and Painting

(1854), 52–3, 102–3, 107–8

These pediments, and stylobates, and architraves never excited a single pleasurable feeling in you—never will, to the end of time. They are evermore dead, lifeless, and useless, in art as in poetry, and though you built as many of them as there are slates on your house-roofs, you will never care for them. They will only remain to later ages as monuments of the patience and pliability with which the people of the nineteenth century sacrificed their feelings to fashions, and their intellects to forms. But on the other hand, that strange and thrilling interest with which such words strike you as are in any wise connected with Gothic architecture—as for instance, Vault, Arch, Spire, Pinnacle, Battlement, Barbican, Porch, and myriads of such others, words everlastingly poetical and powerful whenever they occur,—is a most true and certain index that the things themselves are delightful to you, and will ever continue to be so. Believe me, you do indeed love these things, so far as you care about art at all, so far as you are not ashamed to confess what you feel about them. . . .

Do not be afraid of incongruities—do not think of unities of effect. Introduce your Gothic line by line and stone by stone; never mind mixing it with your present architecture; your existing houses will be none the worse for having little bits of better work fitted to them; build a porch, or point a window, if you can do nothing else; and remember that it is the glory of Gothic architecture that it can do *anything*. Whatever you really and seriously want, Gothic will do for you; but it must be an *earnest* want. It is its pride to accommodate itself to your needs; and the one general law under which it acts is simply this,—find out what will make you comfortable, build that in the strongest and boldest way, and then set your fancy free in the decoration of it. Don't do anything to imitate this cathedral or that, however beautiful. Do what is convenient; and if the form be a new one, so much the better; then set your mason's wits to work, to find out some new way of treating it. Only be steadily determined that, even if you cannot get the best Gothic, at least you will have no Greek; and in a few years' time—in less time than you could learn a new science or a new language thoroughly—the whole art of your native country will be reanimated. . . .

. . . The main gist of the propositions which I desire to maintain may be reduced under six heads.

1. That Gothic or Romanesque construction is nobler than Greek construction.

2. That ornamentation is the principal part of architecture.

3. That ornamentation should be visible.

4. That ornamentation should be natural.

5. That ornamentation should be thoughtful.

6. And that therefore Gothic ornamentation is nobler than Greek ornamentation, and Gothic architecture the only architecture which should now be built.

"Queen Anne" Style

Unadorned red brick (characterised but not inaugurated by the Red House, Bexleyheath, designed in 1859 by Philip Webb for William Morris) was used in place of classical stucco or more elaborate gothic from the early 1850s. However, this so-called "domestic revival" did not mark the abandonment of the gothic style. It was not until the early 1870s that a new style of architecture became fully established. This "Queen Anne" style (really "a mixture of William and Mary with Louis XIII motifs", Nikolaus Pevsner in Peter Ferriday, ed. *Victorian Architecture*, 1963, 239) pointed the way towards the simpler architecture of the future. John J. Stevenson (1831–1908), whose own Red House on Bayswater Road, London (1871, now destroyed), was an important early example of the Queen Anne style, was an architect and architectural writer. Although his lecture (20) may seem almost comically sententious, it is both a major explanation and justification of the Queen Anne style and a statement of some of the forces which were to lead to the modern movement in architecture. The best known of the "Queen Anne" architects was not Stevenson but Richard Norman Shaw (1831–1912).

20 J. J. Stevenson Of the Recent Reaction of Taste in English Architecture
Building News (26 June 1874), 689–90

Both those who favour the reaction and those opposed to it admit that Queen Anne architecture violates Classic rules; and that it is of native growth as much as Gothic is. Nor are the combatants the same as in the old well-fought battle of the styles. The peculiarity of the present movement is that the upholders of this form of Classic are the same men who have hitherto been devotees of Gothic; who thought it, as I confess I used to think it, an abandonment of principle to use any other style, who practised it in its severest forms, and even thought Chartres Cathedral a little too late; some of whom, acting as if they thought the monuments of English history ceased to be of value or interest after the sixteenth century, and, regardless even of what used to be thought the respect due to the memory of the dead, have helped to clear out of the old Churches of England every vestige of what they considered debased Pagan taste with as much zeal as ever Puritan purged Church of idolatrous images. That these men should have been carried away by what Mr. Ruskin calls "the foul torrent of the Renaissance," and polluted themselves with what another writer calls "the abominations of Sir Christopher Wren," and fallen in love with a style which the upholders of Classic and Gothic equally denounced as base, degenerate, and corrupt, seems to require some explanation. Of the fact there can, I think, be no doubt. There has been an awakening in the minds of some men, who formerly cared nothing for any style but Gothic, to the interest and merit in Queen Anne architecture. One architect told me that going back after a long absence to the office where, full of youthful enthusiasm for Gothic, he had served his apprenticeship, he was astonished to find that it contained a most beautiful Georgian staircase, which he at once wished to measure, but which, though he had gone up it every day for five years, he had never before noticed. Another, not an architect, but interested in art, told me that he had lately been surprised and delighted with the beauty of Hampton Court Palace, which on a former visit, some years before, he had found disappointing and uninteresting. We see also buildings in this style, the work of architects brought up on Gothic. Nor is the movement confined to architecture. The pre-Raphaelite School of painters have abandoned the purity and restraint with the stiffness and imperfection of Mediaeval-ism, and glory in the fulness of physical life, and the richness and freedom of Classic ideas. There are, I believe, true evidences of a reaction in taste. The rise in the price of Queen Anne furniture and chimney-pieces, pounds scarcely buying now what shillings bought a few years ago, is evidence merely that the movement has become fashionable, and consequently in danger of becoming vulgarised. Some assert that the whole movement is a mere fashion, first started by Dante Rossetti, and imitated by his followers. As well say the Gothic revival was an imitation of Pugin or of Horace Walpole and his Strawberry Hill. Pioneers like these are not causes, but the first results of the causes which move the waves of the world's history. Their distinction lies in being taller than their fellows, and their eyes being the first to catch the beams of the new light that is rising. In fact the architectural movement in each case is the sequence of a previous religious and literary movement. As in the new light of French Revolution doctrines, the few vestiges of the Middle Ages which had survived the Renaissance were passing away, there revived in the feeling of the time an appreciation of the glory, and chivalry, and adventure of the Middle Ages, of their religion also, and subsequently of their art. In England, this reaction to Middle Age ideas has strongly influenced the more imaginative minds; since the time of Sir Walter Scott, their religion, poetry, and art, have been Mediaeval. It was a natural and living movement, and for this very reason subject to the law of all living things, change, growth, and development. The feeling grew that there are elements of modern life which not Middle Age chivalry nor asceticism, nor Gothic architecture, were fitted to satisfy. The naturalism and emotionalism, the absence of restraint and conventionality, and also of refinement, began to pall, and men turned, as in the sixteenth century the generation trained in the same Mediaeval ideas had turned, for satisfaction of the wants they felt rising in their nature to the treasures of Classic literature, to the Classic conception of life, glorifying in full, healthy, natural outcome, yet moving in measured rhythm, and to the heart which is the manifestation and expression of such life. Minds which have passed through this process found in the forms of Renaissance art, produced under a similar process three centuries before, the expression of their own thoughts and feelings. Correct rigid Classic art had no interest for them.

They had still too much of the life and freedom of Gothic in their souls to submit to be bound down to ready-made lifeless rules. To Classic art in them the infusion of the Gothic spirit gave—what the infusion of Gothic blood had given to the worn-out civilisation of the later Roman Empire—new spirit and new life and the hope of higher development. The springing up of a taste for some form of free Classic architecture is therefore not unnatural, but was to be expected in those who had drunk deeply of Gothic. And the form of free Classic which thus arose was naturally determined by local conditions. Englishmen working in brick, and using sliding sash windows according to the custom of the land (a custom the necessity of complying with which has ever been a thorn in the side of modern domestic Gothic), found the natural expression of their feelings in the brick architecture of the restoration of Queen Anne and the Georges. This architecture has neither the exquisite grace and refinement of Greek, nor the romance and high aspirations of Gothic, but it is perhaps not, therefore, the less suited for the common daily wants of English life.

Voysey and the 1890s

The 1890s witnessed the coming of a more significantly modern style, drawing on both the gothic and classical pasts. The most influential pioneer of the decade was Charles Francis Annesley Voysey (1857–1941), who designed houses which, while in a very English idiom, were characterised by a distinctive and idiosyncratic style of his own. "His work was controlled by his love for simplicity and by his respect for materials and for the customs of the English craftsman" (John Brandon-Jones in Peter Ferriday, ed. *Victorian Architecture*, 1963, 283). Voysey was also a pioneer in the design of furniture, fabric, wallpaper and other fittings, down to cutlery. An artistic journal like *The Studio* gave Voysey its enthusiastic support in the 1890s, rather before the more strictly architectural journals. (The house referred to in Document 21 was designed at Tooting, London.) Charles

Rennie Mackintosh (1868–1928), a more original architect than Voysey, had much less influence in Britain in this period.

21 Horace Townsend   Notes on Country and Suburban Houses Designed by C. F. A. Voysey
The Studio (April 1899), 157–8, 160, 162

It is not so very many years since it was almost a truism among the architectural profession that the architect who wandered from the strait and narrow path and took to designing furniture, wallpapers, and so forth, had committed a species of professional suicide. . . .

The "new architect" nowadays designs the interior, including furniture, hangings, and so forth, of his house, quite as much as he does the exterior. No one in our day, perhaps, has been so completely successful in this respect as Mr. C. F. A. Voysey. To introduce Mr. Voysey to the readers of THE STUDIO were absurd, so familiar are they with what I may almost call, without laying myself open to a charge of exaggeration, his epoch-making work in the decorative field. His furniture, with its broad simple effects, its reliance on proportion, its eschewal of useless ornament, and its strikingly original lines, has helped to form a school of its own, while his wall-papers and textiles strike an equally personal and individual note. Mr. Voysey is a designer who is guided, as one need not study him long to perceive, by very definite and certain principles, and, as the accompanying illustrations will serve to show, his architectural work is to just the same extent subservient to these same principles. Simplicity of thought and perfection of proportion distinguish it from the ordinary architecture of the day. Notable, too, is the deliberate avoidance of style; and here it is that only one or two of contemporary architects at the most are working to the same end as Mr. Voysey, and endeavouring, by an educated distrust of following too closely on the lines laid down by the craftsmen of the past, to so impress what they do with their own individualities, as to present us with a nineteenth-century architecture. Whether they be right or wrong, it seems at least certain that by no slavish adherence to tradition has any living, breathing architectural style of bygone centuries come into existence, valuable and necessary as have been the lessons taught by the artists of previous generations. . . . The long stretch of reposeful roof of green slates, the dressings to windows and doors are of Bath stone, while the walls are of rough-cast. Mr. Voysey's preference for this last-named form of finish—which is marked, by the way—is based, so he tells me, mainly on its economy. He considers a nine-inch brick wall faced with cement rough-cast is as warm and weather-tight as any much more expensive construction; but, at the same time, I imagine he is unconsciously attracted by the artistic value of these great spaces of cream-coloured surface, possessing a texture of their own, and peculiarly lending themselves to Mr. Voysey's stylistic sympathies. . . .

I may say in passing that Mr. Voysey characterises himself as a "stickler for light," though, by those who lend a mere surface consideration to his work, he is often found fault with for the smallness of his windows. He points out, however, that such critics do not take into consideration the size and height of the rooms these long low windows are intended to give light to. In proportion to a lofty room a low room, he avers, needs much less window space. It is not the mere cubic contents which have to be taken into account; the real essential is the amount of reflecting surface in the room itself. In a low room the entire ceiling acts as a reflector, and throws the light downwards into every corner of the interior. This, again, is, as a rule, supplemented by Mr. Voysey through the employment of a deep whitewashed, or otherwise light-tinted, frieze as a feature in his decoration of the wall space. I may say in passing, as might be gathered from the above remarks, that Mr. Voysey is not only an advocate for light, but also for low rooms. They are pleasanter to live in, according to him, they are cheaper, they lend themselves more easily to the securing of pleasing proportion in design, and they are, contrary to general opinion, quite as easily ventilated as lofty ones. One of Mr. Voysey's rare outbursts of temper was directed, while I talked to him recently, against those inconsiderate clients who endeavoured to insist upon his adding a foot or two to the height of a second storey, regardless of the fact that by doing this the entire proportion, that is to say, the main beauty, of their house must be sacrificed.

Theories of Design

Victorians took the theory of design seriously. Conscious that much executed design was of poor quality, they tried by rigid rules to raise standards. Unfortunately, when theorists turned designers, their own work was often little better than that they criticised. Ralph N. Wornum (1812–77) was one of the more influential mid-century writers on the subject; the tenth edition of his book (22) appeared in 1896. With William Morris (1834–96) we come to one of the titans of Victorian art, design, writing and thought (23). His own design, while wholly Victorian in concept and execution, greatly helped to improve standards and had enormous influence in the last third of the nineteenth century. Thus the *Spectator* wrote of Morris: "His power is proved by his many imitators. Nearly all the better kind of designs in the shops are . . . cribs from Morris" (24 November 1883, 1508). Dorothy Peel in *The New Home* (1898) said that Morris was "a man whose glory it is that he first discovered and made war upon the peculiar ugliness of Victorian domesticity. . . . Nothing was too small, too trifling, for his revolutionary zeal" (ix–x). Oscar Wilde (1856–1900) may in this passage (24) be merely engaging in his chief sport, to *épater le bourgeois*, as Sir Nikolaus Pevsner suggests (*Pioneers of Modern Design*, 1960 ed, 27), but an increasing number of architects, designers and writers shared his view of machinery and utility.

22 Ralph N. Wornum   **Analysis of Ornament** (1856), 6, 8, 10–11

Ornament is one of the mind's necessities, which it gratifies by means of the eye; and, in its strictest æsthetic sense, it has a perfect analogy with music, which similarly gratifies the mind, but by the means of a different organ—the ear. . . .

There are two provinces of ornament—the flat and the relieved. In the flat, we have a contrast of light and dark; in the relieved, a contrast of light and shade; in both, a variety of effect for the pure gratification of the sense of vision. Much is common to both; but in the first case, a play of line is the main feature, in the second, a play of masses, and colour may be an auxiliary to either; but it acts with far greater power in the flat, as it is entirely dependent upon light.

Ornament, therefore, is a system of contrasts: the object of study is the order of contrasts. The individual orders may vary to infinity, though the classes are limited, as right-line or curved-line series, series of simple curves or clustered curves, series of mere lines, or natural objects, as flowers, arranged in the orders of these different series. For example, the common scroll is a series of spirals to the right and left alternately; the Roman scroll is the Acanthus plant or brank-ursine, treated in this order of curved series. . . .

Any picture, whatever the subject, which is composed merely on principles of symmetry and contrast becomes an ornament, and any ornamental design in which these two principles have been made subservient to imitation or natural arrangement has departed from the province of ornament into that of the picture or the model, whichever it may be. And in nearly all designs of this kind, applied to useful purposes, you frustrate the very principle of nature, upon which you found your theory, when you represent a natural form in a natural manner, and yet apply it to uses with which it has, in nature, no affinity whatever. Therefore, however you may conform with Nature in little matters, you certainly commit an outrage upon her in great matters.

This is a class of ornament which has much increased of late years in England, and, by way of distinction, we may call it

V.H.—c

the *naturalist* school. The theory appears to be, that as nature is beautiful, ornamental details derived immediately from beautiful natural objects must ensure a beautiful design. This, however, can only be true where the original uses of the details chosen have not been obviously violated; and one peculiar feature of this school is, that it often substitutes the *ornament itself* for the thing to be ornamented, as illustrated in the accompanying examples; in which the natural objects are so mismanaged as to be *principals*: flame proceeding from a flower, a basket on an animal's head to hold a liquid, a bell made of leaves!

23 William Morris   The Beauty of Life
A lecture delivered and published in 1880 as "Labour and Pleasure versus Labour and Sorrow", reprinted in *Hopes and Fears for Art* (1882), 107–10

Believe me if we want art to begin at home, as it must, we must clear our houses of troublesome superfluities that are for ever in our way: conventional comforts that are no real comforts, and do but make work for servants and doctors: if you want a golden rule that will fit everybody, this is it:

"*Have nothing in your houses that you do not know to be useful, or believe to be beautiful.*"

And if we apply that rule strictly, we shall in the first place show the builders and such-like servants of the public what we really want, we shall create a demand for real art, as the phrase goes; and in the second place, we shall surely have more money to pay for decent houses.

Perhaps it will not try your patience too much if I lay before you my idea of the fittings necessary to the sitting-room of a healthy person: a room, I mean, in which he would not have to cook in much, or sleep in generally, or in which he would not have to do any very litter-making manual work.

First a book-case with a great many books in it: next a table that will keep steady when you write or work at it: then several chairs that you can move, and a bench that you can sit or lie upon: next a cupboard with drawers: next, unless either the book-case or the cupboard be very beautiful with painting or carving, you will want pictures or engravings, such as you can afford, only not stop-gaps, but real works of art on the wall; or else the wall itself must be ornamented with some beautiful and restful pattern: we shall also want a vase or two to put flowers in, which latter you must have sometimes, especially if you live in a town. Then there will be the fireplace of course, which in our climate is bound to be the chief object in the room.

That is all we shall want, especially if the floor be good; if it be not, as, by the way in a modern house it is pretty certain not to be, I admit that a small carpet which can be bundled out of the room in two minutes will be useful, and we must also take care that it is beautiful, or it will annoy us terribly.

Now unless we are musical, and need a piano (in which case, as far as beauty is concerned, we are in a bad way), that is quite all we want: and we can add very little to these necessaries without troubling ourselves, and hindering our work, our thought, and our rest.

If these things were done at the least cost for which they could be done well and solidly, they ought not to cost much; and they are so few, that those that could afford to have them at all, could afford to spend some trouble to get them fitting and beautiful: and all those who care about art ought to take great trouble to do so, and to take care that there be no sham art amongst them, nothing that it has degraded a man to make or sell. And I feel sure, that if all who care about art were to take this pains, it would make a great impression upon the public.

This simplicity you may make as costly as you please or can, on the other hand: you may hang your walls with tapestry instead of whitewash or paper; or you may cover them with mosaic, or have them frescoed by a great painter: all this is not luxury, if it be done for beauty's sake, and not for show: it does not break our golden rule: *Have nothing in your houses which you do not know to be useful or believe to be beautiful.*

24 Oscar Wilde Art and the Handicraftsman
(c1882), *Essays and Lectures* (1908; 6th ed, 1928), 175, 177-8

People often talk as if there was an opposition between what is beautiful and what is useful. There is no opposition to beauty except ugliness: all things are either beautiful or ugly, and utility will be always on the side of the beautiful thing, because beautiful decoration is always on the side of the beautiful thing, because beautiful decoration is always an expression of the use you put a thing to and the value placed on it. No workman will beautifully decorate bad work, nor can you possibly get good handicraftsmen or workmen without having beautiful designs. You should be quite sure of that. . . .

Do you think, for instance, that we object to machinery? I tell you we reverence it; we reverence it when it does its proper work, when it relieves man from ignoble and soulless labour, not when it seeks to do that which is valuable only when wrought by the hands and hearts of men. Let us have no machine-made ornament at all; it is all bad and worthless and ugly. . . . All machinery may be beautiful when it is undecorated even. Do not seek to decorate it. We cannot but think all good machinery is graceful, also, the line of strength and the line of beauty being one.

Adornment

Robert Kerr (1823–1904), an architect and leading architectural writer, wrote this highly successful manual (25) for the middle- and upper-class householder. Here we find some words of good advice, intended perhaps for William Langshawe (see 27).

25 Robert Kerr The Gentleman's House; or How to Plan English Residences, from the Parsonage to the Palace
(1864), 99-100

In remarking upon the quality of elegance, it was clearly laid down that English taste amongst the superior orders is averse to rich or sumptuous effects. Excessive adornment, you will be truly told, is almost invariably vulgar, and at the best barbaric. Nevertheless, to let the question rest here, and so repudiate the ornamentation of our dwellings altogether, would be an act of morbid archaicism, which English gentlemen, and still more English ladies, would not approve. Moderation in this, as in all else, is the rule, but nothing less; no exuberance, but no poverty. For there may be even in simplicity an affectation as demonstrative as any other; and when the fastidiousness of excessive refinement takes refuge in a mental blank, it is but an artificial idiocy in taste. A Gentleman's House, in short, whilst it ought to be free of ostentation, ought to be equally free of any opposite extreme. If we see a family of wealth and rank, and of otherwise accomplished taste, dwelling within flat brick walls surmounted by red chimney-pots, we say there is an incongruity here. If we see stately entertainments conducted with all the manifestations of wealth, and with the aids of choice and valuable furniture and plate, paintings, and perhaps sculpture, in rooms whose walls and ceilings are helplessly devoid of decoration, the contrast is absurd. Every one will affirm, therefore, that a Gentleman's House ought to be not merely substantial, comfortable, convenient, and well furnished, but fairly adorned. It ought to exhibit a reasonable amount of intellectual liberality, faithfully keeping on the side of simplicity and moderation, and clinging to the grace of elegance as the beauty which will last the longest; but avoiding none the less that poverty of dress which is not self-denial, but inhospitality.

Description of Design

Documents 26–31 give some idea of Victorian design in practice, from the extravagant gothic popular early in the reign to the much more restrained and simple design favoured by the artistically minded some 50 years later.

Augustus Welby Northmore Pugin (1812–52), designer as well as a leading exponent of gothic architecture, lays vigorously about him, admitting his own "guilt" in the process (26). The Lancashire novelist and historian Elizabeth Stone (27) guys the home of the typical *nouveau riche* millowner whom genteel novelists were fond of snubbing, and certainly her description of the crowded drawing room of William Langshawe contains the ring of truth. *Cassell's Household Guide* (28) was one of the many manuals on household taste; its sensible precepts were somewhat weakened by the pedestrian illustrations which accompanied the article. One of the marked features of mid-Victorian design was the eclectic style about which *Cassell's* had reservations; here Mrs Haweis (1852–98), an artist and popular writer on design, encouraged eclecticism, "a medley, directed with taste" (29). H. J. Jennings (30) describes a style popular shortly before his own period, making gentle fun of the immediately out-dated. But, as he suggests, the heavy designs of the mid-Victorian period moved towards lightness and greater simplicity, and, together with the contrasting but comple-mentary work of the Morris school, the light or subdued colours of the "aesthetic movement" dominated fashionable design in the 1870s and 1880s. Finally, the architect and designer Baillie Scott (1865–1945), a follower of Voysey, describes an interior which, while looking back to Morris and English traditions (with a great hall, timbered walls and a somewhat baronial fireplace), nonetheless points the way to the uncluttered simple bright interiors of the twentieth century (31). It should be noted that English design in the 1890s was distinct from the Art Nouveau style popular on the Continent.

26 A. W. N. Pugin The True Principles of Pointed or Christian Architecture

(1841), 23–4, 40–2

It is impossible to enumerate half the absurdities of modern metal-workers; but all these proceed from the false notion of *disguising* instead of *beautifying* articles of utility. How many objects of ordinary use are rendered monstrous and ridiculous simply because the artist, instead of seeking the *most convenient form*, and *then decorating it*, has embodied some extravagance *to conceal the real purpose for which the article has been made!* If a clock is required, it is not unusual to cast a Roman warrior in a flying chariot, round one of the wheels of which, on close inspection, the hours may be descried; or the whole front of a cathedral church reduced to a few inches in height, with the clock-face occupying the position of a magnificent rose window. Surely the inventor of this patent clock-case could never have reflected that according to the scale on which the edifice was reduced, his clock would be about two hundred feet in circumference, and that such a monster of a dial would crush the proportions of almost any building that could be raised. But this is nothing when compared to what we see continually produced from those inexhaustible mines of bad taste, Birmingham and Sheffield. . . .

The modern admirers of the pointed style have done much injury to its revival by the erroneous and costly system they have pursued: the interiors of their houses are one mass of elaborate work; there is no repose, no solidity, no space left for hangings or simple panels: the whole is covered with trifling details, enormously expensive, and at the same time subversive of good effect. These observations apply equally to furniture;—upholsterers seem to think that nothing can be Gothic unless it is found in some church. Hence your modern man designs a sofa or occasional table from details culled out of Britton's Cathedrals, and all the ordinary articles of furniture, which require to be simple and convenient, are made not only very expensive but very uneasy. We find diminutive flying buttresses about an armchair; every thing is crocketed with angular projections, innumerable mitres, sharp ornaments, and turreted extremities. A man who remains any length of time

in a modern Gothic room, and escapes without being wounded
by some of its minutiæ, may consider himself extremely fortunate. There are often as many pinnacles and gablets about a
pier-glass frame as are to be found in an ordinary church, and
not unfrequently the whole canopy of a tomb has been trans-
ferred for the purpose, as at Strawberry Hill. I have perpetrated
many of these enormities in the furniture I designed some years
ago for Windsor Castle. At that time I had not the least idea
of the principles I am now explaining; all my knowledge of
Pointed Architecture was confined to a tolerably good notion
of details in the abstract; but these I employed with so little
judgment or propriety, that, although the parts were correct
and exceedingly well executed, collectively they appeared a
complete burlesque of pointed design.

27 Elizabeth Stone   William Langshawe, the Cotton Lord
(1842), Vol I, Chapter II

The drawing-room in which Mrs. Langshawe received her
visitors was as splendid as money could make it. The furniture
and the decorations were, however, all good—the best of their
kind; but there was an *elaboration* in the style, and a profuseness
in the ornaments, that savoured more of a heavy purse than a
cultivated taste. The walls were hung with silk damask, finished
off by massive gold cornices and mouldings, or draped round
the magnificent mirrors extending almost from the ceiling to
the ground, which reflected the forms of a fair bevy of ladies,
whose garments were not certainly their least noticeable
appendage. The couches, the ottomans, the bosses, the buhl
timepiece, the profusion of ornamental trifles that glittered
around; the choice exotics in the recesses, the elegant china
ornaments, and the magnificent cut-glass chandelier which
sparkled like diamonds in ten thousand different hues, and,
gleaming in the mirrors, gave the idea of a fairy-land vista
opening on every side—these, each in itself fit for the mansion
of a nobleman—were yet clustered and crowded incongruously.

They were, however, not merely collected, but, comparatively speaking, naturalized in the house of this lowborn and uneducated cotton manufacturer.

28 Principles of Good Taste in Furniture
Cassell's Household Guide, Vol 3 (nd; 1869–71), 77–9

It has long been a common practice . . . to adopt some general style, as Greek, or Gothic, or Renaissance; or some particular branch, as Elizabethan or Louis Quatorze; and to have the building and the furniture all designed in the one style; and by adopting this course, since each style of the past has its own peculiar spirit and characteristics, if these are not departed from, uniformity will necessarily follow. But great want of taste is often manifested by the indiscriminate mixture of various styles of ornament between which there is not the least affinity. Perhaps the wall-paper consists of a diaper in the Moresque style, from which natural forms are strictly excluded, while the carpet design is composed of flowers and foliage naturalistically treated; and maybe, the sideboard is covered with Elizabethan strapwork, while the chairs and mirror are of Renaissance designs. Such inconsistencies are by no means uncommon, and indicate great want of taste and judgment. But in many cases it is not practicable to have the whole of the furniture and enrichments of one style; nor do we believe, as many do, in the desirability of adhering thus rigidly to some particular style, or period, of art, and of reproducing the characteristic details again and again with literal exactness.

Such imitation and repetition have already been overdone, and we much prefer to see uniformity which is not dependent upon the correctness with which ornaments of a past style have been copied, but which arises from some similarity and congruity observable in the general character and treatment of the decoration throughout at least the one apartment, or throughout the whole house.

Let us illustrate our meaning. Suppose, for instance, that our taste inclines us to admire ornament which consists chiefly of natural forms, whether vegetable or animal, like the Gothic artists of the middle or decorated period, who introduced flowers, and foliage and animals, and the human form, in every conceivable combination. Adopting this *naturalism* as our leading principle, we introduce natural forms throughout the enrichments. We choose for our wall-paper a pattern of some simple diaper, consisting of a geometric basis filled in with leaves. For our carpet we choose . . . [a] pattern . . . in which flowers and foliage are also arranged on a geometric basis. We not only thus choose to have geometric forms mixed with the natural forms on our floor and wall, because it is well adapted for distributing the ornament over a large surface, but also because these, being the inferior parts of the decoration, should have the lower class of forms; the higher forms—such as imitations of groups of flowers, fruits, animals, and the human figure—being reserved for the more important features. We choose for our table one with animals crouching underneath, or, if less elaborate, say with animals' feet only; and our chairs have similar terminals to their legs, and a little carved foliage or fruit on the legs and back; and the sofa or couch is designed in the same spirit. In our sideboard or chiffonier, we introduce more richness still. Here the forms may be less conventionalised, and groups of flowers and fruit, of animals or human figures, may be arranged in the panels, or on the back and at the top. At the top of our mirror, and at its lower angles, we have some simple arrangement of natural forms—not too heavy, nor too attractive and fantastic; and the scrolls to the gaselier pendant are foliated, and the balance-balls and globes have neat and appropriate designs, consisting also of natural forms.

Thus there is a harmony and uniformity observable in the whole scheme of decoration, and each object looks as if designed with reference to all the rest. . . .

Again, if our taste incline us towards a more geometric and

conventional kind of ornament, we should in like manner carry the same treatment throughout the furniture and decorations. We must not have in one place a floral design, with all the details carefully copied from Nature, while in another part we have mere geometric forms and conventional foliage, as in the Moresque decorations. . . .

We see two treatments so utterly opposed in spirit that to place them in the same room would show the greatest ignorance of ornament, and want of taste. Each object indicates a distinct style of ornament, and whichever is selected should be accompanied by objects, which both as to their general structure and decoration, are in keeping with it.

The first thing to be considered in the selection of objects of furniture is their suitableness, both as regards size and shape, and these should be regulated by their intended position and use. Fantastic shapes should be studiously avoided; and as simplicity rarely offends, it is far better, as a rule, to select forms which are simple and unassuming. In determining the size, too, it is better to choose furniture which is a little small than such as appears large and cumbrous. A room never looks well when the objects of furniture look disproportionately large. It is best to avoid excess; and it is a better fault not to go far enough than to go too far where the furniture is too large for the room, or too elaborately shaped or decorated or disproportionated to the position and means of the owner, it always has an appearance of vulgarity, which is easily avoided by keeping on the side of simplicity and unpretentiousness.

Some seem to think that you cannot have too much of a good thing, and that the more ornament you can introduce the better. This, however, is a great mistake, for such excess of elaboration marks the degeneracy of most styles of ornament, while in the best periods of art simplicity has generally been one of the leading principles. . . . This leads us to another important consideration: viz., the method of ornamenting furniture. So far as possible, it is best to let the ornament arise out of the construction, and not to appear as if stuck upon the surface without any other connection with the object; but it too often happens that the piece of furniture is regarded only as offering a surface which must be covered with decorations; and ornaments as large in size and quantity as possible are merely spread over it, without any adaptation or thought about suitableness.

29 Mary Haweis   The Art of Decoration
(1881), 201, 206–7

To make a beautiful and artistic room it is not sufficient to collect a mass of good materials, and mix them together. You may spend a fortune at a fashionable decorator's, and make your house look like an upholsterer's showroom; or you may fill your house with antiquities of rare merit and calibre, and make it look like an old curiosity-shop; but it may be most unpleasing all the same.

The furnishing ought to be carried out on some sort of system; and this is especially difficult when the taste is already refined enough to prefer ancient art to new. For it is easy enough to buy cartloads of goods, but the temptations offered by each century in succession, each country in turn, make it impossible to carry out a definite plan without heroic self-control. Old Oriental, genuine old English (say fifteenth century Gothic), early Renascence, Louis XIV., or genuine Queen Anne, and genuine Georgian, all hold out beckoning fingers of welcome.

The aimless conglomeration of totally discordant periods and schools may be utterly confusing and unpleasant; although there *is* a mode of arranging an eclectic style of room which has very great advantages, eclectic and discordant being understood to differ. . . .

An avowedly modern room (one in which modern upholstery prevails) always seems to me injured by the introduction of antiquities, which, like peculiar shades of colour, and certain classes of ornament, always require *carrying out* of the picture.

They injure the modern manufactures by putting out their light (according to the connoisseur), or by 'looking shabby' (according to the Philistine); and after all they almost disappear in their places, lost and overpowered by the more self-asserting shapes and dyes of machine-cutting and distillation, like timid waifs hunted about and pecked to death.

Thus a modern eclectic room may admit modern Oriental objects in sufficiently small quantities, Indian, Chinese, African, and the like, modern German, Swiss, and Russian carving and casts, Italian mosaics, Doulton ware, Minton's china and tiles, and all the best efforts of the nineteenth century. But a medley overstepping the limits of a few hundred years, unless for some very good reason, becomes unpleasant, because the incongruities are powerful enough to strike even the most ignorant.

The distinction between an eclectic room furnished upon some reasonable system, and a room furnished after a given period, must here be noted. The one is really a medley, directed with taste; the other reproduces a scene which a contemporary might have viewed, and must have *no anachronisms*.

30 H. J. Jennings   Our Homes and How to Beautify Them
(1902), 55–6

It was at the beginning of the "eighties" that the extravagances of the pseudo-aesthetic school evoked the pictorial satire of du Maurier and the brilliant ridicule of Gilbert. That the Cimabue Browns, the Postlethwaites, the Maudles, and the Bunthornes, were treated in a spirit of caricature cannot be denied. But the satire was not launched at mere creatures of fiction. The people attacked were real people. The school to which they belonged was a travesty of true aestheticism. Effeminate, invertebrate, sensuous, and mawkish, this school would have ended, if it had not been laughed out of existence, in making the very name of art contemptible. It had its aspostles in the decorative world, who proclaimed with oracular and superfine airs the saving grace of brick reds, sage greens, and peacock blues, of mediaeval furniture, of subdued lights and cunningly arranged draperies. No drawing room under its sanctions was complete without an array of blue and white ginger jars, bowls of lilies, peacocks' feathers, Japanese fans, and—culminating proof of true discipleship—a dado. Yes, the dado became a shrine! Everybody who aspired to be thought somebody, was a worshipper at this shrine. No middle class house was considered perfect without it. Anyone with social aspirations might as well have spoken disrespectfully of the Thirty Nine Articles as have left the dado out of his scheme of decoration. The lady whose rooms had dadoes looked down on the lady whose rooms had none. So rapidly did the cult of the dado spread, that in a little while a movement was seriously started by some society or other for "encouraging" it in the working man's cottage. A caustic wit, scornful of the craze, wrote a set of verses to a plantation air, and lashed the folly with a vitriolic pen. Here are a couple of the verses:

Oh sweet adornment for the cottage wall,
  Dado, dado;
Oh poverty's sure solace whatso'er befall,
  Dado, dado, da;
To dream of thee all night,
To gaze on thee by day,
Is the proletarian's supreme delight;
  Dado, dado, da.

When the grate is empty and the cupboard bare,
  Dado, dado;
When the Briton's tugging at his wife's back hair,
  Dado, dado, da;
How rapturous to mark
Thy grades of green and gray,
Where the farthing dip dispels the dense, dim, dark;
  Dado, dado, da.

It says a good deal for the merits of the dado that it should have survived the extravagant and indiscreet advocacy which provoked these lines. It would have been no great wonder if, as a consequence of its appearance in the cheap suburban villa, the dado had by this time become as extinct as the dodo.

Gone is the so-called "aesthetic movement" with all its fantastic folly. Its affectations no longer flourish. Its once popular drawing rooms, with their peacock's feathers and Japanese tea trays no longer exist. Blue and white teapots are no longer "Intense"; the gospel of the "Too, Too" falls no more on receptive ears; society has forsworn the creed that "the Incongruous is the expression of the Utter".

But it must in fairness be admitted that the aesthetic movement, of which this craze was but the rank growth, sowed precious seed. People began to realise that it was possible to make their homes more beautiful. William Morris, Walter Crane, and other greater designers devoted their skill to the improvement of decorative art. The Century Guild led the way in an appreciation of the best examples of 18th Century English furniture. A return to the ugliness of the Early Victorian period—a return even to the artificial Gothic revival—was made impossible.

31 M. H. Baillie Scott   An Ideal Suburban House
The Studio (January 1895), 128–31

Passing from the hall into the drawing-room, we find ourselves in a long low room, which, in the delicacy and daintiness of its treatment, presents a pleasing contrast to the broad and homely character of the hall. The woodwork is here all finished white, and the walls are covered with a wallpaper of soft green leafage, amongst which glows golden fruit with the blue sky between. Above is a broad frieze where, amid flowing leafage, blooms the flower that never grew on sea or shore.

The furniture is simple and dainty in design, and everything in the room is disposed with quiet dignity of effect, while conspicuously absent are the host of so-called decorative articles which make locomotion perilous in so many drawing-rooms, and which tempt one to exclaim with the carpenter through the looking-glass, "If these were only cleared away, oh, wouldn't it be grand!" The pictures are few and choice, not dotted over the walls, but carefully grouped. Everything, in short, appears to have been specially designed to fit its particular position in the room, and we feel that the aim has been not to try and get as many pretty things as possible crowded together, but rather to eliminate as far as possible everything which is unnecessary. Here again simplicity is hand in hand with economy, and the price of the thousand and one nicknacks which destroy the repose of the average drawing-room is saved.

And here one may insist that the great advantage of a well-designed house is that it requires none of that palliative furniture which becomes a necessity in the average house to hide defects of proportion and construction. There are no large expanses of plate-glass windows to shroud in curtains, and no handsome marble mantelpiece to drape. Our object is, in fact, rather to display the beauties than hide the defects of the house, and so a far less amount of furniture is required than is usually considered necessary. The dining-room next claims our attention, and here we have a treatment more in character with the hall. In the fireplace we have revived the old-fashioned chimney-corner, with the addition of a hood of hammered copper to take the smoke from the fire. The whole of the back of the recess which forms the chimney-corner is in red brick, the joints not too neatly finished, and the brick-work not too uniform in tint. On the wide hearth a wood fire may be made, or a fire-basket in wrought-iron may be used for coal. A small window high enough up to prevent draughts is to give light at the fireside, and ventilation if required.

The seats at the sides of the fireplace are made sufficiently wide and low for comfort, and are fixed at just the right distance from the fire. On the beam over the chimney-corner is carved an appropriate motto, and in the half-timber-work frieze above is framed a mezzotint portrait. The ceiling shows the joists with a central massive beam, while the sideboard is specially designed for its position in the recess at the side of the fireplace. A separate door near the sideboard may be used for serving. The dining-room as well as the hall and drawing-room is floored with oak and pitch pine in narrow boards laid alternately, and these are covered in the drawing-room with a carpet and in the hall and dining-room with rugs. The contrast between the oak and pitch pine boards tends to emphasise the lines formed by their edges, and thus adds to the perspective effect of the vista when the movable screens between the rooms are taken down. . . .

The staircase is carried out in the same homely and picturesque style as the hall and corridor. . . . To the right and left extend passages from which the bedrooms open.

In the treatment of the bedrooms, of which there are five on this floor, it is suggested that as much variety as possible should be introduced. One bedroom may be finished in white enamel, with perhaps a blue wall-paper; another may be treated in golden yellows or flame tints; while a third may suggest the homely character of the hall. In any case, it must be borne in mind that a definite final effect should be aimed at, and the room should not present the usual accumulation of articles, which, however pretty in themselves, bear no actual relation to a definitely conceived scheme. In selecting the furniture, it is easier to point out what to avoid than what to choose. On the one hand, we have the handsome mahogany suite; on the other, the "Art" suite in painted deal, neither possessing the quality of simple dignity which is regarded as essential. The use of "fitments" will often result in a very good effect, but they should be used with due consideration of their limitations in rooms which are sufficiently broken up in their outline to suggest this method of furnishing.

SANITATION AND WATER SUPPLY

Water supply, pipes and drains form one of the most important and least known aspects of the Victorian home. However, analysis of change is not always easy, since what was being preached at the start of the period was often still not practised at its end. Thus we have that fascinating character John Claudius Loudon (1783–1843), landscape gardener, writer and architect, discussing baths (32) in 1838, many years before they were common even in wealthy families. J. H. Walsh discusses baths and water closets (33) growing in use if not in efficiency in the mid-century. His readers must have raised their eyebrows to learn that baths were "fixed in most good houses" and that constant hot water had become "almost a necessary in all well-regulated families". Lord Ernest Hamilton (1858–1939), son of the first Duke of Abercorn, shows that indifference to plumbing was common in aristocratic circles in his youth (34). The Rev Henry Moule (1801–80) was the inventor (in 1860) and fervent enthusiast for the earth closet (35), which he makes sound almost attractive; and the difficulties involved in house plumbing are graphically illustrated by the letter in *The Scotsman* (36), which also indicates the contemporary concern with ventilation. To some writers, indeed, ventilation seemed almost to be an adequate substitute for sanitation.

S. Stevens Hellyer, a leading plumber and writer of sanitary texts, attacks the then outdated but still common pan water closet, and discusses the reluctance of middle-class families to install baths (37). The section on water closets was newly written for the third edition of his book, and as late as the sixth edition, in 1900, Hellyer was still hotly attacking the pan closet which, though condemned by the Local Government Board, was still being produced. The section on baths was written for the first edition, in 1877; the significant footnote was added to the third edition.

The familiar gas "geyser" was first produced in the later 1860s; here (38) *The Builder* gives optimistic details of an improved version. Finally, H. J. Jennings, writing in 1902, takes the bath for granted and makes suggestions for decorating the bathroom (39).

32 J. C. Loudon   The Suburban Gardener and Villa Companion
(1838), 675–6

The Bath-room, when for the use of the family generally, may be on the ground floor, or on the bed-room floor of the house, as may be most convenient; but a bath should never be placed either in a bed-room or in a sitting-room, because, when a hot bath is used, the quantity of steam produced fills the atmosphere of the room, and, condensing on whatever furniture it may contain, necessarily renders it damp. The advantage of having the bath-room on the ground floor is, that hot water may be more conveniently supplied to the bath from the cistern at the back of the kitchen fireplace; and the advantage of having it on the bed-room floor is, the convenience and saving of time in using the bath in the morning before dressing, or at night before going to bed. Where there are dressing-rooms to the bed-rooms, a bath may be placed in each of these, or in such of them as may be thought necessary; and the water may be heated in the room by a fireplace and small boiler, properly constructed for that purpose; or it may be pumped up from the boiler at the back of the kitchen fireplace, or brought down in pipes from a boiler placed in a room in the floor above, or in a garret. . . .

The size of the bath-room need not be large, because it is not understood to contain a swimming-bath, but only one for immersion. For this purpose, as the bath need not be larger than 8 ft. in length and 3 ft. in breadth, a room 8 ft. by 10 ft. in the clear might suffice, the bath being along the narrowest end, the fireplace on one side, a window on that opposite, and a door on the side opposite the bath. A room 10 ft. or 12 ft. square, however, will be more convenient.

33 J. H. Walsh A Manual of Domestic Economy
(2nd ed, 1857), 61, 63

Water-closets are now fixed at all prices, and of a countless
variety of forms. Nothing, however, in my opinion, comes up
to the construction which has been so many years in use, and
which is called the *pan closet*. But, though very few people are able
to superintend this part of the work, and it is better left to the
supervision of a respectable plumber, where such a man can
be trusted, yet the general principles of constructing this
article, so subservient to our comfort, should be known by all
those who undertake the building of a house.

. . . Baths are fixed in most good houses of the present day,
and are either supplied with hot and cold water from an
apparatus of their own, or else from a boiler and cistern used
for other purposes. The bath itself is either of tin, galvanized
iron, copper, or marble,—or sometimes of slate, or of composition, or of earthenware, which are now rapidly coming
into use. The price of these varies greatly, from the galvanized
iron—costing about 30s.—to the marble bath, which may be
calculated at 1s. 6d. per foot super. (veined marble being
almost always used), in addition to the cost of laying in
cement. The composition bath is a very clean and useful
material, and superior to marble, it being free from all danger of
breakage. Its cost is about £4 or £5, according to the distance
from the seat of manufacture. The best and cheapest mode of
supplying these baths, when often wanted to be used with hot
water, is to attach a wrought-iron boiler to the back of the
kitchen fire; this communicates with a copper cistern placed
above the level of the bath by means of two pipes, one of
which opens into the top, and the other into the bottom of
both the boiler and the cistern. From the constant interchange
of particles which takes place in water submitted to the action
of heat, it follows that there is a continual stream of hot water
ascending through one pipe, and cold descending through the
other; and in this way the water in the cistern, if favourably

placed, may be made to boil at a distance of thirty feet from the kitchen fire; and of course this is sufficient to supply any bath with its hot water. But there is one objection, in point of economy, where coals are dear. The continual supply of hot water at a distance necessarily takes off a great quantity of caloric from the fire, which must therefore be kept larger by means of more coals than if wanted for no other purpose than cooking. Consequently, when a bath is only occasionally required, and yet the hot water is always kept ready, it is a very expensive mode of supplying this luxury of life; and it is cheaper in such a case to have a small copper and flue expressly for heating the water. Here, again, however, there is often great difficulty in finding room up-stairs for the purpose; and, on the whole, I believe the boiler at the back of the kitchen fire is in most houses the best method of furnishing the bath with warm water. Besides which, the constant supply of hot water has now become almost a necessary in all well-regulated families, whose wants in this respect therefore demand a daily and liberal allowance, and not a scanty and occasional one.

34 Ernest Hamilton   Old Days and New
(nd; 1923), 87–8

There were no such things as hot baths in the modern sense. Every big country house, it is true, boasted one or more large iron tanks encased in mahogany, evidently designed to do duty as baths and—judging from their size—designed to accommodate several people at once. At one end of these tanks was a brass dial on which were inscribed the words "hot," "cold" and "waste," and a revolving handle manoeuvred an indicator into position opposite such of these inscriptions as a prospective bather might be attracted to. When the indicator pointed to "cold," there was a free response in the shape of a flow of clear, clean water, which made its appearance through a small circle of perforated holes in the bottom of the bath. A call on the hot water supply, however, did not meet with an effusive or even a warm response. A succession of sepulchral rumblings was succeeded by the appearance of a small geyser of rust-coloured water, heavily charged with dead earwigs and bluebottles. This continued for a couple of minutes or so and then entirely ceased. The only perceptible difference between the hot water and the cold lay in its colour and in the cargo of defunct life which the former bore on its bosom. Both were stone cold.

In the face of such uninviting conditions, it can readily be understood that these huge enamelled iron tanks were not popular as instruments of cleanliness. In fact, although Eastwell and Barons Court, two big country houses in which much of my early youth was passed, each boasted two of such baths, I have never heard of any of the four being used for the purposes for which they were no doubt originally designed. As boys, my brother and I found the lower bath at Eastwell admirably suited to the trial trips of our toy boats; and at Barons Court, where we had no toy boats, it was our practice to use the ground floor bath as an occasional aquarium.

35 Henry Moule   The Advantages of the Dry-Earth System in the Disposal of Sewage and Excreta

Transactions of the National Association for the Promotion of Social Science (1870), 429–30, 432

(*a*.) The first and fundamental principle, is the now well-known property of earth or clay, and especially of dry and sifted or powdered earth or clay, to deodorise extreta and other offensive matter, and to stay or check putrefaction. (*b*.) In connection with this, however, there is another principle, not so well-known, though of almost equal importance, namely, the limit of this power of deodorisation. This I affirm to be the saturation of the earth used by the vapour and liquid of the excreta, &c. For within an hour or two after the earth in the

receptacle of a closet should become so saturated with urine
as to approach at all to the consistency of mud, the escape of
ammonia, which with a proper use of earth is not to be per-
ceived, would in that case be distinctly perceptible. (c.) A
third principle, of vast importance—especially in the event of
the introduction of the dry-earth system into towns—a principle,
however, which, although discovered and published ten years
ago, is still to many incredible is this, apparently so opposite to
the former principle—that dry earth possesses for purposes of
deodorisation, and of restraint of putrefaction, the capability
of repeated action or use. When after use in a closet it becomes
thoroughly mixed with the excreta and is dry, its deodorising
power is then as great as ever, and it may so be used, with
equal efficacy, five, ten, or twenty times. In the introduction
of the system into towns, the advantage arising from this must
be self-evident; since the requisite supply for any given town
for a twelvemonth may thus, by four uses during that period,
be reduced 75 per cent. . . .

Take a population of 1000 souls, and compare the systems
with respect to this. For its sewerage there would be required
about 30,000 gallons of water daily. That volume of water has
no deodorising power. All that it does in the way of cleansing
is to shift the nuisance from the individual premises. Subsequent
to this it aids in the generation of foul gases in the sewers, and
these may find their way back into every house that is furnished
with a water-closet or a sink. It then is worse than wasted,
either in the pollution of some stream, or now, perhaps, of
some tract of land. Now mark the contrast, and the twofold
advantage here of the dry earth system. The excreta of a
population of 1000 souls shall, if it be passed through dry-earth
closets, be not just shifted from the house and premises into
the sewer, there to become more offensive; but there shall be
complete deodorisation and inoffensive removal, and all shall
be kept out of the sewers, and prevented from polluting rivers
and fields, *by the use of two tons of earth a day!* Mark it; two tons
of earth against 30,000 gallons of water a day!

36 House Drainage

Pseudonymous letter by 'J' in *The Scotsman* (21 August 1877), 3,
reprinted in *The British Architect* (24 August 1877), 98

Sir,—Last winter I bought a large and expensive house in
the west end of Edinburgh. It was newly built and thoroughly
ready for occupation. Before purchasing, I had it inspected by
a first-rate professional man, who pronounced it in all respects,
so far as he could see, excellent in material and workmanship. Its architects are of the first rank; the tradesmen were
all pronounced first-class. Naturally I was a pleased proprietor.

Not many weeks, however, had we been in occupation when
we became conscious of an objectionable smell in several of the
apartments. Clerk of works and other experts pronounced it an
escape of gas; and after much searching among the always
carefully hidden pipes, a leakage caused by a nail driven
through one of them was found, and stopped. Still the smell
continued; at times faint, at times well-nigh intolerable; a
subtle and evasive smell, sometimes worst at one place, sometimes at another. New wood, new varnish, new plaster, new
furniture, new paint and papers, were all suggested as causes;
but comparisons of like material in rooms where there was no
smell ultimately shut off all plausibilities of that kind. From
the first I had felt pretty certain that the evil which we had to
deal with was a drain smell, an influx of sewage gases. But
from a peculiarity of the place where the smell usually most
strongly asserted itself—it would be tedious to explain that
peculiarity minutely here—I was at first almost baffled in
maintaining my belief; for the place indicated had no communication with drains. At last, however, by patient examination we *nosed* out the main defect; as King Jamie did the
Gunpowder Plot—not exactly in a cellar, but in an under
floor. Finding so serious a flaw in the arrangements of a
pronounced perfect mansion, I determined on a complete
personal inspection of cisterns, closets, and of the water, soil, and

ventilation pipes all through the house. In the course of that inspection we discovered:—

1. Of five cisterns, not one was ventilated.

2. Of those five, three supplied water at once to water-closets and for cooking and drinking purposes.

3. That two water-closet cesspools were ventilated by a pipe carried up to the roof, past sitting-rooms and bed-rooms, *in the inside of the house.*

4. That the two great drain pipes—one carrying only rain water from the roof, the other carrying the whole of the water used within the house, and half the roof rain water also—ventilated themselves, *and the sewers*, by opening, one at the slates under the eaves, the other flush with the flat portion of the roof. In spite of traps, both of course stank abominably.

5. That one of the cisterns was so placed that, in case of anything going wrong with a water-closet right above it, the foul water must fall into the cistern beneath—a general supply one.

6. That none of the water-closets had any provision against an overflow arising from accidental derangement of wires, valves, or the like. One has twice overflowed, and saturated the ceiling below.

Here, surely, were causes enough for any amount of smells, for any number of perils by water, and for intolerable apprehension of more serious mischief from sewage air.

37 S. Stevens Hellyer   The Plumber and Sanitary Houses

(1877; 3rd ed, 1884), 176–7, 188, 192, 234–5

No water-closet is perfect which does not get rid of every vestige of excrement after usage by one pull of the closet handle, *i.e.*, a water-closet which is not completely cleansed together with its trap and soil-pipe by a fair flush of water—say three gallons—is not a perfect closet. And yet if the water-closets throughout the United Kingdom were examined, not

ten in a hundred would be found to free themselves, and their
traps, much less their soil-pipes, of every piece of paper, and
every particle of excrement, after being used, by one pull of
their handles. . . .

A water-closet to be perfectly wholesome must have all its
belongings made sanitary. Some imagine that an offensive
closet can be remedied by changing the apparatus. As well
might a policeman put a new hat upon a drunkard's head and
expect it to make him sober, as for a plumber to put a new
water-closet apparatus upon a foul or defective trap and expect
thus to make a wholesome water-closet. "What's bred in the
bone will come out in the flesh" is an old adage; and what's
bred in the trap or soil-pipe will come out into the closet. . . .

It has always been a puzzle to me to understand how such
a water-closet as a pan-closet should become so great a favourite
with architects, plumbers, and the public. The only "bliss"
that the public can have about so foul a thing is "ignorance"
of its nature, but what excuse to make for architects and
plumbers I know not, except that it was the custom of their
fathers to specify and to fix pan-closets, and this has become a
law with them. . . .

The pan-closet dies hard, for notwithstanding all that has
been said and written upon its unsanitariness, it is still largely
used both in London and the Provinces. "You see, sir, the
stuff is out of the pan so quickly, and I have fixed 'em all my
life." . . .

Instead of a bath in a house being the exception, it ought to
be the rule. But one may as well look for a fountain in a desert
as for a bath in any of our old English houses.* It is not too
much to say that there are scores of villages in England without
a single bath in the entire village, except perhaps in the rector's

* English people are beginning to see the value and comfort of full-sized
baths with hot and cold water, and no *new* house *now* in London and the
suburbs is considered complete without this modern "luxury". I consider
that no house, of any fair size, is complete unless it has at least two baths,
one for the family and one for the domestics.

or squire's house. And many of our towns are scarcely better off, I am afraid, in this respect.

To mention a bath-room to a landlord or householder is to paint before his mind's eye, in a single word, the Bankruptcy Court. And to talk about having hot-water circulation throughout a house is to plunge landlord and tenant into *hot water*. And yet it is astonishing how far a sovereign will go, especially when drawn out into a thin gold wire. Instead of having to pay £30 or £40 for fitting up a bath, as many imagine, this can be done at any cost between £10 and £100.

If a West of England broadcloth is too expensive, fall back upon fustian, for any coat is better than no coat at all. And if a luxurious bath-room, with all its convenient appurtenances, cannot be afforded, have a *make-shift* one; for "cleanliness is next to godliness," and any kind of bath is better than none at all.

Everybody should be induced to cultivate a habit of personal cleanliness by a bath fitted up with hot as well as cold water. And the poorer the family the greater the need, perhaps, for such a bath.

38 A New Water-Heater
The Builder (2 July 1892), 11

There is no doubt about the utility of the Rapid Water-Heater, or "Geyser," as it is very commonly called, but notwithstanding the useful part it fulfils, there is a prejudice against them amongst the general public, due wholly to their having been accountable for some rather serious mishaps from time to time. This was when they were first introduced, and before being as well understood as now; but, of course, prejudices of this kind are slow to die. Of the accidents that occurred, there were two or three causes discovered which naturally led people to suppose that the articles were unusually productive of danger, but now the accidents have occurred, and the causes are known, it is hardly likely that opportunity will be given for similar mishaps to occur again. The chief sources of trouble were—firstly, the possibility of having the heating chamber, where the gas-burners are, full of gas before the match was applied, so that a more or less violent explosion occurred at ignition. This is remedied in various ways by making ignition only possible when the burners are drawn out from the chamber in question. Secondly, and what has proved most disastrous, is the free escape of all burnt gases, products of combustion which are of a dangerously poisonous character, into the room. Many bath-rooms are small, and could very quickly become dangerously full of these products, as the quantity from such a number of burners is large, and possibly the little room may have no fireplace to ventilate it. What fatalities have occurred were due to conditions such as these. Every rapid water-heater should have a flue, and the flue must be effective, otherwise the results may very possibly be more harmful than if no flue existed.

We have received a prospectus of the "Calda" rapid water-heater, of a somewhat new design, made by Mr. G. Shrewsbury. It is almost entirely made of copper, and is of the kind that does not have the heat imparted to the water direct, but has the water separated from the source of heat by the sheet copper of which it is composed (the direct and indirect methods are matter of much discussion). Another point in its favour, as against some of the other makes, is that it cannot, without special trouble, be emptied of water. It will be understood that if a "Geyser" can be quite emptied of water, and then the gas is ignited before turning the water on, that there may be some disagreeable phenomena and possible injury to the apparatus. As this heater discharges water from its top, it can be placed down on the floor if desired instead of over the end of the bath. It is quite adequate as regards the rapidity with which the water is heated, and the necessary element of safety in lighting is provided for, but Mr. Shrewsbury considers that no flue is required with his creation, and this is where we disagree. His heater can be made with a flue if desired, so purchasers have every opportunity of ensuring this element of safety if they desire, and we should strongly recommend everyone who thinks of using a *rapid* water-heater to have it connected or provided with an efficient chimney. With that caution, this heater may be safely recommended.

39 H. J. Jennings   Our Homes and How to Beautify Them
(1902), 236, 239

At a pinch it might be possible to live a tranquil, and even a useful, life without a drawing room. It might be possible, under the stress of circumstances, to make one room serve the purposes of both breakfast room and dining room. But there is a room which no self-respecting householder can do without, and that is the bath room. One can only marvel at the astounding fact that, prior to twenty or thirty years back, the majority of small and medium-sized houses, and perhaps fifty per cent. of the larger ones, were built without bath rooms. If there be any truth in the proverb "Cleanliness is next to Godliness," what an ungodly time it must have been before the new order of things. For although a bath room is not absolutely indispensable to cleanliness, it distinctly encourages it. The morning "tub" is much more inviting when you have a comfortable room, properly fitted up, in which to take it. And a bath room should be not only properly fitted up, but appropriately decorated as well. It is outside the scope of this book to go into details of sanitary appliances, or to discuss the various improvements which scientific sanitation has effected. My duty is confined to the decorative possibilities of the bath room, and let me say at once that simplicity should be the keynote. You can have the walls covered with washable paper, or with glazed tiles. You can have the floor covered with linoleum in a tile design, or with cork carpet. Nothing more is wanted: anything more would be superfluous. Everything in the bath room should, on sanitary grounds, be easily cleaned; for this reason glazed tiles are the very best treatment. If, however, you live in a rented house, and do not care to go to the expense of improving the landlord's property, the tiles may be dispensed with, and a serviceable bath-room paper, in a tile pattern, used for the walls instead.

HEAT AND LIGHT

Early Versions of Central Heating

As with plumbing, with heating precept outran practice. J. C. Loudon (40) and Samuel Brooks (41) discuss versions of central heating, and Loudon indicates some of the difficulties. He concluded both prophetically and pessimistically: "The time, doubtless, will come, when a heating apparatus will be considered as an essential part of all houses of a certain size; and for smaller houses in streets, along a railroad, or at no great distance from one another, warm air may be supplied, as gas and water are now, by public establishments; but these improvements are too far distant for any practical use to be made of them in this work" (p 61). Early and mid-Victorian schemes for central heating were common enough, but in practice the difficulties were almost always insurmountable. (See Mark Girouard. *The Victorian Country House*, 1971, 15–16.) William Strutt (1756–1830), millowner and inventor, devised the Belper stove in 1806; it is described in Charles Sylvester's *The Philosophy of Domestic Economy* (1819).

40 J. C. Loudon　The Suburban Gardener and Villa Companion
(1838), 58–9

Various plans have been adopted, within the last twenty years, for adding to the comfort of houses, both in town and country, by the introduction of some general system of warming and ventilating them, so as to supersede, in a great measure, if thought desirable, the use of open fireplaces. The objects in

view are, generally, a more equal diffusion of heat, and a
saving of fuel; and both have, in many instances, been attained,
in connexion with the renewal of the air, so as to render the
houses so heated as wholesome to live in as those heated by
open fireplaces; though, in by far the greater number of cases,
the heating, and the economy of fuel, have been effected without
due regard to ventilation, and the result has, consequently,
proved injurious to the health of the occupants of the house.
Up to 1814 and 1815, almost the only mode for warming the
temperature of the air of halls and staircases was by the placing
of German or Swedish stoves in them; the former being built
of brick, and generally covered with Dutch tiles; and the latter
being wholly of cast iron. The first grand improvement upon
this mode was made by Mr. Strutt of Belper, near Derby,
about 1807; who, soon afterwards, introduced this improved
system of heating into his manufactories, the Derby Infirmary,
and his own dwelling-house in Derby. It was afterwards made
public by Mr. Sylvester, in 1820, in his work entitled the
Philosophy of Domestic Economy. Mr. Strutt's apparatus was
placed in the lowest part of the house or building to be heated,
and consisted of an immense iron pot (called a cockle, from the
circuitous passages formed round it for the passage of the air
to be heated), placed in an inverted position, with the fire
under it, and a constant stream of fresh air from the atmosphere
passing over it. This air, being heated to 80° or 90°, was carried
by air-flues into all the principal rooms of the house; while,
the fireplaces being left open, a portion of the air in the rooms
escaped by the chimneys, equal to that thrown in by the
heating apparatus. It would occupy too much space in this
work, to enter much into detail on this subject; otherwise, it
would be easy to show that Mr. Strutt's principle, that of
introducing fresh air along with fresh supplies of heat, is the
only principle which combines a due regard to the health of
the occupants of the house, with the other objects in view. Mr.
Strutt's mode of heating (or, as it is generally called, Sylvester's
mode) has been introduced into numerous private houses, with

different degrees of success; but, partly from the management of the apparatus not being thoroughly understood; partly from the difficulty of introducing it, so as to be thoroughly effective, in houses already built; and partly from the difficulty of getting servants to attend regularly to apparatus of this, or of any other description; but chiefly to another mode of heating (by hot water) having come into fashion; it is now very generally given up. Another reason why it has been given up is, the liability of this plan to overheat the air, and deprive it of its moisture; more especially in cases where the persons managing the stove do not understand that, when an increased temperature is wanted in the rooms heated, it is not to be produced by raising the temperature of the air introduced (which is always understood to be about 80°, or a few degrees more or less), but by introducing the air in greater quantities, which is done by producing a more rapid current.

41 Samuel H. Brooks Designs for Cottage and Villa Architecture
(nd; 1839), 130, 133

Of all conductors, the metals are the best, and consequently, if they are brought into connection with any body hotter than themselves, they will receive a portion of its heat by conduction. We have an instance of this, in the method of heating buildings by the circulation of hot water, or hot air, in iron pipes. The water being raised to a temperature of 212 degrees, and continually circulating, imparts a considerable amount of its heat to the pipe through which it flows. The air is in contact with the external surface of the pipe, and is also heated by conduction. A certain number of particles of air, if we may so speak, surround the pipe, and receiving an increased temperature by contact, expand and rise. Another series of cold particles then take their place, and in the same manner are heated. It is thus by a rapid change of particles round the centre of heat, that the whole atmosphere is in a short time brought to a higher temperature, and made suitable to the wants or comforts of those who are to live in it. . . .

Of the conduction of heat we have an excellent example in the system of heating buildings by hot water or steam circulating through metallic pipes. All hot-air stoves produce their effects by the principle of conduction; for air being made to circulate through a space in which it is acted upon by some source of heat, escapes into the apartment in which they are placed at a temperature much higher than that it has under common circumstances.

Open or Closed Stoves?

The disadvantages of closed stoves are summarised here, though perhaps the "air-tight" and central heating were not quite so injurious to patriotism as Nathaniel Hawthorne and Mrs Stowe seemed to think (43). The *Illustrated London News* refers to stoves displayed at the Great Exhibition (42).

42 Heat, and its Application
Illustrated London News (24 May 1851), 460

From the nature of the fuel, we are led to consider the contrivances in which the fuel is burnt, and the Exhibition is particularly rich in stoves of various denominations. For ordinary dwelling apartments great advances have been made in modern times, the tendency being to place the fire almost level with the feet, with the unsightly ashpit completely concealed from view. These stoves, whilst they are in the highest degree elegant, are costly in their construction, and great care should be taken that they be not placed sufficiently near any woodwork to cause its ignition. We remember to have seen Sir Robert Peel, within a few days of his death, studying one of these stoves with great interest, at the *soirée* of the Civil Engineers, and he took away one of the papers with him to study it more at ease. We shall certainly recommend no person who can afford it to be without this form of stove; for the heat

V.H.—D

being applied at the very bottom of the room, is diffused more genially through the apartment; and the lower parts of the body, which, with long sitting, are so particularly liable to feel cold, derive warmth more readily than with the ordinary grates. These stoves are furnished with bright, reflecting surfaces, to throw the heat into the room; and in one case we noticed the fire-place to be placed about the focus of a parabolic reflector, which distributed the rays of heat in a parallel manner.

In our opinion, the simple radiating and reflecting stove is incomparably superior to any other form for rooms in which persons ordinarily dwell. There is a form exhibited by Mr. Pierce, which he terms the pyro-pneumatic stove, which has not only an open fire-place, but which has a contrivance by which air is admitted from without and circulates through the room. The objection we raise to all these stoves is the effect which they have in causing currents of over-dry air to pass through the apartment, and which have somewhat the effect of a blighting easterly wind. The regulation of the moisture of the air by such contrivances is possible, but difficult; and, therefore, upon medical grounds, we do not admire their use in ordinary dwelling apartments. For churches, halls, and other places where extensive areas have to be warmed, and the room is only used for a short time, they may, doubtless, in many cases, be adopted with advantage.

We must consider, for many reasons, that any close stove is perfectly abominable for dwelling-rooms. In the first place, the blazing fire is lost to view; then, the radiant heat, acting upon the skin in a cooler room, has a different and more salutary effect than warmer air without the radiant heat.

43 Harriet Beecher Stowe   Sunny Memories of Foreign Lands
(1854), 145

As I have spoken of stoves, I will here remark that I have not yet seen one in England; neither, so far as I can remember, have I seen a house warmed by a furnace. Bright coal fires, in grates of polished steel, are as yet the lares and penates of old England. If I am inclined to mourn over any defection in my own country, it is the closing up of the cheerful open fire, with its bright lights and dancing shadows, and the planting on our domestic hearth of that sullen, stifling gnome, the air-tight. I agree with Hawthorne in thinking the movement fatal to patriotism; for who would fight for an air-tight?

English or American Heating?

The American practice of scoffing at British plumbing and heating, now at last beginning to die out, has an old lineage. Here Stephen Fiske (1840–1916), the drama critic, producer and author, and only American of these three writers, has some harsh things to say about British practice (44), while J. J. Stevenson (45) and Mrs Haweis (46) defend British "adherence to old customs" and in particular the cheerful open fire. It may be questioned how often American rooms reached 100°F or how many English people were happy at 55°F.

44 Stephen Fiske   English Photographs
(1869), 192–3, 196–7

There is an excellent chance for some speculative showman—some British Barnum—to realise a moderate fortune by importing to this country, erecting and exhibiting, an American house. I do not mean a specimen of the log-cabins in which a large proportion of my countrymen are supposed to reside, nor a model of the modest White House, at Washington, which is made to serve as a poor substitute for a Presidential palace; but I mean an average American house, such as those which are erected in all the cities of the United States for the residences of the middle-class population. Compared with a dwelling of this kind, the middle-class houses in England seem destitute equally of comfort and convenience, although those who have never been accustomed to anything different or better consider them quite comfortable and convenient enough for all practical purposes. But then different people have different minds. An Englishman absolutely believes that he can warm a room by building a grate-fire at one end of it. An American visiting this country is in a continual shiver, his face being scorched and his back cold, or *vice versâ*, until he becomes thoroughly acclimated, and learns that the most healthy warmth is that which exercise in the open air imparts to the blood. . . .

If there be a bath-room in an English house, it must answer for the whole household. If there be a lift, it stops at the dining-room floor, although coals and water have to be carried to the higher stories. If hot and cold water be laid on, it is only in certain select apartments. Ventilators are almost unknown, except, perhaps, that antiquated sort which are let into the windows. Heated air is considered unhealthy, and so the ladies and children sit before the grate-fires with shawls over their shoulders, and catch cold in order to prevent injuring their lungs. Gas is making its way into all English houses now, but is still forbidden to be used in sleeping-apartments, although the smoke from even a wax-candle is hardly preferable to the odour of the small amount of gas which can possibly escape. No stranger can live for a week in an English house and not be ill from exposure to the chilly halls and stairways, even if he succeed in making himself comfortable before the fire. The English wrap themselves up to cross the hall as though they were going out of doors. Refrigerators are comparatively a new invention here. Iced water is vetoed as injurious to the teeth. It is true that in England one generally has no trouble to keep cool; the trouble is ever to get warm.

45 J. J. Stevenson   House Architecture
Vol II (1880), 212–13, 217–18

For heating English houses the best system, on the whole, is the old one of open fires. No doubt it is unscientific: it produces dust, which by other systems might be avoided; and it is wasteful, as a fraction of the fuel in a close fire would produce the same heat in the room which in an open fire goes mostly up the chimney. But it has the advantage that we are used to it, and that every one understands it: it is a tolerably efficient mode of ventilation, and it is so cheery and pleasant that we are not likely to abandon it, as long as the coal lasts. . . .

Open fires in all these forms are wasteful. A great part of the heat goes up the chimney, and is lost in warming the external atmosphere.

By other methods about twice or thrice as much heat could be obtained from the same amount of fuel; but for ordinary dwelling-rooms no other method has been found so pleasant and satisfactory or so healthy; and, notwithstanding that the wastefulness of the system has been demonstrated again and again, our houses are likely to continue to be built with a fire-place in each room. . . .

In American houses and hotels there is one fire for the whole building for heating air, which is led by ducts in the walls and pipes to each room, where it enters by a grating which can be opened or closed at the pleasure of the occupant. The dust of open fires, and the trouble of making them and of cleaning grates, is avoided.

Our adherence to old customs has never permitted us to carry out to this extent the system of heating our houses by hot air. We have contented ourselves with using a general system of heating in houses as a supplement merely to open fires. Many English people cannot bear the American mode of heating, and prefer to shut the hot air inlet into the room and keep themselves warm by putting on more clothing.

But even the comparatively low temperature of the heated air in English houses is to some people unbearable. It makes them feel enervated and listless. In America, where the evil has been greatest, the system of heating our bodies and our rooms by the air which we have to breathe has begun to be questioned, and by some Americans has been denounced in

strong terms. The air supplied to the rooms is sometimes
heated to 100° or more.

46 Mary Haweis The Art of Decoration
(1881), 339-42

The fault of most fires is that they do not warm the room,
while they do drain the pocket. Modern science is seeking to
provide a thin, vertical fire, about four or five inches from back
to front, which presents in fact the smallest possible face to the
chimney and the largest to the room, thus economising fuel
and gaining heat. How to keep such a fire from going out, and
how to make the surrounding machinery picturesque, is, I
think, hardly yet a *fait accompli*. Most people are giving up the
large circular burnished eyesores which drive a conscientious
housemaid wild, and yet at present this kind of stove, well
filled, throws out the most warmth. It does so, however, only
at a cost repugnant to intelligence—the waste of two-thirds of
the heat of the fuel. . . .

Were it not that the beauty of a burning fire is too valuable
to get rid of, even from the æsthetic point of view, I would
recommend gas stoves and hot pipes as far more comfortable,
after the American fashion. A big fire is either so hot that you
cannot sit beside it—and to sit anywhere else seems inconsistent
when there *is* a fire—or else it has a way of toasting bits of you
and leaving the other bits in the power of "Jack Frost." It is
horrible to have a cold nose and a burning hand; it is more
horrible to have a burning nose and cold hands. Fried toes
alone are small comfort, so is one hot ear, yet it is really not
possible to be equally warm all round beside a fire.

The ideal condition of things would probably be a small fire
whereby one can sit sociably, whilst the rest of the room is
moderately warmed by pipes. Moderately, I say advisedly,
since most people who use pipes accustom themselves to a
temperature which is very apt to cause congestion of the lungs
on entering it after a cold walk. In my opinion, a sitting room

over 55° Fahrenheit is unhealthy, and extremely likely to induce colds.

Gas Stoves

Gas stoves were not new in 1895, but Charlotte Humphry (?1843–1925), author and journalist, illustrates and attacks (47) a then still common prejudice against them. The penny-in-the-slot gas meter, an innovation when Mrs Humphry wrote, considerably encouraged the use of gas stoves in middle-class homes. It also enabled gas to be introduced for the first time into the homes of the less prosperous working classes.

47 Charlotte Humphry   Are Gas Stoves Advisable?
Windsor Magazine (April 1895), 470

Are gas stoves advisable? When the coal strike was at its height and coal was 30s. a ton, and wretched, dirty stuff even at that price, I asked the above question of everybody who was likely to know the answer to it.

"Awfully extravagant things," said one. "Most unhealthy," said another. "Your flowers will all die," said a third, one of those lovable people to whom life without flower friends is just a little worth living, but not so much as it might be. All the answers were dead against the gas, so I went on buying bad coal at a huge price, and it went on filling up the grates with rusty cinders and the rooms with a sticky, nasty, floating ash that made everything disagreeable to the touch.

The housemaid complained that she was for ever dusting, and my beloved books and papers were far more eloquent in their silence under a film of coal dust. So one day I paid a visit to the gas inspector, and, being well aware that it was his business, almost his duty, to present gas fires in as glowing and agreeable a light as possible, I carefully discounted in the recesses of my own mind all that he said in their favour, and added on to what he had the fairness to urge against them.

All the time a vision of ever-clean grates and rooms free from dust after the one vigorous application of brush and duster in the morning filled my consciousness, and eventually I gave him the order to put gas stoves on hire from the company in two rooms of our house. I have never regretted the decision. We have had endless comfort out of those stoves. But before I enlarge on this side of the question I must deal with the three objections made by the friends whom I had consulted.

The gas stoves are certainly dearer than coal fires; that is, when coal is at its normal price. I have calculated the expense as equal to about a third as much again. In this way: for those who keep large fires, and reckoning coal at the rate of 24s. a ton, the gas stoves cost 30s. for the same period as the ton of coal would last.

As to the unhealthiness, we have proved very satisfactorily that there is nothing in that. The health of the family is quite as good as it was during the domestic era of coal fires, and, if anything, better. The family temper has much improved, but of that more anon. As to the flowers, they last as long as ever they did, look as lovely, smell as sweet, and are to all appearance as healthy. But then we do not burn gas in our dwelling-rooms as an illuminant, preferring lamps, and the fumes of the stoves escape up the chimney.

Problems of Gas Lighting

Before the coming of electric light the Victorians suffered severe difficulties over lighting. Gas, though widely used, could be dangerous and also had aesthetic problems. This was especially true before the invention of the incandescent gas mantle in the middle 1880s, for that caused less discomfort and was far more efficient than earlier forms of gas lighting. Lewis Day (1845–1910), a progressive designer and writer, illustrates the disadvantages of gas in a drawing room (48), and he was echoed by many writers. J. J. Stevenson wrote: "In burning it produces noxious vapours, which kill plants, tarnish metal, and destroy colouring, and its flame is often unsteady and hurtful to the eyes" (*House Architecture*, II, 1880, 254). In a lecture written about 1879 William Morris advised against the use of gas, "which will indeed soon reduce all your decorations to a pretty general average" ("Making the Best of It", *Hopes and Fears for Art*, 1882, 135), and as late as 1895 M. H. Baillie Scott, assuming the absence of electricity, wrote: "There is no glaring gas, but here and there lamps and candles throw a soft suffused light" ("An Ideal Suburban House", *The Studio*, January 1895, 128).

48 Lewis F. Day   Every-day Art
(1882), 205

As it is chiefly in the evening that this room will be inhabited, care must be taken not to make it too dark. That would involve difficulty in the way of illumination; which means gas; which means heat, foul air, heaviness, and general discomfort. If a moderator or duplex lamp or two do not sufficiently illuminate it, it will be too dark. On the other hand, it must not be too light, or we shall lose the feeling of repose, that we most want. Call to mind the cosiest rooms you can think of, and you will find that none of them are in a very light key. They are not white-and-gold drawing-rooms, but sober morning-rooms, or dining-rooms (so-called) that are really living-rooms. The tone of the room then is determined, not so dark as to necessitate gas, not so light as to appear cold or naked. The tint is a matter of choice, to be settled according to preference, or perhaps with reference to the other rooms; one does not want to have all the rooms in the house of a colour. The doctor will be at one with the artist on that point.

Electric Light
At the end of the nineteenth century electric lighting was hardly out of its infancy. Cragside, the dramatically situated country house near Rothbury designed by Norman Shaw,

was lighted by electricity as early as 1880, and a number of
public buildings soon followed—the House of Commons in
1881, and the British Museum, Mansion House and Royal
Academy in 1882. The third Marquess of Salisbury (1830–
1903), whom we shall meet again as a politician concerned
with the housing of the poor, was an enthusiastic amateur
scientist, and his experiments with electricity in 1880–1 are
here ruefully recalled (49) by his daughter, Lady Gwendolen
Cecil (1860–1945). However, even in wealthy homes,
electricity was unusual before 1900, and when Dorothy Peel
herself moved to a new home (50) in an expensive part of
London at the turn of the century she had to install electric
light. She installed a single bathroom also (*Life's Enchanted
Cup*, 1933, 125), but in *The New Home* she advocated (p 20)
a bathroom on each of the upper floors.

49 Gwendolen Cecil   Life of Robert, Marquess of Salisbury
Vol III (1931), 3–4, 6–7

At the time that he left office, the invention of the incandescent lamp, by which electric lighting was at length controlled
to practical usefulness, had just been announced. Lord Salisbury had been for some time impatient for the development.
He had erected some *Jablokhoff* are lights outside his house at
Hatfield—mainly for the benefit of his guests' coachmen on
the occasion of the annual county ball—and had tried to
introduce them into the interior. For a brief period his family
and guests were compelled to eat their dinners under the
vibrating glare of one of these lamps fixed in the centre of the
dining-hall ceiling. No exertion of goodwill or courtesy could
silence the plaintive protests of his lady visitors, and he would
gird with growing despondency at the obstructions which
feminine vanity offered to the conquests of science. He was
saved from humiliating defeat by the timely appearance of the
Edison-Swan lamp. . . .

These experiments found their expression in a series of experiences which for a year or two relieved the monotony of domestic life at Hatfield. There were evenings when the household had to grope about in semi-darkness, illuminated only by a dim red glow such as comes from a half-extinct fire; there were others when a perilous brilliancy culminated in miniature storms of lightning, ending in complete collapse. One group of lamps after another would blaze and expire in rapid succession, like stars in conflagration, till the rooms were left in pitchy blackness, and the evening's entertainment had to be concluded in the light of hastily collected bed-candles. The necessity of fuses was not yet recognised, and one evening a party of guests, on entering the Long Gallery after dinner, found the carved panelling near the ceiling bursting into flames under the contact of an overheated wire. It was happily a shooting party in which young men formed a substantial element. They rose joyfully to the occasion, and, with well-directed volleys of sofa cushions, rendered the summoning of a fire-engine unnecessary.

These various catastrophes were greeted by the master of the house with a purely detached interest. When the lights collapsed, his voice could be heard through the darkness amidst the general outcry of laughter and dismay, commenting meditatively upon the answer thus supplied to some as yet undetermined problem of current and resistance.

50 Dorothy Peel   The New Home
(1898), 38, 41

There is undoubtedly no light which in any way comes up to electric light. In any place where the electric mains are in the same street it is not an expensive matter to have the house wired and connected. . . .

The economy of electric light is due chiefly to two causes: the first being the extreme facility with which the switches can be turned off and on. When gas is used, it is the custom to keep a small jet constantly burning in order to avoid the trouble of finding a match-box, striking a match and lighting the gas. In a house where there are often ten or twelve of these small jets alight the whole evening, the cost of consumption soon mounts up, whereas electric light is switched off directly the light is no longer required. The second cause is to be found in the fact that the electric light is absolutely cleanly, thus a great saving is effected in labour and in the cost of re-papering, painting, white-washing, and cleaning of curtains and chair covers. In a house lighted by gas the ceilings require cleaning each year. The upper portions of the curtains suffer much from the effect of the gas, which also has a fatal effect on gilt of any description and upon oil paintings.

PART TWO

The Homes of the
Working Classes

THE URBAN POOR: DESCRIPTION

The Sanitary Period

It was hardly earlier than the beginning of Victoria's reign that doctors, writers and politicians began to realise that they were living in an age of cities and that the cities contained huge numbers of badly housed poor people. Until about 1850 there was intense interest in the homes of the poor, partly because bad housing conditions bred disease which spread to all social classes, partly because of working-class movements, the most obvious of which was Chartism. Working-class housing was looked upon as an aspect of public health. Accordingly, it was medical men like W. H. Duncan (1805–63, Liverpool and Britain's first Medical Officer of Health), and sanitary reformers like Edwin Chadwick (1800–90), who were responsible in the early years for discovering the state of housing among the poor. Duncan's estimates (51) of the numbers of cellar and court dwellers were subsequently revised to a lower figure, but whichever figure is correct they indicate horrifying conditions. John Glyde (1823–1905) was a bookseller and social reformer (52), who had abandoned much of his former radicalism by 1850. (See the useful introduction by A. F. J. Brown to the 1971 reprint of his book.) The famous *Morning Chronicle* series on "Labour and the Poor" has received much attention in recent years, though the many articles by other correspondents have been less noticed than those by the

colourful Henry Mayhew (1812–87), the "Metropolitan
Commissioner". The passage printed here (53) draws on
Mayhew's investigations for the *Chronicle* in 1849–50 and his
subsequent independent publications.

It is not easy to summarise the enormous mass of writing,
official and individual, on the homes of the poor during this
period. Three points should perhaps be made. First, the
extraordinary abundance of evidence should have destroyed
any excuse on the part of the wealthy and influential for
ignorance of social conditions. Second, urban slums were
not restricted by size of city or by geographical location.
And finally, in the worst slums observers found attempts at
cleanliness and cheer which encouraged some of them to
think that all the very poor could live better if they only
tried hard enough.

51 Select Committee on the Health of Towns
Evidence of Dr W. H. Duncan on Liverpool
PP, Vol XI (1840), 141–2, 145

2374. . . . I have data on which I have estimated the
number of the working population at 175,000 out of 250,000;
I calculate that out of that number 38,000 live in cellars; that
is allowing rather less than five inhabitants, four-and-three-
quarters, in each cellar, for which I have also statistical data. . . .

2380. . . . Six years ago I counted the number of courts
printed in the Directory of Liverpool; at that time there were
considerably upwards of 2,000; I estimate that now there are
2,400.

2381. Courts of the description referred to, with only one
outlet?—Yes, generally speaking; there are some which have
two outlets, but the great majority, particularly of the old
courts, have only one communication with the street through
a narrow archway of three feet wide, the upper part of which
is generally built up; the width between the two rows of houses

varies from perhaps nine to 15 feet; I have a diagram here to explain the structure of the courts.

2382. It is unnecessary to ask you much of the construction of the courts; is that extremely injurious to health?—There can be no doubt of it; it prevents proper ventilation.

2383. Not only is the end of the court built up, but the end which is open is considerably narrower than the court itself?—Generally speaking, in the great majority of courts; very few have an entrance wider than four feet, and that is usually by an archway covered over; the houses in front of the street are generally built over it.

2384. The width of the courts is, you say, from nine to 15 feet between the rows?—Yes; there are many only six feet.

2385. The construction would appear almost as if it was contrived for the purpose of preventing ventilation?—Yes; further on (in the diagram) there is another court; the backs of the houses in this court are built against the backs of the houses in the other court.

2386. There are courts in which not only there is this construction followed, but the houses in rows, forming the court, are back to back with the houses forming other courts?—Yes, that is the case in the majority of instances.

2387. So that no ventilation can pass through the court?—No; and at the further end there is generally a privy, or two privies, with an ash-pit between the two privies, and those are generally in a very bad state; there are frequently no covers to the ash-pit, and no doors to the privies; they are in the most abominable state of filth.

2388. Mr. *Cowper.*] Are those the only conveniences in the whole court?—Yes; and in some instances not only to the whole court, but to the whole street, for the inhabitants of the whole street frequently make use of those privies, having none of their own.

2389. *Chairman.*] Is it generally the case that the outlet to those courts is only a passage under a house?—In most of the older courts that is the case.

2390. So that that one outlet admits very little air to the court?—Yes; but in many of the courts more recently built the entrance is wider and not built over.

2391. It is unnecessary to ask you whether a construction could be contrived more likely to be prejudicial to the health of the inhabitants of those courts?—It is scarcely possible to conceive of any, considering the population of those courts.

2392. What is the average population of those courts?—I think the average is between six and seven inhabitants to each house, and calculating the number of houses in each court at six, that would make about 36 or rather more in each court; so that on that estimate there will be 86,400 of the inhabitants of Liverpool living in those courts.

2393. Are those chiefly of the working classes?—Entirely; except, perhaps, that a few of the better kind of courts in Liverpool may be inhabited by shopmen and small shop-keepers, and persons of that class.

2394. In addition to the 38,000 and upwards living in underground cellars, there are 86,000 of the working classes living in those close courts in Liverpool?—Yes.

2395. Lord *James Stuart.*] Is there any communication by drains to the common sewer?—None; I do not know of any court in which there is an underground drain; I frequently made the inquiry, from having been led to notice the state of filth in which most of the courts were; in fact, in the main streets, in the greater number of those inhabited by the working classes, there are no sewers.

2396. *Chairman.*] Are the Committee to understand that there are neither sewers nor underground drains in those courts?—None whatever. . . .

2440. Do the owners of those small dwellings derive from them a very considerable rent?—The cottage owners, as they are termed, are generally considered a very wealthy class of individuals; I think the average rent of houses in courts is about 3*s.* a week.

2441. Are they generally taken by the week?—Yes, almost

always; in the front houses in streets, the rent is perhaps 3s. 6d. a week.

2442. Lord J. Stuart.] Do the landlords or the tenants pay for the water?—The landlords pay for the water, and the tenants pay 3d. a week, perhaps, in addition to the rent, for the water; and the poor complain that if one of the landlords is in arrear, the whole supply is stopped, or if the pipes go out of order.

2443. They may be without a supply for days or weeks?— Yes, frequently they are so, and have to borrow it from their neighbours, or go into the adjoining courts, or get it the best way they can.

2444. Chairman.] Is it not generally considered that investments in this small species of cottage property pay a very high interest?—It is generally conceived so.

2445. So that it is a very profitable and tempting investment? —Very much so.

52 John Glyde, Jun   The Moral, Social and Religious Condition of Ipswich in the Middle of the Nineteenth Century
(1850), 36, 47–9

There are 106 courts in the town, containing 627 houses. The drainage from some of these is very defective. In some instances all the refuse water has to be carried to a dead well, situated either in the middle or at the end of the yard. In others, the water course is very badly paved, and stagnant water is the consequence. The demoralizing practice of providing but one convenience for several houses is here seen in full force. No less than 67 courts, containing 358 houses, are in this position; giving an average of one to every five houses. The courts are also equally deficient in accommodation for the washing of clothes. Many of the inhabitants have to perform that operation in their dwellings, to the serious injury of their health and destruction of their comfort. The supply of water to the courts is also of a defective character. Ten of them are without any supply, to 4 the water they require is fetched from wells, and to 21 from pumps. The difficulty and the labour attending the procuration of this needful article, must have a deteriorating influence on the character of the inhabitants, and prevent the formation of those habits of cleanliness so essential to the health, comfort, and moral elevation of the poorer classes. The ventilation of the courts is bad, their situation often very confined, and the entrance in some instances narrow. Some of their houses are situated back to back. Above 500 of them have no back doors; and, in the major portion, the rooms are so small that, where they are occupied by families, they cannot fail of being *crowded* in the sleeping apartments. . . .

The deficiency of private receptacles for refuse must tend greatly to deteriorate the moral habits of the community. Numerous are the cases in which the out office is common to several houses, in one case to twelve houses. Are not these circumstances sufficient to destroy all modesty, to blight the beauty of the female character, and to banish all feelings of self-respect from the human mind; and do they not militate most powerfully against the comfort, decency, and morality of the labouring population of the town? The insufficient number and consequent indiscriminate use of sleeping apartments is another great cause of demoralization. When we find a father, mother, and 5 children sleeping in one room, (a girl of 13 and a boy older) can we wonder at the depravity which must be the result? We do not say that such is invariably the case; but must not such herding together tend to destroy all the finer feelings of our nature? Can common decency be preserved under such circumstances? Is it not hopeless to expect moral improvement of the working classes, until the means of preventing such evils are provided? The poor creatures are so situated that they cannot help themselves; they cannot of themselves improve the wretched accommodations they are obliged to put up with; and it is clearly our duty therefore to assist them. The bad ventilation of courts, houses, and rooms, has a great effect on the nervous energies, and so acts upon the system as to induce a desire for stimulants, and lay the foundation for disorderly habits.

In the midst of all these disadvantages, the visitor of the poor meets with numerous instances of determined struggles for cleanliness and general purity of character, and even of moral heroism of a high cast. The intense suffering and privations which many of these poor creatures undergo, not merely excite the commiseration of the class above them in society, but act as a stimulus to personal improvement. The clean bricks in front, the whitened door step, and the white muslin window blind, at some of these court-bound dwellings—situated as they are at a distance from any water pipe or pump, and having no drainage for the refuse—are indeed strong proofs of a moral feeling which even the deteriorating circumstances around have been unable to crush. On entering such dwellings (of which a proportion, we think, of seven to ten will be found), the geranium, the balsam, or the musk plant will be seen in the room, whilst the piece of ground in front will be carefully cultivated. The scarlet runner is a favourite plant with them. Common painted wood engravings and a small looking glass hang on the walls, and a copy of the Bible or perchance a Prayer Book, on the table, in front of the best tea tray; on the mantel-piece there is a pair of shells, a well-polished brass candlestick, a small china ornament or two, or perhaps a pair of singular looking drinking glasses. All these things show us that taste and simple elegance have still an abode in these humble dwellings. In some, the desire to keep a "better suit" indicate that there is an effort to stem the general effects of poverty, and that commendable self-respect is not worn out.

53 Henry Mayhew   Of the Homes of the Costermongers

London Labour and the London Poor, Vol I (1851), 47–8

The costermongers usually reside in the courts and alleys in the neighbourhood of the different street-markets. . . .

The homes of the costermongers in these places, may be divided into three classes; firstly, those who, by having a regular trade or by prudent economy, are enabled to live in comparative ease and plenty; secondly, those who, from having a large family or by imprudent expenditure, are, as it were, struggling with the world; and thirdly, those who for want of stock-money, or ill success in trade are nearly destitute.

The first home I visited was that of an old woman, who with the assistance of her son and girls, contrived to live in a most praiseworthy and comfortable manner. She and all her family were teetotallers, and may be taken as a fair type of the thriving costermonger.

As I ascended a dark flight of stairs, a savory smell of stew grew stronger at each step I mounted. The woman lived in a large airy room on the first floor ("the drawing-room" as she told me laughing at her own joke), well lighted by a clean window, and I found her laying out the savory smelling dinner looking most temptingly clean. The floor was as white as if it had been newly planed, the coke fire was bright and warm, making the lid of the tin saucepan on it rattle up and down as the steam rushed out. The wall over the fire-place was patched up to the ceiling with little square pictures of saints, and on the mantel-piece, between a row of bright tumblers and wine glasses filled with odds and ends, stood glazed crockeryware images of Prince Albert and M. Jullien. Against the walls, which were papered with "hangings" of four different patterns and colours, were hung several warm shawls, and in the band-box, which stood on the stained chest of drawers, you could tell that the Sunday bonnet was stowed safely away from the dust. A turn-up bedstead thrown back, and covered with a many-coloured patch-work quilt, stood opposite to a long dresser with its mugs and cups dangling from the hooks, and the clean blue plates and dishes ranged in order at the back. There were a few bushel baskets piled up in one corner, "but

the apples smelt so," she said, "they left them in a stable at
night". . . .

On taking my leave I was told by the mother that their silver
gilt Dutch clock—with its glass face and blackleaded weights—
"was the best one in London, and might be relied on with the
greatest safety."

As a specimen of the dwellings of the struggling costers, the
following may be cited:

The man, a tall, thick-built, almost good-looking fellow,
with a large fur cap on his head, lived with his family in a
front kitchen, and as there were, with his mother-in-law, five
persons, and only one bed, I was somewhat puzzled to know
where they could *all* sleep. The barrow standing on the railings
over the window, half shut out the light, and when any one
passed there was a momentary shadow thrown over the room,
and a loud rattling of the iron gratings above that completely
prevented all conversation. When I entered, the mother-in-law
was reading aloud one of the threepenny papers to her son, who
lolled on the bed, that with its curtains nearly filled the room.
There was the usual attempt to make the fireside comfortable.
The stone sides had been well whitened, and the mantel-piece
decorated with its small tin trays, tumblers, and a piece of
looking-glass. A cat with a kitten were seated on the hearth-rug
in front. "They keeps the varmint away," said the woman,
stroking the "puss," "and gives a look of home." By the drawers
were piled up four bushel baskets, and in a dark corner near
the bed stood a tall measure full of apples that scented the
room. Over the head, on a string that stretched from wall to
wall, dangled a couple of newly-washed shirts, and by the
window were two stone barrels, for lemonade, when the coster
visited the fairs and races.

Whilst we were talking, the man's little girl came home. For
a poor man's child she was dressed to perfection; her pinafore
was clean, her face shone with soap, and her tidy cotton print
gown had clearly been newly put on that morning. She
brought news that "Janey" was coming home from auntey's,

and instantly a pink cotton dress was placed by the mother-in-law before the fire to air. (It appeared that Janey was out at service, and came home once a week to see her parents and take back a clean frock.) Although these people were living, so to speak, in a cellar, still every endeavour had been made to give the home a look of comfort. The window, with its paper-patched panes, had a clean calico blind. The side-table was dressed up with yellow jugs and cups and saucers, and the band-boxes had been stowed away on the flat top of the bedstead. All the chairs, which were old fashioned mahogany ones, had sound backs and bottoms.

Of the third class, or the very poor, I chose the following "type" out of the many others that presented themselves. The family here lived in a small slanting-roofed house, partly stripped of its tiles. More than one half of the small leaden squares of the first-floor window were covered with brown paper, puffing out and crackling in the wind, while through the greater part of the others were thrust out ball-shaped bundles of rags, to keep out the breeze. The panes that did remain were of all shapes and sizes, and at a distance had the appearance of yellow glass, they were so stained with dirt. I opened a door with a number chalked on it, and groped my way up a broken tottering staircase.

It took me some time after I had entered the apartment before I could get accustomed to the smoke, that came pouring into the room from the chimney. The place was filled with it, curling in the light, and making every thing so indistinct that I could with difficulty see the white mugs ranged in the corner-cupboard, not three yards from me. When the wind was in the north, or when it rained, it was always that way, I was told, "but otherwise," said an old dame about sixty, with long grisly hair spreading over her black shawl, "it is pretty good for that."

On a mattrass, on the floor, lay-a-pale-faced girl—"eighteen years old last twelfth-cake day"—her drawn-up form showing in the patch-work counterpane that covered her. She had just been confined, and the child had died! A little straw, stuffed into an old tick, was all she had to lie upon, and even that had been given up to her by the mother until she was well enough to work again. To shield her from the light of the window, a cloak had been fastened up slantingly across the panes; and on a string that ran along the wall was tied, amongst the bonnets, a clean nightcap—"against the doctor came," as the mother, curtsying, informed me. By the side of the bed, almost hidden in the dark shade, was a pile of sieve baskets, crowned by the flat shallow that the mother "worked" with.

The room was about nine feet square, and furnished a home for three women. The ceiling slanted like that of a garret, and was the colour of old leather, excepting a few rough white patches, where the tenants had rudely mended it. The white light was easily seen through the laths, and in one corner a large patch of the paper looped down from the wall. One night the family had been startled from their sleep by a large mass of mortar—just where the roof bulged in—falling into the room. "We never want rain water," the woman told me, "for we can catch plenty just over the chimney-place."

They had made a carpet out of three or four old mats. They were "obligated to it, for fear of dropping anything through the boards into the donkey stables in the parlour underneath. But we only pay ninepence a week rent," said the old woman, "and mustn't grumble."

The only ornament in the place was on the mantel-piece— an old earthenware sugar-basin, well silvered over, that had been given by the eldest girl when she died, as a remembrance to her mother. Two cracked tea-cups, on their inverted saucers, stood on each side, and dressed up the fire-side into something like tidiness. The chair I sat on was by far the best out of the three in the room, and that had no back, and only half its quantity of straw.

The parish, the old woman told me, allowed her 1s. a week and two loaves. But the doctor ordered her girl to take sago and milk, and she was many a time sorely puzzled to get it.

The neighbours helped her a good deal, and often sent her part of their unsold greens;—even if it was only the outer leaves of the cabbages, she was thankful for them. Her other girl—a big-boned wench, with a red shawl crossed over her bosom, and her black hair parted on one side—did all she could, and so they lived on. "As long as they kept out of the 'big house' (the workhouse) she would not complain."

I never yet beheld so much destitution borne with so much content. Verily the acted philosophy of the poor is a thing to make those who write and preach about it hide their heads.

The Middle Period

Social problems, while not ignored, received less attention during the third quarter of the nineteenth century than during the 1840s. There is no simple explanation, but clearly the initial shock experienced by the wealthier classes wore off after a period. Mid-Victorian prosperity and the decreased militancy of the Labour movement are also part of the pattern. Nonetheless, there is abundant material on slum housing between 1850 and 1880. Isabella Bird (1831–1904), later Mrs Bishop, a famous traveller and writer, describes (54) the slums of Edinburgh, whose conditions were made worse by the high buildings in which the poor lived. William Holms published as a pamphlet (55) letters which had previously appeared in the *Glasgow Herald*. He explains the ticket system, which was introduced under a local Act of 1862, but did little to stop overcrowding. The docility of the Glasgow poor at interruptions in the middle of the night was noted also by the Rev Lord Sidney Godolphin Osborne (1808–89), a well known advocate of social reform, writing in *Meliora* (2nd series, ed Viscount Ingestre, 1853). "On the ground as the rule", Osborne wrote, "on rotten besteads as the exception, lay human beings of all ages and sexes." Dogs and cats were "to all appearance, the cleanliest creatures we saw" (p 9). The article from the *Daily Telegraph* (56) takes us to Merthyr Tydfil, to an investigation of the homes of the locked-out miners, who lived, like most miners, in particularly abominable conditions.

54 [Isabella Bird]   Notes on Old Edinburgh

(1869), 10–11, largely reprinted in John Ruskin. *Fors Clavigera*, letter 40, "The Scottish Fireside", *Library Edition of the Works of John Ruskin*, Vol XXVIII (1907), 73–4

We entered the first room by descending two steps. It seemed to be an old coal-cellar, with an earthen floor, shining in many places from damp, and from a greenish ooze which drained through the wall from a noxious collection of garbage outside, upon which a small window could have looked had it not been filled up with brown paper and rags. There was no grate, but a small fire smouldered on the floor, surrounded by heaps of ashes. The roof was unceiled, the walls were rough and broken, the only light came in from the open door, which let in unwholesome smells and sounds. No cow or horse could thrive in such a hole. It was abominable. It measured eleven feet by six feet, and the rent was 10d. per week, paid in advance. It was nearly dark at noon, even with the door open; but as my eyes became accustomed to the dimness, I saw that the plenishings consisted of an old bed, a barrel with a flagstone on the top of it for a table, a three-legged stool, and an iron pot. A very ragged girl, sorely afflicted with ophthalmia, stood among the ashes doing nothing. She had never been inside a school or church. She did not know how to do anything, but "did for her father and brother." On a heap of straw, partly covered with sacking, which was the bed in which father, son, and daughter slept, the brother, ill with rheumatism and sore legs, was lying moaning from under a heap of filthy rags. He had been a baker "over in the New Town," but seemed not very likely to recover. It looked as if the sick man had crept into his dark, damp lair, just to die of hopelessness. The father was past work, but "sometimes got an odd job to do." The sick man had supported the three. It was hard to be godly, impossible to be cleanly, impossible to be healthy in such circumstances.

The next room was entered by a low, dark, impeded passage about twelve feet long, too filthy to be traversed without a light. At the extremity of this was a dark winding stair which led up to four superincumbent storeys of crowded subdivided rooms; and beyond this, to the right, a pitch-dark passage with a "room" on either side. It was not possible to believe that the most grinding greed could extort money from human beings for the tenancy of such dens as those to which this passage led. They were lairs into which a starving dog might creep to die, but nothing more. Opening a dilapidated door, we found ourselves in a recess nearly 6 feet high, and 9 feet in length by 5 in breadth. It was not absolutely dark, yet matches aided our investigations even at noon-day. There was an earthen floor full of holes, in some of which water had collected. The walls were black and rotten, and alive with wood-lice. There was no grate. The rent paid for this evil den, which was only ventilated by the chimney, is 1s. per week, or £2, 12s. annually! The occupier was a mason's labourer, with a wife and three children. He had come to Edinburgh in search of work, and could not afford a "higher rent." The wife said that her husband took the "wee drap." So would the President of the Temperance League himself if he were hidden away in such a hole. The contents of this lair on our first visit were a great heap of ashes and other refuse in one corner, some damp musty straw in another, a broken box in the third, with a battered tin pannikin upon it, and nothing else of any kind, saving two small children, nearly nude, covered with running sores, and pitiable from some eye disease. Their hair was not long, but felted into wisps, and alive with vermin. When we went in they were sitting among the ashes of an extinct fire, and blinked at the light from our matches. Here a neighbour said they sat all day, unless their mother was merciful enough to turn them into the gutter. We were there at eleven the following night, and found the mother, a decent, tidy body, at "*hame.*" There was a small fire then, but no other light. She complained of little besides the darkness of the house, and said, in a tone of dull discontent, she supposed it was "as good as such as they could expect in Edinburgh." The two children we had seen before were crouching near the embers, blinking at a light we carried, and on the musty straw in the corner a third, about ten years old, was doubled up. This child had not a particle of clothing, but was partially covered with a rag of carpet. She was ill of scrofula, and the straw she lay on seemed to be considered a luxury. Three adults (including a respectable-looking grandmother) and three children slept on that unwhole-some floor, in a room, be it remembered, 9 by 5, and under 6 feet high. We allow each convict 500 cubic feet of air in his cell.

55 William Holms House-overcrowding and Mortality in Glasgow
(1869), 6–7

I visited about fifty dwellings; commencing at half-past 10 o'clock, p.m., and completing my round of visits about 3 o'clock of the following morning.

With one exception, we were received by the occupants of the various houses with an amount of civility which surprised me, considering the very unseasonable hour we had chosen to break in upon their repose.

That the deficiency in the amount of air to each inmate of the houses visited may be better understood, it should be borne in mind, that from 500 to 600 cubic feet is usually regarded as the minimum quantity for an adult. The inspectors of prisons in England recommend not less than 1000 cubic feet "for every prisoner," as being "essential to health and ventilation." In these houses which have been ticketed by order of the magis-trates, the required allowance is only 300 cubic feet for each inmate. I presume that it was found necessary to be content with this most inadequate allowance, as otherwise more than half of the inhabitants of those dwellings must have been dislodged and driven to the streets. I shall now briefly refer to some of the houses which I saw. We proceeded to 157 Bridgegate. The first house we entered consisted of a kitchen and two small rooms, the former about 14 feet long, 12 feet wide, and 7½ feet high,—equal to 1260 cubic feet of air space. Here were seven adults and one child. The rooms were each about 10 feet long and 6 feet wide, equal to 450 cubic feet. In each of them we found four labouring men asleep. As the doors and windows were closed, the atmosphere was so sickening as to be almost intolerable. In the same close we found fourteen adults in a house with 2254 cubic feet; and on the upper floor, a two-roomed dwelling ticketed 1581·5—the former number indicating the cubic contents of the house, the latter figure denoting the number of adults permitted by the police to sleep in the premises. In this miserable dwelling we found a poor old tailor, who, with his family, slept at night in the same apartment in which he worked during the day; while a still smaller room was let to lodgers, the total occupants being seven adults and six children. We next went to 147 Bridgegate, which is a long, narrow, dark, ill-ventilated close. Here we found a house of one apartment, ticketed 1392·4, in which were ten men and women. I need scarcely say that the air was most offensive and unwholesome. In another one-roomed house, ticketed 797·2, we found four adults and two children. We next visited No. 11 St. Margaret's Place, off Bridgegate. The first house we entered appeared to have concentrated all the evils likely to produce disease. It was dark and dirty; and although ticketed 1643·5, contained seven adults and seven children; most of them lying on the floor, with no other bed clothing than the clothes they were in the habit of wearing during the day: the excuse made for this overcrowding was, that the lodgers were people who had been turned out of their houses owing to the formation of the Union Railway; and being unable to get accommodation elsewhere at a suitable rent, had taken one of the two apartments in this wretched dwelling.

Our next visit was to the Back Wynd, off Trongate, where we

found another Union Railway family huddled together, as lodgers, with the regular occupants of the house, making in all five adults and four children, sleeping in a room about 12 feet long, 11½ feet wide, and eight feet high. This house was ticketed 1100·3. In the adjoining house, with 1292 cubic feet, we found nine adults and one child, most of them sleeping on the floor. From this we went to 183 New Wynd, and entered a common lodging—in an upper room of which, with about 1600 cubic feet, were eight men and women. We now proceeded to 30 Princes Street, where we found the most dreadful instance of overcrowding we had yet witnessed. The attic floor contained several one-roomed dwellings, to reach which, as the passage is at the side of the house, where the roof is low, we had to stoop and grope our way. The centre room, lighted from the roof, was ticketed 700·2; it was kept by an old woman, who had nine lodgers, so that actually ten human beings were crowded into a space insufficient even for two. It will assist the reader to realize this if he will imagine his parlour or dining-room, say 20 feet long, 16 feet wide, and 10 feet high, inhabited by forty-five persons. I had felt the passage to be badly ventilated, but the effluvia in this apartment was so abominable, that I left the obliging inspectors to complete the enumeration of human beings, and retreated to the door, where now, by contrast, the outer air seemed sweet and pure.

56 The Lock-out in Wales
Daily Telegraph (12 February 1875), 3

It strikes a visitor to almost every mining district as all but unaccountably strange that men who make so much money as colliers and ironworkers should be housed worse and be content to live in more unsanitary conditions than other classes of labourers in towns and villages who do not earn half their wages. It seems to me that the men in many cases would act far more wisely if they struck for better houses rather than for higher pay, and the employers themselves would be vastly the gainers by the moral and social improvement which superior dwellings would bring about among their men. And this, it so happens, is precisely what the Rev. John Griffith, rector of Marthyr, has just been saying in a sermon preached at the parish church. "Let the masters," said he, "prove that they have another interest in the men besides that of mere money— mere payment of wages, and then we shall never have any of these strikes. Let them do something to win the men out of the public-houses. Let them spare some of their enormous gains to build places of amusement and recreation during leisure hours. Let them give them better houses to live in, with better conveniences for privacy and decency, and better streets." Leaving for the present the question of amusement and recreation which pitmen of all classes of workers most certainly need, and which they will have of a bad sort if they are not provided with good, let me for the present say a few words on the subject of better houses.

As I have already had occasion to communicate, I have visited many of the surrounding districts, including Dowlais, and certainly here and there I have discovered much to shock the sensitive investigator. I have explored "China", the most terrible spot in all Merthyr, and essentially like what in the bad old times Tiger Bay, Shadwell, was. But Tiger Bay had never a very dreadful entrance, whereas the way to "China" is down a steep of broken steps which lead to a kind of hole in the wall, and then one finds himself in the midst of the Celestial region, a maze of ramshackle crazy-looking houses, or rather one-storied hovels. These are all painted yellow, with doors half unhung, and roofs from which the slates have slipped, exposing the blackened rafter-ribs beneath, in patches, with broken windows and flagstone floors, cracked and hillocky, and seemingly set in the native mud. As for the inhabitants, who are chiefly of the gentle sex, I will only say that compared with their surroundings they have nothing to complain of on the score of unfitness. As to drainage, there appears to be none in this awful underground, unlit nest of a hundred and fifty homes or so; indeed, it would seem to be as little known by the inhabitants as by the sanitary inspector, "China" being, as I was given to understand, chiefly used as a holiday resort for a certain class of colliers of the neighbouring district when money is flush with them. I thought that having seen this spot South Wales could have nothing more ugly in the way of human habitations to show me; but I was mistaken. The gentleman to whom I applied on the subject appeared to be considerably amused at my ignorance. "China is bad enough," said he, "and so is Wind-street, and Horse-street, and Pigeon-row, and a dozen other places I might mention; but if you wish to see a bit of real old Merthyr you must go a little farther afield; you must go to Gas-row, at Dowlais, or Back o' Plough, as it is commonly called." Bearing in mind the preaching at the parish church, I thought that a bit of real old Merthyr might not prove an unseasonable sight, and accordingly by noon I was at Dowlais, and following the clue my friend had provided me with, proceeded to discover Back o' Plough.

Having seen it, I feel compelled to state that Back o' Plough may justly claim the title of being the most hideous spot in England or Wales. I am tolerably acquainted with London's ugliest parts—with Jack Ketch's Warren, with Mint and Kent-street, with Flower and Dean-street, and Keate-street, great and small; but for everything that is repulsive and appalling Gas-row is their peer. They seem to be pit labourers who live here—industrious folk enough, and willing to live decent lives if they were enabled to; but under existing circumstances they might as well attempt to do so in a pigstye. If Merthyr of old was all like it, I say it is a marvel that the plague didn't sweep off its sooty surface every man, woman, and child, some deep shaft serving as their common grave. The houses are rubble-built, and contain generally four rooms. But such rooms!—about 11 ft. square would be the dimensions of each, with a floor of small stones, up from between which the black ooze squelches when the foot falls unevenly on them—with walls of the colour of an underground vault, and low

wooden ceilings, the beams of which are shaggy with a coat of
sooty cobwebs, which the hair of a tall man would brush off
were he not to take the precaution to stoop. This is the living-
room for the man and his wife and as many children as there
may happen to be; and what with the sole ventilation being the
chimney and the housedoor, and the enormous fire, fed with
pickings from the pit-heaps, the air is of a quality not soon to
be forgotten when once tasted. In one such place I entered, in
which resided a family of seven souls, daylight could be seen
through the walls, down which on one side water was trickling.
The woman opened the door which led to the upper den that
served as a bed-room; and on the stairs, which were rotten and
hollowed out, there were pools of water deep enough almost to
cover the foot of a child. This, however, the mother explained
was not invariably the case; it was only during the winter
months, and was owing to part of the bed-room roof having
fallen in. Another place—next door, in fact—there resided I
should not like to say how many people, big and little, but
certainly as many appeared to crowd the fireplace side of the
apartment as sheep are sometimes seen to crowd in a market
pen. A horribly dirty family this, and no wonder! The smoke
seemingly declined to go up the chimney at all, and the place
was literally as black as night in consequence. Had it not been
for the great glowing fire, one could not have seen across the
room; but presently out of the suffocating haze there came
forward a man, wheezing and speaking so hoarsely that his
wife had to interpret what he said to explain that he found the
smoke "orful bad for his asthma". Here, as at No. 1, the walls
were reeking and the floor unfit even for a washhouse. The
man was an out-of-work pit labourer and the rent he had to
pay was 6s. a month. I had not yet seen a "Black o' Plough"
bed-room, but my curiosity was presently to be gratified.
"Come up here," exclaimed a woman whose jaws were bound
up in a dirty white cloth. She hailed me at the top of a flight
of stone steps, which I at once ascended. "If you are one of
them gentlemen as can say something to make 'em put us a

bit right, I wish to the Lord you would," said the woman; and really her desire could not be called an unreasonable one. In the weather-stained and filthy ceiling, at the fireplace side, there was a hole through which, excepting for the intervening laths, a Newfoundland dog might have passed easily, and again there were the reeking walls and the saturated floor. This, seemingly, was where the family lived as well as slept. There was a bedstead, at all events, one of the truckle kind, overspread with a few loose, dirty rags and sunk amongst them, with his tattered old coat serving for sheets and blankets, was the woman's sick husband, with a bad foot and unable to rise. A crazy old table and a chair or two composed the whole of the remainder of the furniture.

The "Bitter Cry" and the Aftermath

In 1883 there appeared the most famous and possibly the most influential pamphlet ever written on slum housing. This was *The Bitter Cry of Outcast London* (57), itself influenced by the publication earlier in the year of *How the Poor Live*, by George R. Sims (1847–1922), reprinted from the *Pictorial World*. Sims is the "recent and reliable explorer" quoted towards the end of the extract. Andrew Mearns (1837–1925) was a minister and secretary of the London Congregational Union from 1876 until 1906. He concluded that non-attendance at worship was due to "the condition in which they live". W. T. Stead's *Pall Mall Gazette* popularised the *Bitter Cry*, which was discussed in newspapers up and down the country and in the monthly and quarterly journals, and similar enquiries were undertaken in a number of other towns. James Crosby was a journalist on the *Bristol Mercury*, which printed the articles later republished as *The Homes of The Bristol Poor* (58). *Homes of the People* was a report (59), reprinted from the *Eastern Morning News*, of a conference held in Hull on 1 February 1884. The speaker here reprinted was a prominent local figure, the Rev J. Malet Lambert (1853–1931). The revelations of 1883–4 led, in addition to

V.H.—E

much sensationalism, to the Royal Commission on Housing (1884–5) and the revival of serious concern over slum conditions.

57 [Andrew Mearns] The Bitter Cry of Outcast London (1883), 4–7

We do not say the conditions of their homes, for how can those places be called homes, compared with which the lair of a wild beast would be a comfortable and healthy spot? Few who will read these pages have any conception of what these pestilential human rookeries are, where tens of thousands are crowded amidst horrors which call to mind what we have heard of the middle passage of the slave ship. To get into them you have to penetrate courts reeking with poisonous and malodorous gases arising from accumulations of sewage and refuse scattered in all directions and often flowing beneath your feet; courts, many of them which the sun never penetrates, which are never visited by a breath of fresh air, and which rarely know the virtues of a drop of cleansing water. You have to ascend rotten staircases, which threaten to give way beneath every step, and which, in some places, have already broken down, leaving gaps that imperil the limbs and lives of the unwary. You have to grope your way along dark and filthy passages swarming with vermin. Then, if you are not driven back by the intolerable stench, you may gain admittance to the dens in which these thousands of beings who belong, as much as you, to the race for whom Christ died, herd together. Have you pitied the poor creatures who sleep under railway arches, in carts or casks, or under any shelter which they can find in the open air? You will see that they are to be envied in comparison with those whose lot is to seek refuge here. Eight feet square—that is about the average size of very many of these rooms. Walls and ceiling are black with the accretions of filth which have gathered upon them through long years of neglect. It is exuding through cracks in the boards overhead;

it is running down the walls; it is everywhere. What goes by the name of a window is half of it stuffed with rags or covered by boards to keep out wind and rain; the rest is so begrimed and obscured that scarcely can light enter or anything be seen outside. Should you have ascended to the attic, where at least some approach to fresh air might be expected to enter from open or broken window, you look out upon the roofs and ledges of lower tenements, and discover that the sickly air which finds its way into the room has to pass over the putrefying carcases of dead cats or birds, or viler abominations still. The buildings are in such miserable repair as to suggest the thought that if the wind could only reach them they would soon be toppling about the heads of their occupants. As to furniture—you may perchance discover a broken chair, the tottering relics of an old bedstead, or the mere fragment of a table; but more commonly you will find rude substitutes for these things in the shape of rough boards resting upon bricks, an old hamper or box turned upside down, or more frequently still, nothing but rubbish and rags.

Every room in these rotten and reeking tenements houses a family, often two. In one cellar a sanitary inspector reports finding a father, mother, three children and four pigs! In another room a missionary found a man ill with small pox, his wife just recovering from her eighth confinement, and the children running about half naked and covered with dirt. Here are seven people living in one underground kitchen, and a little dead child lying in the same room. Elsewhere is a poor widow, her three children, and a child who had been dead thirteen days. Her husband, who was a cabman, had shortly before committed suicide. Here lives a widow and her six children, including one daughter of 29, another of 21, and a son of 27. Another apartment contains father, mother and six children, two of whom are ill with scarlet fever. In another nine brothers and sisters, from 29 years of age downwards, live, eat and sleep together. Here is a mother who turns her children into the street in the early evening because she lets her room for immoral purposes until long after midnight, when the poor little wretches creep back again if they have not found some miserable shelter elsewhere. Where there are beds they are simply heaps of dirty rags, shavings or straw, but for the most part these miserable beings huddle together upon the filthy boards. The tenant of this room is a widow, who herself occupies the only bed, and lets the floor to a married couple for 2s. 6d. per week. In many cases matters are made worse by the unhealthy occupations followed by those who dwell in these habitations. Here you are choked as you enter by the air laden with particles of the superfluous fur pulled from the skins of rabbits, rats, dogs and other animals in their preparation for the furrier. Here the smell of paste and of drying match-boxes, mingling with other sickly odours, overpowers you; or it may be the fragrance of stale fish or vegetables, not sold on the previous day, and kept in the room overnight. Even when it is possible to do so the people seldom open their windows, but if they did it is questionable whether much would be gained, for the external air is scarcely less heavily charged with poison than the atmosphere within.

Wretched as these rooms are they are beyond the means of many who wander about all day, picking up a living as they can, and then take refuge at night in one of the common lodging-houses that abound. These are often the resorts of thieves and vagabonds of the lowest types, and some are kept by receivers of stolen goods. In the kitchen men and women may be seen cooking their food, washing their clothes, or lolling about smoking and gambling. In the sleeping room are long rows of beds on each side, sometimes 60 or 80 in one room. In many cases both sexes are allowed to herd together without any attempt to preserve the commonest decency. But there is a lower depth still. Hundreds cannot even scrape together the two-pence required to secure them the privilege of herding in those sweltering common sleeping rooms, and so they huddle together upon the stairs and landings, where it is no uncommon thing to find six or eight in the early morning.

That people condemned to exist under such conditions take to drink and fall into sin is surely a matter for little surprise. We may rather say, as does one recent and reliable explorer, that they are "entitled to credit for not being twenty times more depraved than they are." One of the saddest results of this over-crowding is the inevitable association of honest people with criminals. Often is the family of an honest working man compelled to take refuge in a thieves' kitchen; in the houses where they live their rooms are frequently side by side, and continual contact with the very worst of those who have come out of our gaols is a matter of necessity. There can be no question that numbers of habitual criminals would never have become such, had they not by force of circumstances been packed together in these slums with those who were hardened in crime. Who can wonder that every evil flourishes in such hotbeds of vice and disease? Who can wonder that little children taken from these hovels to the hospital cry, when they are well, through dread of being sent back to their former misery? Who can wonder that young girls wander off into a life of immorality, which promises release from such conditions? Who can wonder that the public-house is "the Elysian field of the tired toiler?"

58 [James Crosby] The Homes of the Bristol Poor (1884), 11–12, 14–15

Within a stone's throw is the open space of the Haymarket, and close to that the well-kept carpet-like turf of the pleasure garden into which kind-hearted, philanthropic persons of the parish have changed the old churchyard of St. James's. On a dull day, you would pass the narrow, door-like entrance of this alley without becoming aware of its existence. Entering, we find ourselves in a court of six or eight three-story houses—the exteriors wearing a generally battered and depressing appearance, hemmed in as these dwellings are in what is known as a "blind court," narrow and without through ventilation. These are "tenement houses"—let room by room to families at 1s. 6d. per week—nearly all blank and miserable-looking homes of the very type specially to be dealt with in any future effort for the improvement of the dwellings of the poor. As one enters them the unsavoury mephitic air peculiar to rooms where people sleep and live in common, seldom wash and rarely change their clothes, is offensive enough, and inside, in the rooms themselves, and on the narrow, dark unventilated staircases, the noxious exhaltations make one long for the outer air and the vitalising oxygen. The occupants—labourers, quay rangers, hawkers, and men in uncertain employment—would with difficulty be induced to pay more than 1s. 6d. per week to be "housed" at night. They do not attempt to make "a home." A bedstead without a bed, or in default a piece of sacking with a bundle of rags on the floor, two shattered chairs, the fragment of a table, and a saucepan, are their household goods. The breadwinner goes out in the morning, and returns to sleep at night—the children of school age are mercifully looked after by the School Board, the one gleam of light and hope in the gloomy social outlook; while the whole family of five or six live and sleep in one room. "How many have you here, mother?" asks my companion as he familiarly addresses the occupant of a lower apartment. "Oh, there's two lone women in the top rooms; husband and wife and three children next room; husband, wife and three children next; husband, wife and three children next, with an extra room; husband, wife and two children next, and myself and son down here; that's all!" One of the two old ladies at the top of the house said she had occupied the dreary apartment eleven years, paying 1s. 6d. per week for it. This "rookery" was a sample of the rest—from thirteen to sixteen or seventeen persons in a house, and in some instances husband, wife, and four children living and sleeping in one room. . . .

We notice—however wretched the neighbourhood—the marked difference for the better directly the one-room limit is overstepped. The air, too, is not so fetid, and the scenes are not so depressing, but the primary conditions of morality and decency are often wanting: the crowding of a whole family in one small bedroom must be deplorable, and the desolation of some of the homes where everything has been parted with for food is quite sufficient to account for the sullen misery into which some seem to have settled down. The rent varies from 2s. 6d. a week for two-roomed houses to 2s. 9d. or 3s. for three rooms, all of them very small. One house, with two rooms up and one down, is occupied by a labourer, his wife, and five children. The eldest boy, 15 years, sells newspapers, and it is well that he thus helps the weekly income, as the father has only earned 1s. up to Friday morning, and 2s. 9d. had to be paid for the week's rent. The youngest child, a baby a few months old, was on a pillow bed on two chairs by the fire when we visited the place, and in this small sitting room, about nine feet square, was the only closet for the house—in a cupboard within a couple of yards of the hearth. There was an air of tidiness and cleanliness about the house, the wife was a most industrious woman, and, in addition to attention to the household, she washed for her neighbours. We learnt that there are other houses there where the closets are similarly situated in the sitting-rooms; in other instances they are in blocks at the ends of the courts or outside the front doors, and in one court they are constructed in the frontages, the doors of the closets alternating with the entrance doors of the several dwellings. The "street doors" open directly into the living room, and where the house is crowded both sitting rooms and upstairs rooms are used for sleeping, though amongst the kitchen requisites and such sitting-room furniture as can be procured there is little space for the bedstead, especially as all stick chopping (for sale as firewood) has now to be done inside the door and not in the court as formerly. In one court some of the rooms directly off the flags are two feet below the level, and blank and miserable looking are some of these dwellings, for which the rent is 2s. 6d. a week.

59 Homes of the People
(Hull, 1884), 5–9

Our first attention is naturally directed to the town within the docks. To get a bird's eye view of the whole it will be as well to ascend the tower of Holy Trinity Church and look down on the roofs below. The building customs of our fore-fathers are at once apparent. Along the main streets new or rather mostly modernised places of business face the road. You can see them like lines of veneer running down Whitefriar-gate, Lowgate, and the Market-place. In the centre are the old red tiles of another generation. The whole area, in fact, between Lowgate, the Market-place, and Queen-street, as one line, and High-street as another, is crowded as closely as it can be packed with dwelling-houses, the only unalterable law of construction and arrangement having apparently been that a passage—wide enough for a human being—must be left somewhere to afford communication with the outer world. The same may be said, though not to the same extent, of the rest of the area within the docks. Thousands who pass and re-pass the main streets day by day know nothing of the domestic habits of the people whose homes are reached by these narrow archways, like entries to a beehive, which perforate the sub-stantial front line of shops and offices. A few examples will show of what kind these homes are. . . .

Immediately opposite the front steps of this Town Hall, not a stone's throw from where we are, is the entrance to a narrow passage known as Dixon's-entry. Let anyone who wants to know how some people live in Hull take a few minutes' walk thither. Now you may do it with impunity, at least by day, ten years ago it was otherwise. Here are from 40 to 50 houses under the shadow of the Town Hall, which are a disgrace to civilisa-tion. It is a colony distinct from the Hull we know. It has its own shops, its own customs, almost its own language. There are about 10 houses in each block built back to back, partly without drainage of any kind, in great part rotten and filthy, the woodwork decayed, the windows often partly gone and replaced with old mats and hay. No wonder will be felt when I add that there are to be found there people, some of whom are as sad a disgrace to humanity as their dwellings are to the town in the centre of which they stand. This is one of the worst cases in the old town. It may be nearly equalled in several places, but not excelled. It is common for terraces of wretched houses to be found facing each other from 5 to 6 feet across. Of such Hay's-entry, Chapel-lane, is an example, and not the worst. In the corner of Scale-lane and High-street, on the north side, is a court called Broad-entry, off this again is another of about 10 houses built facing each other at not more than 4 feet distance. In Hale's-entry, off High-street is the backway to two public-houses. Union-court, off Church-lane, contains a number of dilapidated miserable tenements, mostly let off in single or double rooms. Little-lane, containing about twenty houses, between Humber-street and Blackfriargate, is about seven feet across, with a public house at each end. In the Market-place, at the back of sumptuous shops, are to be found houses with four privies all within six or seven feet from the front door. Kirkus's-buildings, Sewer-lane, have the privies about four feet from the front doors, and immediately opposite. At 4, Sewer-lane is a house containing several families, with the two open privies between the front door and the stair bottom. Robinson-row has some filthy and rotten tenements, reeking with every form of disease both physical and moral. I will not recite more names to weary you, as I have given enough to justify the general statement and to place the facts beyond the possibility of contradiction. But before I pass now to the districts outside the docks let me ask you, gentlemen, to consider for a moment what these facts explain. Foul language or brutal crime sometimes startles us as we come from our decent homes; but place your children in a narrow court six feet wide, inhabited by 70 or 80 people, who live a life apart from that of the outer world. Let there be a drunkard on the upper floor, let decency by the position of your dwellings be impossible, let a house three or four doors away be a den of drunken and degraded women, and your bright child would issue forth in a year or two an adept in curses, and possibly already initiated in crime. Yet these are the conditions actually surrounding many of the would-be decent poor. The shadow of Wilberforce seems to call us to free them from a tyranny as awful as that which degraded the negro of other days. . . .

If anyone should take the trouble of mounting to the first floor above the bell chamber in St. Stephen's Church steeple, the whole mass of small red tiled courts is seen at a glance clearly distinguished from the surrounding houses. Fresh air or sanitary convenience apparently never entered the heads of those who planned these houses. There they stand a crowded beehive of humanity, with nothing to break the monotony of courts except an occasional substantial house, which turns out to be a public-house or else a towering school. Such is the general construction of this district, shaped like a triangle between Prospect-street on the one hand and the station on the other. Coming down and inspecting the streets and courts more closely, we shall find no cause to change our impression. Here, as in all the older parts of Hull the entrances to the courts are closed up by a house fronting the street, and the interior presents the appearance of a long box without a lid. . . .

Some courts are fairly habitable. If you will take the trouble, as I have done, to go the round, you will find many which cannot be called fit to be the homes of the thousands of working men's families who inhabit them. Here the men who work at Hull's standard industry retire when the night or the morning brings them cessation from toil. From reeking, whirring mills they go to 10 feet rooms, shadowed by the houses opposite, crowded, perhaps, with children, with every domestic arrangement of the 100 people in the boxed-up court within the sight and hearing of the front and only door, the whole too often pervaded with the stench of uncleaned drains or middens. Here are courts which branch off into other and narrower ones again, and many single houses literally built in the backyards of the front ones. Darley's-place has the privies 4 feet from the front door, and immediately opposite them.

The Late Period

After the shocks of the early 1880s there was no let-up in the revelations of bad housing which poured forth. Robert Blatchford (1851–1943), the most famous of socialist journalists, writing as "Nunquam", was led to socialism in part by his investigation of the slums of Manchester, the "Modern Athens" (60). The other extracts do something to add a quantitative dimension to urban poverty. The 1891 Census (61) was the first to investigate overcrowding, which it defined as more than two occupants living in one room. Only homes with fewer than five rooms were assumed to be overcrowded, and on this basis 11·23 per cent of the population of England and Wales was overcrowded in 1891. The percentage in London was 19·71 and in Scotland, with its long traditions of overcrowding, no less than 48·2. (See J. H. Clapham. *An Economic History of Modern Britain*, Vol III, 1938, reprinted 1951, 460–4.) By 1901 improvement was discernible everywhere, but overcrowding remained very bad. The pioneering first study of York (62) by Seebohm Rowntree (1871–1954) found that a quarter of the York working class was living in conditions which often degenerated into slums. Only the "well-to-do artisans", 12 per cent of the working class, normally lived in homes equipped with (outside) water closets.

60 "Nunquam" (Robert Blatchford) Modern Athens, A City of Slums
Sunday Chronicle, Manchester (5 May 1889), 2

Mr. Gladstone called Manchester the Modern Athens. I will call it a city of slums. The ex-Mayor of Manchester boasted of town halls and libraries, and temples for the worship of the fine arts! I will tell you of courts and alleys, of filth and squalor, of misery and gloom, and of rascality and imposition.

The ex-Mayor said no city had done so much for the health of the people as had Manchester; and the present Mayor says the death-rate is only 26. I say no city of like size and of like extremity of need has done so little for the health of its people as has this Modern Athens. I say that the death-rate is nearly 29, and is the highest death-rate in England; I say that the working-class dwellings of this city are unfit for human habitation, and that their sanitary surroundings are abominable.

I will arrange my charges under two heads:

1. Insanitary Dwellings.
2. Insanitary Surroundings.

And I shall try to show how vast and dire these two evils are, and how they blast the health, the comfort, and the morality of an intelligent, industrious, and noble people.

Since I began my investigations, I have been often asked by friends, "Where are the slums of Manchester?" and I have answered, "They are everywhere. Manchester is a city of slums." And, so far as the working-class dwellings are concerned, this is no exaggeration; and one may say deliberately that the working-class dwellings are the slums, and that the slums are the working-class dwellings. It is, indeed, the terrible extent of this evil that makes it so appalling. Were there but a few bad streets in a few poor districts, one might turn away in the belief that only the criminal and vicious classes resided in them. But here we are, face to face with the fact that the bulk of the working people of one of the richest and busiest cities in the world are cooped up in styes too vile to harbour brutes. . . .

How shall I attempt to paint the shame of Modern Athens— the dwellings of her people? The miles of narrow, murky streets, the involuted labyrinths of courts and passages and covered ways, where a devilish ingenuity seems to have striven with triumphant success to shut out light and air; the broken pavements, the ill-set roads, where filth is scattered broadcast and the stagnant water lies in pools; the ash-pits filled to overflowing, and shedding their foul contents upon the sloppy walks, close to the cottage doors; the dark, narrow, dilapidated, built-in hovels; the rotten bricks, the ruptured cave-spouts, the sinking roofs, the stone floors laid upon the sodden earth; the perished woodwork, the damp and blackened walls, the filthy ceilings! How shall I bring to the reader's mind a conception of life in these courts, and alleys, where children play in mud and stench, and where the slaves of the sweater toil and gasp in the close, mephitic air, straining their eyes in the ill-lit rooms and growing prematurely old with labour and care and exhaustion of the vital powers? It is a place accursed and miserable, this Modern Athens, and one to which no language can do justice.

In the covered passages, leading from closed courts, the air is palpable to the touch. The stench can be *felt*. The darkness, the smoke, and the gloom come down upon the spirit like a pall, and stifle hope and gaiety. The misery and destitution that here hide and crouch would sear a heart of flint. No man with a man's feeling can pass through such scenes without depression; only an iron physique can come away from them unscathed. Our artist was ill after his first expedition; I have come home many times quite prostrated; and even our guide, himself a denizen of the slums and long inured to their miseries and discomforts, has suffered in both mind and body.

The houses are not only unhealthy from their construction and surroundings; they are also shamefully out of repair. The paper is black with the grease and grime of years, the plaster is cracked and crumbling, the ceilings are rent and swollen and foul, the woodwork is paintless, the roofs are broken, the walls damp, the doors and windows warped and shrunken, the rotted bricks and lath and plaster are reeking with pollution and, in fact, if twenty thousand of these styes were demolished to-morrow the materials of which they are composed would not be worth the cost of cartage.

Many of the ceilings are only six feet high; none are over eight. The average size of the rooms is about ten feet square—many not eight feet square. There are no boilers in the kitchen in which to wash the clothes, and the usual drying ground is the roadway of the street or court. In winter time these dens are damp and cold, draughty and dark, and the brick or cobble floors of the courts are filled with puddles of water and liquid filth. In summer time the rooms are like ovens; the close courts are hot and stifling, and the stench from the ash pits and pans becomes poisonous and unbearable. The houses, too, are infested with vermin, and in the hot nights the poor people may be seen sitting out on the flags and steps, sleep being for them almost impossible.

61 1891 Census   General Report
PP, Vol CVI (1893–4), 23

These differences are of course such as might be expected, as being the natural results of the greater costliness of space in towns. But less easy is it to explain the extraordinary differences between the towns themselves when compared with each other. The figures for the 33 great towns that are included in the Registrar-General's weekly returns are given in Table 30 of Appendix A, and on examining that table it will be seen that the proportion of the population living in an overcrowded condition, as previously defined, varies as much as from 1·74 to 40·78 per cent. without any very apparent explanation.

The six great towns in which the percentages of overcrowded persons were the highest were as follows:—

Gateshead - - - -	40·78
Newcastle upon Tyne - -	35·08
Sunderland - - -	32·85
Plymouth - - - -	26·27
Halifax - - - -	21·31
Bradford - - - -	20·61

On the other hand, the six towns with the lowest percentages were these:—

Preston	-	-	-	-	4·13
Nottingham	-	-	-	3·62
Croydon	-	-	-	-	2·76
Derby	-	-	-	-	2·69
Leicester	-	-	-	-	2·22
Portsmouth -	-	-	-	1·74

Portsmouth and Plymouth would appear to be towns having much resemblance to each other in their general character; yet in Portsmouth less than 2 per cent. of the population are apparently overcrowded, while in Plymouth the percentage is over 26. Leicester and Bradford again are two large industrial towns, both engaged in textile manufactures; for the former the percentage is 2·22, and for the latter 20·61, or nearly 10 times as high. Possibly accurate local knowledge may be able to account for such remarkable contrasts; but there is nothing in the data supplied by the Census that, so far as we can discover, throws light on it.

Similarly wide differences are presented by the figures for different registration counties; the six with most overcrowding (London omitted) and the six with least, and their several percentages, being as follows:—

Northumberland -	-	-	38·69
Durham	-	-	-	34·03
West Riding of Yorkshire	-	16·49
Pembroke -	-	-	-	14·33
Cumberland	-	-	-	13·02
Warwickshire	-	-	-	11·82
Herefordshire	-	-	-	3·65
Kent -	-	-	-	-	3·00
Sussex	-	-	-	-	2·90
Radnorshire	-	-	-	2·79
Surrey	-	-	-	-	2·70
Hampshire -	-	-	-	2·58

These differences are not quite so unintelligible as those between the towns; the overcrowded counties, as a rule, are industrial and especially mining counties, and contain large towns; while the least overcrowding is, as a rule, in the counties where there are neither large manufactures nor large industrial towns.

Speaking generally, it would appear that the coalbearing counties are those where the crowding of dwellings is most severe. Northumberland and Durham, if the figures are to be trusted, are far away the worst in this respect. Nor can this be attributed merely to the presence of Newcastle and Tynemouth in the former, and of Gateshead and Sunderland in the latter. For even when these towns, and all other urban sanitary districts that have more than 15,000 inhabitants, are taken out of the account, the figures that represent the amount of over-crowding in the residue of the counties are still excessively high, indeed are slightly higher than when the towns are included.

62 B. Seebohm Rowntree   Poverty, A Study of Town Life

(1901), 147, 152–4

The houses occupied by the working-class population may be roughly divided into three classes—(1) the comfortable houses of the well-to-do artisans; (2) houses, for the most part four-roomed, principally occupied by families in receipt of moderate but regular wages; (3) houses in the poorest disticts, many of which are typical "slum" dwellings. Of course no clear dividing line marks off the three classes, for although the difference between houses in Classes 1 and 3 is obvious, it is often difficult to decide whether a house shall be placed in the second class; nevertheless it may be roughly stated that houses occupied by 1466 families belong to Class 1, others occupied by 7145 families to Class 2, and others occupied by 2949 families to Class 3. . . .

CLASS 3.—*Occupied by about 2949 Families, equal to 26 per cent of the Working-Class Families in York.*

This class comprises all houses which are not good enough to be included in Classes 1 and 2. They may be roughly divided into two grades—first, the houses which are only slightly inferior to those in Class 2, and second, the slum houses. The houses in the first grade are less uniform in general plan than those in Class 2. Many have only two or three rooms, and scarcely any more than four. Their dingy walls add gloom to the narrow streets, and the absence of all architectural relief conveys a sense of depression. Inside a few are clean and tidy, but most are dirty and overcrowded. Generally speaking, it may be said that they are occupied by the struggling poor, who pay rents varying from 2s. or 2s. 6d. for a two-roomed house (usually called "an oop-an'-a-doon") to 4s. or 4s. 6d. for a house with four rooms, the landlord paying all rates. Often the closet accommodation is both inadequate and insanitary.

From these houses we descend by degrees to the typical slum dwellings. They were mostly built long before Public Health Acts or bye-laws regulating the width of streets and the construction of houses were heard of. They are generally small, few of them having as many as four rooms. Some are situated in narrow alleys paved with cobbles, others in confined courts which admit sadly too little sunlight and air, and which are often separated from the main street by dark covered passages three or four feet wide.

Overcrowding and insanitary conditions of all kinds abound in the slums, and back-to-back houses in which through ventilation is impossible are common in them. The water-supply is very inadequate, one tap being often the sole supply for a large number of houses. In some cases the tap which supplies the drinking water is fixed in the wall of the water-closet. Pantries and water-closets are sometimes separated by a wall only one brick in thickness. Many of the ashpits are over-flowing, and heaps of all kinds of rubbish are distributed promiscuously over the yard or court. . . . Midden privies are usual, and these, like the water-taps, are in many cases shared by several houses. They are particularly offensive in these over-populated and under-ventilated districts. A number of slaughter-houses situated in the midst of the slum districts form another unsatisfactory feature. Even in the poorest districts some of the houses, to the great credit of the tenants, are kept tidy and clean, but the majority exhibit the usual characteristics of slum property. They have dirty windows, broken panes are frequently stuffed with rags or pasted over with brown paper, and a general appearance of dilapidation and carelessness reveals the condition and character of the tenants.

Inside the rooms are often dark and damp, and almost always dirty. Many of the floors are of red bricks, or of bricks that would be red if they were washed. They are often uneven and much broken, having been laid on to the earth with no concrete or other foundation. On washing-days pools of water collect which gradually percolate through to the damp and unsavoury soil below.

DEMOLITION

The destruction of the homes of the working classes—by railways, streets, public buildings and "improvement" schemes aimed simply at getting rid of the poor—is so important a matter as to need a section to itself. The very poor tended to be migratory in their habits in any case, but constant demolition of their homes increased this tendency. Lord Shaftesbury (1801–85) was concerned throughout a long lifetime with the homes of the poor. When he and a future Prime Minister, Lord Derby (1799–1869), tried (not for the first time) in 1861 to stop the destruction of working-class houses, the comment of *The Times* (63) showed a remarkable lack of either perceptiveness or humanity. Friedrich Engels (1820–95) shows (64) that, although the demolition problem was above all metropolitan, other large cities had a similar approach to this early type of "town planning". William Gilbert (1804–90), doctor, author and father of the dramatist, was a champion of the poor, and in this extract (65) and elsewhere his hostility towards those who dispossessed them was made clear.

The official enquiries of the 1880s showed that, while there was something to be gained from breaking up slum areas and creating open space, the effect on the people who lost their homes was catastrophic. Andrew Young was a surveyor who was employed by the London School Board and also had a private practice. He told the Royal Commission of 1884–5 (66) that some of the worst properties with which he had to deal were those bought by the School Board, which necessarily had to build schools where population was thickest.

Until the end of the period and beyond the problem of demolition continued (though the outstanding difficulty of the railways abated as railway building declined), and little was done to rehouse the poor. The London School Board, for example, while giving *ex gratia* payments to those evicted, built no houses to replace those destroyed until 1899.

63 The Times   Leading Article on Housing
(2 March 1861), 8–9

[We refer to] those frightful truths which are already sufficiently known—and nothing can be so discreditable to a civilized country—that human beings are huddled together in filth and squalor, and without distinction of age or sex, in ill-ventilated, ill-repaired, ill-drained, and ill-roofed dwellings. Unhappily, this is but too true. Why it should be so no one can tell. It cannot be from any special convenience in the locality, for these people must be labourers, whose work must lie in all parts of the great metropolis. It cannot be for cheapness, for the returns show that the inhabitants of these rickety dens pay upon an average a rent of 6*l.* a-year for a space of a thousand cubic feet, which, in proportion, is as much as a nobleman pays for his mansion in Belgrave-square. Perhaps it is the attraction of misery to misery and dirt to dirt. Such aggregations cannot be favourable either to public or to private morality. They must tend, not only to harbour, but to generate, dangerous classes. As we cut nicks through our woods, and roads through our forests, so it should be our policy to divide these thick jungles of crime and misery. Much already has been done to tempt these people to purer air and better habits. Thousands of cottages are springing up yearly in the suburbs which fringe the metropolis; model lodging-houses are being built; capitalists are well aware that there is no customer so profitable as the labouring man; but the multitudes, for bad reasons or for no reasons, cling to their old habits and to their old impenetrable haunts. The singular complaint of Lord DERBY and Lord SHAFTESBURY is not that these districts of wretchedness should be allowed to exist, but that Railways should be allowed to come in to open them up or to sweep them away. That a clergyman, who has passed his life in ministrations amid such a population should complain that a Railway proposed to turn his whole parish into Railway lines, and to make him a sinecure pensioner, is not unnatural. He looks at the subject with the short sight of a man accustomed to live in darkness; but that Lord DERBY should call upon the Legislature to interfere to protect these fever preserves and these crime converts is indeed strange. Stranger still does it sound to hear Lord SHAFTESBURY bemoaning the destruction of that dreadful rookery by Field-lane, which was the safe refuge of every London thief, and through the mysterious recesses of which the black volumes of the uncovered Fleet Ditch rolled, ready at any moment to hide the evidence of deadly crime. These are the dwellings of the labouring classes which we have heard two influential Peers describe in all their grossness, and yet desire to save. These are the dwellings which they would preserve, and for the preservation of which they would keep Railways out of London. Can anything be more absurd! Now that the centre of London is no longer the centre of manu-factures, now that employment is dispersed over the great metropolitan province, it is convenient, and it is even necessary, that the habitations of the labourers should be likewise dis-persed; and the Railways which come to thin these neighbour-hoods are even more beneficial to the labouring man than they are to the classes above him. If there be a grievance, it is to that numerous class in London which lives by plunder alone, and which may be compelled to quit its accustomed haunts for others less hidden from the eyes of the police. If lodging a poor man did not pay, there might be danger that the labourer might be straitened for a lodging; but, while he pays the builder a better percentage upon his money than can be got out of a Prince, there can be no fear that the labourer will be unable to find a roof, even if a Railway should take his old house for a Station.

64 Friedrich Engels   The Housing Question
(1872; first English ed, nd; 1935), 75–7

In *The Condition of the Working Class in England* I gave a description of Manchester as it looked in 1843 and 1844. Since then the construction of railways through the centre of the town, the laying out of new streets, and the erection of great public and private buildings have broken through, laid bare and improved some of the worst districts described in my book, others have been abolished altogether, but many of them are still, apart from the fact that official sanitary inspection has since become stricter, in the same state or in an even worse state of dilapidation than they were then. On the other hand, however, thanks to the enormous extension of the town, whose population has increased since then by more than half, districts which were at that time still airy and clean are now just as excessively built upon, just as dirty and overcrowded as the most ill-famed parts of the town formerly were.

Here is just one example: On page 80 and the following pages of my book I describe a group of houses situated in the valley bottom of the river Medlock, which under the name of Little Ireland was for years one of the worst blots on Manchester. Little Ireland has long ago disappeared and on its site there now stands a railway station built on a high foundation. The bourgeoisie pointed with pride to the happy and final abolition of Little Ireland as to a great triumph. Now last summer a great inundation took place, as in general the rivers embanked in our big towns cause extensive floods year after year owing to easily understood causes. And it was then revealed that Little Ireland had not been abolished at all, but had simply been shifted from the south side of Oxford Road to the north side, and that it still continues to flourish. . . .

This is a striking example of how the bourgeoisie solves the housing question in practice. The breeding places of disease, the infamous holes and cellars in which the capitalist mode of production confines our workers night after night, are not abolished; they are merely *shifted elsewhere!* The same economic necessity which produced them in the first place, produces them in the next place also. As long as the capitalist mode of production continues to exist, it is folly to hope for an isolated solution of the housing question or of any other social question affecting the fate of the workers. The solution lies in the abolition of the capitalist mode of production and the appropriation of all the means of life and labour by the working class itself.

65 William Gilbert　The Dwellings of the London Poor
Good Words (1872), 458–62

Let us commence with the West-end, because the earliest destruction of the dwellings of the London poor, which has been carried on so energetically for the last forty or fifty years, took place in that portion of London. When the war with France terminated, and the idea of improving the metropolis occupied the attention of Government, Regent Street was projected, and one great reason for its formation in the line it took was that it would destroy an immense number of poor dwellings. The inhabitants were ejected in crowds; but no provision was made for their reception. In the western districts land was too valuable for them to find a home; and they migrated towards the Strand, to Westminster, and in many instances into Lambeth. The improvements in the Strand and Trafalgar Square followed, when the same reason that was urged on the formation of Regent

Street was again brought forward. The poor were too crowded; their dwellings were unsightly and unhealthy. The work of destruction recommenced. Westminster increased in population considerably; Lambeth still more so. St. Giles's, already too crowded, received a great accession of inhabitants. In this last instance, to such a pitch had the misery and overcrowding come, that the whole parish was threatened with an overwhelming mass of pauperism. At last the attention of Government was called to its condition; and the usual panacea of municipal legislation in cases of the kind was applied. Acres of ground covered with densely inhabited dwellings of the poor were laid waste, and New Oxford Street, Endell Street, and several others were formed; but no accommodation was provided for the poor who were driven away.

In the meantime Westminster had not been inactive in this work of ejectment. The Five Fields at Pimlico, the whole of the present locality of Belgravia, were formerly occupied by a comparatively sparse population. In order to form the present region of palaces these poorer inhabitants were necessarily driven away, either into Chelsea or into Westminster; and the result was that certain spots in the last-named district became so crowded, and the rates so burdensome, that improvements, or relief in some shape, were loudly called for. Many were the attempts made to induce the Dean and Chapter to enter into some arrangements. But the demands of that body rendered it impossible to effect any improvement, unless houses of such size and appearance were built as would utterly preclude the possibility of the poor residing there. Victoria Street was in consequence projected, and an immense mass of poor people were driven away, with this result, that up to the present time not more than one-half of the space formerly covered by dwellings of the poor has been built over. One great object, however, had been attained—the poor had been ejected. . . .

. . . The Metropolitan Board of Works resolved on the formation of a new street to connect Westminster with the Borough. Here, again, parochial influence was strong, and, instead of making the line by the shortest and cheapest road, as well as the one which would have ejected fewest inhabitants, it was taken through Stamford Street, solely on account of the improvement (?) which it was urged would be effected by the destruction of the squalid hovels and densely-inhabited dwellings of the poor in that locality. But this does not exhaust the injustice inflicted on the poor in the locality. The Charing Cross line to Cannon Street had to be carried out. And here again followed an enormous destruction of the dwellings of the working classes, who were turned out of their houses: and, with the exception of the re-burnishing of gin-shops in the neighbourhoods of St. George's, Southwark, and Walworth (the two localities into which they were driven), not the slightest notice appeared to be taken of the transaction. . . .

. . . We will now return to the Middlesex side of the water, and, starting from Charing Cross, continue our way up the Strand into the City. The first object we come on connected with our subject is the site of the new Law Courts. Some six or seven years since the whole of this immense space was covered with dwellings. Of these many were used for attorneys' offices, others of them formerly (a century or more ago) had been respectable dwelling-houses; but by far the greater portion were occupied by the poorest classes.

One of the great tests of the poverty of a district is infant mortality. While the births in London were at an average 30 per cent. greater than the deaths, in this parish of St. Clement's Danes, the death-rate from excessive infant mortality, was greater than the births. When it was proposed that the Law Courts should be built in this parish, more than four thousand poor creatures were ejected from their dwellings to find a home where they could, no provision being made for their reception elsewhere. Nor is this all. They were positively driven away before it was absolutely decided that the new Law Courts should be built here. And while the promoters of the scheme were wrangling among themselves whether, after all, this was the best spot, the ground remained utterly useless and unoccupied. Just look at the appearance it now presents. Would it be possible to imagine a more complete picture of desolation? And yet you may judge from the foundations of the houses lately rising above the surface of the ground how densely populated the whole space must formerly have been.

We have lately been reading lamentable accounts of the destruction in those portions of the city of Strasbourg which, during the siege, were principally exposed to the fire of the German artillery, but the houses there destroyed would probably not form one tithe of those of the dwellings of the poor who have been driven out of this one locality. There is, however, one difference to be remarked in the comparison. No sooner had the Germans entered Strasbourg than one of their first cares was to erect new dwellings in place of those which had been destroyed. But as I have before mentioned, not a house has been erected to shelter those helpless creatures who have here been driven away. . . .

. . . Doubtless the reader will ask whether in the wholesale destruction of the dwellings of the working classes, the civic authorities, with their enormous wealth, did not give some consideration to the welfare and convenience of these poorer citizens. They did; and in a manner very characteristic of the management of the charitable operations by the Corporation of the City of London. In the formation of the Farringdon Street Wastes, as they were formerly called (the many acres of ground cleared by the destruction of the houses of the working classes in that neighbourhood), they were appealed to by certain philanthropists to make some provision for a portion of the poor people ejected. Nor was the appeal without its effect, although perhaps the manner in which it was responded to will hardly meet with the reader's approbation. The City authorities met, and resolved that a certain sum of money, £20,000 we believe, should be set aside to build model lodging houses for the reception of the better class of the poor, and that when these houses were filled, others should be commenced. On making this determination public, the Corporation were complimented in the highest manner, and these compliments were received by them as just reward for their efforts in the cause of the poor.

Their virtuous determination then gradually fell asleep. Not a word more was said about the model lodging-houses; public indignation either faded out, or the public interest diverted to other subjects, and some twenty years elapsed without even the foundation of a house being commenced. The spot of ground was then sold (some say at a considerable profit) to the Metropolitan Railway Company, and the whole affair is now almost forgotten.

66 Royal Commission on the Housing of the Working Classes   Evidence of Andrew Young
PP, Vol XXX (1884–5), 193–4

5940. Had you much difficulty in getting the occupants to quit?—Very great difficulty, more than I have had in any other site. After quitting they came back again.

5941. Did you give them compensation for going?—Yes, some compensation was given them.

5942. How much would they get?—Those having one room might have from 5*s.* to 1*l.*

5943. And they came back at night, I understand from you? —Yes, after they had given us the key, and had given up possession, they came back at night and took possession again.

5944. With regard to the Tower Street, St. Giles', case, that was very overcrowded, was it not?—Yes, it was.

5945. That site you cleared about 10 years ago, I think?— Yes.

5946. Have you any facts within your own knowledge which lead you to know that overcrowding has increased or decreased in that neighbourhood?—I have recently sold for a client to the Metropolitan Board of Works for a new street about 40 houses close by these. I visited the various rooms on the spot, and was very much struck with the increased overcrowding from the time of purchasing for the school board site to the present time.

5947. What has been the cause of the overcrowding?—I take it that it has been in consequence of the general clearances around the heart of London.

5948. In the case of the Great Wild Street, Drury Lane, site, that is a very overcrowded district, is it not?—Yes, I think that was even more so than the Tower Street site, and the remaining houses, I have reason to know, are quite as bad as those that we removed.

5949. That site was overcrowded, perhaps, in consequence of the demolitions for the erection of the Drury Lane Peabody Buildings?—There is no doubt of it.

5950. That is a costermonger population, is it not?—There are a large number of costermongers and porters at the Covent Garden Market living just about there.

5951. Are they a class of people that would get into the Peabody Buildings?—No, they are the class of people who are kept out. . . .

5960. Did you have great difficulty in getting rid of your tenants there?—Yes, we had great difficulty in doing so.

5961. Did that arise from the difficulty the tenants experienced in finding fresh accommodation?—It did. It was only by giving them a couple of months, allowing them to go one family or one house at a time, that we could do it.

5962. Were they people whose work made it necessary for them to live in the neighbourhood?—Yes, they were all people gaining their living or engaged in the immediate neighbourhood, either in Covent Garden or the neighbourhood.

5963. Some of them, I believe, rather than leave the neighbourhood, sold their furniture and went into common lodging-houses?—They did not sell it—they broke it up. For one or two nights it was quite a painful scene to see them.

5964. (*The Marquess of Salisbury.*) The people broke the furniture up and burnt it, did they not?—Yes, they broke it up and burnt it It was not furniture that they could sell; it answered their purpose, but no broker would touch it.

DISCUSSION: THE CAUSES OF URBAN SLUMS

The Law and its Administrators

Instead of being designed to facilitate the better housing of the working classes, the law appeared to be aimed at preventing it. Where the law was adequate the aims or methods of those who carried it out were suspect. Indifference and hostility to public expenditure were rightly blamed for lack of progress in housing. Joseph Chamberlain (1836–1914) was writing (67) in the immediate aftermath of the furore over the *Bitter Cry of Outcast London*. As a then Radical politician he was concerned with the enormous profits made from scandalously over-generous compensation, and advocated a "betterment" tax on those whose property was improved by public clearance schemes. (Chamberlain refers in his first line to the promoters of housing legislation in and after 1875.) Lord Salisbury, the Conservative leader, had written an article with the same title as Chamberlain's in the *National Review* in November 1883, suggesting that public money should be lent to organisations intending to erect working-class dwellings. The Cross Acts (1875, 1879, 1882) dealt with the clearing and rebuilding of large urban areas, while Torrens' Acts (1868, 1879) were concerned with single properties. Although the clearing was done by local authorities, rebuilding was left to private enterprise in almost all cases. Bodies like the Metropolitan Board of Works (predecessor of the London County Council) found that they could only sell land to charitable bodies such as the Peabody Trust (see 113) at an enormous loss, since land had to be bought at its market value and sold at the much lower value which prevailed for working-class housing (68). In one scheme in 1876–82 alone, involving fewer than 4,000 people, the Board spent £391,303 on the purchase and clearance of the property, and received income of £76,360, of which £36,781 15s od was from the Peabody Trust (C. J. Stewart, ed. *The Housing Question in London, 1855–1900* [nd; 1901], 137, 142). *Punch* (69) puts its finger on the cause of much suffering, at the time of a Local Government Board Circular urging local authorities to use existing powers to improve working-class homes. (Sir Charles Dilke, 1843–1911, was then the President of the Local Government Board; Hugh Owen, 1835–1916, his Permanent Secretary.) The Royal Commission explains more fully some of the inadequacies and evasions of the law (70). Despite improvements made by the Housing Act of 1890, the law remained cumbersome and expensive to would-be housing reformers until well beyond the end of the century.

67 Joseph Chamberlain   Labourers' and Artisans' Dwellings
Fortnightly Review (December 1883), 767–8

The intention of the promoters was excellent. The local authority was to be empowered to reconstruct large areas where they were found to be so occupied as to be injurious to the moral and physical welfare of the people, and where from want of light, air, ventilation, and proper conveniences they had become unfit for habitation and injurious to the health of the surrounding population. For this purpose they were to exercise compulsory powers of purchase, and the property was to be acquired at the fair market value as estimated at the time of valuation, having regard to its nature and condition, and with no allowance for compulsory purchase or prospective value.

Nothing could be fairer in theory, but what has been the result in practice? The owners of this class of property, whose greed and neglect have rendered interference necessary, have in every case obtained from the public, under the guise of compensation, amounts altogether and demonstrably in excess of the market value of their property even on the most favourable computation. Surely the sound principle of compensation in such cases should be the real value of the land and buildings used under legitimate conditions, and not the exorbitant value arising from criminal practices. To take an instance: there is a certain class of property always found in these unhealthy areas, and used for immoral purposes actually prohibited by the law. The illegal occupation is, however, the justification of the exorbitant rents demanded from the wretched occupants by the persons who trade in their vices. A house which for honest occupation is worth £50 a year will bring in double or treble to an owner who winks at the traffic which it is permitted to shelter. When this house is required by the local authority, the demand for compensation is based, and often allowed, on an income which represents not a fair return for an investment, but the profit on complicity with vice. The same result obtains where tenements which could properly accommodate a single family are made to do duty for three or four times as many persons as can be decently housed in them. The income derived is proportionately increased, and compensation follows as a premium on evil practices.

Accordingly men are found to speculate on the probability of interference, and they buy up in anticipation property which is likely to provoke the action of the local authority. If they succeed in aggravating the nuisance till it is intolerable, their fortunes are made. The ratepayers at large must bear the cost of putting an end to this detestable business, and are expected at the same time to reward munificently all who have been engaged in it.

The proposals of Lord Salisbury, taken by themselves, would only intensify the evil. The owner who has neglected his most obvious duty is to have the taxes to draw upon as well as the rates. The individual wrong-doer is to remain unpunished— retribution for his sins is to be exacted from the whole community. What the total cost may be it is impossible to estimate accurately, but some idea of the nature of the liability which is to be slipped from the shoulders of the landowner and placed on the backs of the ratepayers may be gathered from the experience of existing legislation.

The report of the Committee of the House of Commons (June,

1882), presided over by Sir Richard Cross, gives a full account of the operations in the metropolis under the Acts of 1875 and 1879. The Metropolitan Board of Works have dealt in all with forty-two acres of land inhabited by 20,335 persons. The net loss on the improvement is estimated at £1,211,336, or about £60 per head of the population assumed to be benefited. The cost of the land required has been about 17s. per square foot. The price obtainable for the same land, if sold with the obligation to build workmen's dwellings, is 3s. 4d. per foot on the average, but its value for commercial purposes is stated to be 10s. per foot.

The inference from these figures is most important, but, strangely enough, the Committee do not seem to have drawn it. Under Sir R. Cross's Acts, which were "intended to guard against any excessive valuation of the property dealt with," it appears that the owners of houses, courts, and alleys which had been declared by the proper authority unfit for human habitation, received 17s. per foot for land which could not be valued, even after the improvements had been made and new streets laid out, at more than 10s. per foot for commercial purposes, or more than 3s. 4d. per foot for artisans' dwellings. In other words, the effect of expropriation in the case of those owners, whose lâches and criminal neglect had brought about the state of things which required State intervention, was that they made a profit of 7s. per foot on the ordinary market value of their property under the most favourable circumstances, and that they obtained 13s. 8d. per foot more than their land was fairly worth for the special purpose for which they had been employing it.

It is not surprising, under these circumstances, that the Committee report that "The difficulty in carrying out the provisions of these Acts obviously arises from the great cost of doing so." In fact, the Acts as at present worked offer a premium for neglect and wilful indifference to sanitary provisions.

They say, in effect, to the bad landlord, "Allow your property to fall into disrepair, to become a nest of disease, and a centre of crime and immorality, and then we will step in and buy it from you at a price seventy per cent. above what you could obtain in the ordinary market if you attempted to dispose of it without our assistance."

68 [Lewis Dibdin] Dwellings of the Poor
Quarterly Review (January 1884), 164

In round figures, the Metropolitan Board have cleared away forty acres of buildings. Of these, twenty-three are still, at this moment, vacant. Some of the sites have been lying useless and waste for years, with the result that the overcrowding of London is aggravated by some 10,000 people having been squeezed into houses already full to overflowing. The fact is, that rebuilding has not kept pace with pulling down. Notwithstanding the enormous sacrifice at which the Metropolitan Board of Works is forced to offer sites for sale, purchasers cannot be found. Artizans' dwellings, built according to the Board's plans and under its supervision, are not a promising speculation. Even the great building companies are not attracted. There is no competition. Of eight sites put up to auction last June, only three were sold. But for the Peabody Trustees, who have found in Cross's Acts the solution of what was their great difficulty—how to procure sites, most of the seventeen acres bought under these Acts, and now covered with model dwellings, would probably be still lying waste. Until a remedy has been found for this reluctance to build, the prosecution of fresh schemes under Cross's Acts is a matter of very doubtful expediency, and even safety. Unemployed areas, such as at present exist, mean a ruinous waste of income to the ratepayers, and a serious amount of suffering, discontent, and injury, to the poor. Happily the need for wholesale clearances, though still great, is not so pressing as it was in 1875. There is far greater scope for the application of Torrens's Acts to single houses.

69 The Bitter Cry of Bumbledom
Punch (12 January 1884), 18

Wot rubbige it is, all this muck about labourers' dwellings!

Wheresomever the poor is there's bound to be breakages, dirt, and bad smellings.

Poor thrives on 'em. Ask them as knows,—not your Parsons, and scribblers, and Presidents,

As goes sniffin' round in the slums, to the jolly disgust of the residents;

But proper Porochial parties, as knows that the labouring classes

Are half of 'em regular prigs, and the rest noisy Radical asses.

Us to blame? That's a capital notion! Drat them and their "statutes" and "digests".

"Convenience of reference." Ah! that is one of their imperent sly jests.

The Westries and Boards don't want woritting. Worrit is just my abhorrence.

We know all about their fine Acts, whether cooked up by CROSS or by TORRENS.

But to act upon Acts at full drive, as though *we* was mere waifs in a Workus.

A-doing our bit on compulsion,—they might as well treadmill or burke us!

Permissive they're all werry well, leaving *us* to be starters and judges;

But puttin' the screw on like this is just making us porper-like drudges.

Removal of Noosances? Yah! If we started on *that* lay, per-miskers,

There's more than a few in the Westries 'ud feel suthin' singin' their wiskers,

Or BUMBLE'S a Dutchman. Their Cir'clar—it's mighty obliging—defines 'em,

The Noosances namely; I wonder if parties *reads* Cir'clars as signs 'em,

If so, Local Government Boarders must be most *on*commonly knowin',

V.H.—F

And I'd like to 'eave bricks at that DILKE and his long-winded
myrmidon, OWEN.

The Public's got Slums on the brain, and with sanitary bun-
kum's half busted.

We make a more wigorous use of the powers with which we're
intrusted?

Wy, if we are at it all day with their drains, ashpits, roofs, walls,
and windies,

Wot time shall we 'ave for our feeds and our little porochial
shindies?

70 Royal Commission on the Housing of the Working Classes   First Report
PP, Vol XXX (1884–5), 21–3

Two more alleged causes of overcrowding and of sanitary
evils in the metropolis remain for examination. The one is the
relation between owners of property upon which the dwellings
of the poor stand and the tenants of those dwellings, the other is
the default of local authorities in using their legitimate powers.

The freeholder of a building estate appears to be in practice
not the responsible owner of the property for sanitary purposes.
The terms of the leases provide that the tenant shall keep the
house in repair, but the stringent conditions of the leases fall
into disuse; the difficulty of personal supervision of the property
is apt to grow greater, and the relations between the ground
landlord and the tenant who occupies the house grow less and
less. The multiplicity of interests involved in a single house and
the number of hands through which the rent has to pass, causes
the greatest doubt as to who is the person who ought to be
called upon to execute repairs or to look after the condition of
the premises. This is especially the case when building has taken
place for which no trace of sanction can be found on the part of
the ground landlord, the erections under such circumstances
being often crowded on gardens or courts, the preservation of

which would have been for the sanitary benefit of the existing houses.

Much evidence has also been given as to the system of middlemen, of house jobbers, house farmers, or house knackers, for by all those titles are designated those persons who stand between the freeholder and the occupier, and who fix and receive the rent of the tenement houses.

In dealing with this system, Your Majesty's Commissioners are not founding their report on the evidence of those clergy, philanthropists, and local and other reformers, who have agreed in condemning it; they have preferred to confine themselves to the testimony of two witnesses who are intimately connected with the leasehold system. The first, Lord William Compton, is the son of the owner of one of the largest properties in London on which middlemen are found; the second is Mr. Boodle, the agent to the Northampton as well as to the Westminster estate. From the evidence of these two witnesses it appears that the existence of the system of house farmers is in some measure owing to the preference for middlemen on the part of both the landlord and his man of business. Moreover, this evidence shows that there is an indisposition on the part of landlords to avail themselves stringently of the provisoes in their leases for re-entry and for the troublesome and costly process of ejectment of tenants in case of breach of covenant, the covenants usually including external and internal repairing, cleaning and painting, and the keeping in order of drains. Again, it was pointed out that landlords like to give short leases of decaying property, so that they may fall in when long leases expire, and the property can be dealt with as a whole more satisfactorily than it could be piecemeal. All these considerations appear to favour the middleman system, to which is attributed by Mr. Boodle the breaking up of houses built for single families into tenements, with all the evil and inconvenience attending that arrangement. This is also said to be the cause in a great measure of the enormous rents charged for the single rooms in tenement houses in which it has been seen the poor chiefly live in the worst parts of

London. On the Clerkenwell Estate Lord William Compton went very carefully into some of the figures relating to houses leased from the Marquess of Northampton by certain house farmers. In Queen Street he ascertained the exact rents received by and paid to two persons of this class, who are also members of the Vestry of Clerkenwell. At No. 10, for instance, he found that the weekly rent of the front room was 12*s.*, of the back room 4*s.* 6*d.*, of the kitchen 3*s.*, of the first floor 13*s.*, and of the second floor 7*s.* This amounted to about 100*l.* a year, and the rent which the house jobber paid to Lord Northampton was 20*l.* a year. The agent to the Northampton Estate allows that a middleman might in a particular instance be making 150 per cent. per annum, not counting his outlay for repairs, but that the repairs are only wanted once in three or four years, and therefore in the other years he makes his 150 per cent. In what manner the repairs are carried out has already been shown in the evidence which described the condition of the houses in this and other poor quarters of the town. The house farmer is not at all anxious to encroach upon his profits, whether they are at the rate of 50 per cent. or 150 per cent., by periodical repairs. Lord William Compton stated that he shrank from calling to account the middleman for neglecting to repair, fearing that a rise in the rents would be the consequence of such a proceeding. The average income of the tenants has already been mentioned, so it is not surprising that sometimes the middlemen find a difficulty in collecting the rents on a Monday morning, and their remedy in that case seems to be a threat to raise them still higher. It was stated by witnesses that if there were more official supervision, by means of improved local government to prevent overcrowding and to enforce sanitary requirements it would be impossible for middlemen to make the large percentages they at present secure. This leads to the other great remaining cause of evil, the remissness of local authorities. . . .

The vestries and district boards have under 18 & 19 Vict. c. 120. power of appointing medical officers of health and inspectors of nuisances who are in no way subject to the Local Government Board or any other public department, either as to tenure of office or as to salary. These powerful governing bodies are elected by parishioners rated to the relief of the poor; but little interest is, as a rule, taken in the election by the inhabitants, instances having been known of vestrymen in populous parishes being returned by two votes on a show of hands. The fact that only two authorities out of 38, the vestry of Chelsea and the district board of works of Hackney, have in the past been energetically taking action under the provisions of the Sanitary Act in respect of tenement houses, may be fairly taken as presumptive proof of supineness on the part of many of the metropolitan local authorities in sanitary matters, at all events as regards parishes which contain large numbers of such houses as would come under the Act. The proportion of inspectoral staff which is considered adequate to the population in various parts of the metropolis may also be taken as evidence of similar laxity of administration on the part of some of the local authorities. In Islington there is one inspector to 56,000 inhabitants; in St. Pancras, one to 59,000; in Greenwich, one to 65,000; in Bermondsey, one to 86,000; and in Mile End, one to 105,000. Clerkenwell, with a population of 69,000, employs the services of two sanitary inspectors, with an assistant, who is, however, also sexton and coroner's officer; it cannot, therefore, be considered as an extreme instance of inactivity in this respect. Standing, as it does, half way between the least inspected of the districts cited, and the case of St. James's, Westminster, which has one inspector to every 9,000 population, it will not be unfair to examine shortly the constitution of the vestry of that parish as one of the local authorities which have the sanitary condition of London in their keeping. This vestry consists of 72 members, of whom the average attendance is stated by Mr. Paget, the vestry clerk, to be from 25 to 30. There are on the vestry 13 or 14 persons who are interested in bad or doubtful property, and they include several of the middlemen already referred to. There are, moreover, 10 publicans on the vestry, who, with the exception of one or two, have in this parish the reputation of working with the party who trade in insanitary property, and accordingly this party commands a working majority on the vestry. Taking the house farmers alone, it is found, from Mr. Paget's evidence, that they preponderate in very undue proportion on the most important committees of the vestry. On the works committee there are 10 out of the 14 house farmers referred to, on the assessment committee seven out of the 14 appear. Enough has been said about the condition of the dwellings of the poor in this parish. It will suffice, therefore, to mention that when the sanitary committee of the vestry (which was greatly influenced by its active chairman, whose zeal is said to have caused his subsequent dismissal from it) recommended the enforcement of the tenement provisions of the Sanitary Act, the opposition of the vestry was sufficiently strong to indefinitely postpone the consideration of the recommendations. It is not surprising to find that the sanitary inspectors whose tenure of office and salary is subject to such a body should show indisposition to activity. The state of the homes of the working classes in Clerkenwell, the overcrowding and other evils which act and re-act on one another must be attributed in a large measure to the default of the responsible local authority. Clerkenwell does not stand alone; from various parts of London the same complaints are heard of insanitary property being owned by members of the vestries and district boards, and of sanitary inspection being inefficiently done, because many of the persons whose duty it is to see that a better state of things should exist are those who are interested in keeping things as they are.

The Jerry-builder Again

The jerry-builder, of course, did not confine his operations to the homes of the middle classes. With few articulate and influential voices to speak on their behalf, the working classes were by far the greater sufferers. Writing in the 1840s Engels shows (71) that many houses in Manchester were rotten when they were built, while Walter Besant (1836–1901) indicates (72) that even at the end of Victoria's reign the problem was by no means solved. One cause of bad building was that the builder was often a town councillor, a theme taken up a few years later with deadly effect by Robert Tressell (Robert Noonan) in his novel *The Ragged Trousered Philanthropists* (published 1914).

71 Friedrich Engels   The Condition of the Working-Class in England in 1844
(1845; first English ed, 1892), 57-8

Farther to the north-east lie many newly-built-up streets; here the cottages look neat and cleanly, doors and windows are new and freshly painted, the rooms within newly whitewashed; the streets themselves are better aired, the vacant building lots between them larger and more numerous. But this can be said of a minority of the houses only, while cellar dwellings are to be found under almost every cottage; many streets are unpaved and without sewers; and, worse than all, this neat appearance is all pretence, a pretence which vanishes within the first ten years. For the construction of the cottages individually is no less to be condemned than the plan of the streets. All such cottages look neat and substantial at first; their massive brick walls deceive the eye, and, on passing through a *newly-built* working-men's street, without remembering the back alleys and the construction of the houses themselves, one is inclined to agree with the assertion of the Liberal manufacturers that the working population is nowhere so well housed as in England. But on closer examination, it becomes evident that the walls of these cottages are as thin as it is possible to make them. The outer walls, those of the cellar, which bear the weight of the ground floor and roof, are one whole brick thick at most, the bricks lying with their long sides touching; but I have seen many a cottage of the same height, some in process of building, whose outer walls were but one-half brick thick, the bricks lying not sidewise but lengthwise, their narrow ends touching. The object of this is to spare material, but there is also another reason for it; namely, the fact that the contractors never own the land but lease it, according to the English custom, for twenty, thirty, forty, fifty, or ninety-nine years, at the expiration of which time it falls, with everything upon it, back into the possession of the original holder, who pays nothing in return for improvements upon it. The improvements are therefore so calculated by the lessee as to be worth as little as possible at the expiration of the stipulated term. And as such cottages are often built but twenty or thirty years before the expiration of the term, it may easily be imagined that the contractors make no unnecessary expenditures upon them. Moreover, these contractors, usually carpenters and builders, or manufacturers, spend little or nothing in repairs, partly to avoid diminishing their rent receipts, and partly in view of the approaching surrender of the improvement to the landowner; while in consequence of commercial crises and the loss of work that follows them, whole streets often stand empty, the cottages falling rapidly into ruin and uninhabitableness. It is calculated in general that working-men's cottages last only forty years on the average. This sounds strangely enough when one sees the beautiful, massive walls of newly-built ones, which seem to give promise of lasting a couple of centuries; but the fact remains that the niggardliness of the original expenditure, the neglect of all repairs, the frequent periods of emptiness, the constant change of inhabitants, and the destruction carried on by the dwellers during the final ten years, usually Irish families, who do not hesitate to use the wooden portions for fire-wood—all this, taken together, accomplishes the complete ruin of the cottages by the end of forty years. Hence it comes that Ancoats, built chiefly since the sudden growth of manufacture, chiefly indeed within the present century, contains a vast number of ruinous houses, most of them being, in fact, in the last stages of inhabitableness.

72 Walter Besant   East London

(1901), 220–1

Another cause of overcrowding springs from the bad building of the workmen's houses. It is not only the foundation that is rotten: the house itself is built of bad brick laid in single courses, the woodwork is unseasoned and shrinks, zinc is used instead of lead, the stairs are of matchboard—only the cheapest and worst materials are used. There are laws, there always have been laws, against bad building; there are inspectors, yet the bad building continues. A man who had been an apprentice in the building trade told me how this surprising result of our laws and our inspectors used to be possible twenty-five years ago. "It is this way," he said; "I was a boy when these houses were built. For a house like this it was £15 to the inspector; for one of the smaller houses it was £10." We must not believe it possible for such a thing to happen now; one's faith in human nature would suffer too severe a blow, but when one looks around in certain quarters that little transaction between the honest builder and the faithful inspector recurs to my unwilling memory.

In course of time authority interposes. The houses are condemned. Out go the people, with their sticks into the street; the houses are boarded up, the boys throw stones at the windows; the place is deserted. But where are the people to go?

High Rents

High rents were increasingly realised to be a vitally important aspect of slum housing during the last 20 years of the nineteenth century. The Royal Commission on Housing (73) took a somewhat complacent view of provincial rents; following its Report rents continued to rise, and more rapidly in the large provincial towns than in London. (See Board of Trade. *Second Series of Memoranda . . . on British and Foreign Trade and Industrial Conditions*, *PP*, Vol LXXXIV, 1905, 35.) George Haw (b 1871?), journalist and author, deals (74) with the problem in London, where rents were higher than anywhere else.

73 Royal Commission on the Housing of the Working Classes First Report
PP, Vol XXX (1884–5), 17–18

Rents in the congested districts of London are getting gradually higher, and wages are not rising, and there is a prospect, therefore, of the disproportion between rent and wages growing still greater. . . .

In South St. Pancras, for instance, 4*s.* a week was paid for one room, 10 feet by 7, at 10, Prospect Terrace; the same was the case at 3, Derry Street. At 22, Wood Street 5*s.* was paid for a single room, and if cheaper quarters were needed, an underground kitchen must be sought which commanded a rent in this neighbourhood of 2*s.* 6*d.* a week. At 8, Stephen Street, Tottenham Court Road, 5*s.* a week was paid for a single room in a state of great decay. In Chapel Row and Wilmington Place, Clerkenwell, 3*s.* 9*d.*, 4*s.* 6*d.*, and 5*s.* were the rents for single rooms. In Spitalfields the average rental for one room was from 4*s.* 6*d.* to 6*s.* a week. Most of these quotations are for unfurnished rooms. In Notting Hill 4*s.* or 5*s.* a week per room was said to be the rent of furnished rooms, and in the Mint 4*s.* 6*d.* for the same accommodation; but the character of the furniture is, as a rule, in its wretchedness beyond description. Instances might be multiplied from the metropolitan evidence, but enough has been quoted. It is only necessary to add, that many of the tenements just cited are the dwellings which have been referred to as instances of extreme overcrowding.

In the provinces the rents of houses and of tenements are much lower than in London. Three shillings a week was quoted as being paid in one instance for a single cellar in Newcastle, and 2*s.* 6*d.* was said to be the usual price of a single room in that city, but rents, as a rule, for obvious reasons, such as the comparative cheapness of land and building, run much lower in provincial towns than in London. . . .

High rents are due to competition for houses and to the scarcity of accommodation in proportion to the population. It might be asked why cannot the pressure be relieved by a distribution of the now crowded masses over the area of the metropolis, inasmuch as it is a well known fact that for various causes certain districts contain a large number of uninhabited houses, many of which are suitable for the working classes. The answer to this query, which will have to be referred to again when the question of suburban residence is dealt with, is that an enormous proportion of the dwellers in the overcrowded quarters are necessarily compelled to live close to their work, no matter what the price charged or what the condition of the property they inhabit. It has been seen how crowded the poor central districts of London are, and one reason is that for a large class of labourers it is necessary to live as nearly as possible in the middle of the town, because they then command the labour market of the whole metropolis from a convenient centre. Sometimes they hear of casual work to be had at a certain place provided they are there by 6 o'clock the next morning, so they must choose a central position from which no part of the town is inaccessible.

74 [George Haw]   No Room to Live
(1900), 53–5

How the Heavy-rented endure it all amazes me the more I think of it. How widows working fourteen hours a day, for eight or nine shillings a week, can contrive to pay half their earnings, and sometimes more than half, for a one-roomed hovel, is a perfect mystery to me. Through all their thankless toil the ever-present thought, like a spur to the laggard, is "the rent, the rent, only let me earn the rent". They are not really free creatures till they see the rent assured; for they well know how speedily they would be turned out were a fraction of the full amount to be wanting when the collector calls.

The property-sweater is bleeding his victims all over London. In the Mayfair district there are single rooms, twelve feet by ten, fetching as much as a pound a week each. A Vestryman of the neighbourhood has stated in public that he found eight people living in one of these pound-a-week rooms.

In the adjoining district of Soho the very houses which were the town mansions of the nobility a century ago are to-day inhabited, for the most part, from basement to attic, by the Heavy-rented. The very attics are rented as high as eight shillings a week, and some of the basements run to ten. . . .

. . . But in the East End the Heavy-rented are seen in a worse plight still. A few months ago my attention was drawn to some dozen two-roomed houses in a Spitalfields street. Last July the tenants were paying four-and-six; by the end of August they were paying seven-and-six, and all new comers had to pay a deposit of two pounds for the key; two months later, half of the houses having been sold again, the rents had reached eight shillings.

In a street off Beaumont Square, Mile End, all the houses in which were bought last summer by a notorious property-sweater, the rents were raised from sixteen shillings a week to thirty-one and sixpence a week at one bound. In the same neighbourhood, and about the same time, whole streets of smaller houses had the rents raised from eight-and-six to sixteen shillings. When a protest was made to one of the landlords he replied callously that other property would go the same way soon. And it did.

The property-sweater . . . will buy up some slum property, perhaps a whole court or street, and contrive indirectly to draw the attention of the local authority to its unhealthy state. The local authority then obtain a magistrate's closing order, describing the houses as "unfit for human habitation". The unhappy tenants, all the time paying the usual rent, are thereupon turned out under the compulsion of the law. Forthwith the property-sweater has the shoddiest repairs carried out, so as to induce the local authority to withdraw the closing order, and with little loss of time the houses are thrown open again. A new class of people rush in at double the rents, glad to get housed at any price.

The poor pay more in rent than any other class. And, observe, I don't simply mean more in proportion to their income; for this is a fact which has long been recognised. What I mean is that on the total of London's rent-roll it will be found that the largest amounts come from properties inhabited by the working people and the struggling poor. . . .

. . . Yes, the hovels of the poor are very profitable investments. The poor pay several millions a year in rent, and enrich thousands of families. . . . The properties in slum-neighbourhoods fetch far more than villas in pretty suburbs. Many a six-roomed house in a Bermondsey back-lane or a Bethnal Green court is fetching six shillings a room, or £93 a year, while on the heights of Highgate or in Dulwich lanes the rents and rates combined of well-built eight-roomed villa houses, fitted with baths, with gardens front and back, do not exceed £50 a year. It seems to be a rule, as Canon Scott Holland has pointed out, "that the law of rent should so work itself out, under present conditions, that as a district grows poorer its rents should rise." Such a practice as the Canon remarks, is intolerable.

Public Indifference

There is no doubt that if an aroused public had demanded improved working-class housing, reforms would have come far more quickly. Yet only small numbers in any given section of the community concerned themselves with the problem. George R. Sims ("Dagonet") was for many years a campaigner for social reform; his "In the Workhouse: Christmas Day" (1877) was rightly looked on not as a joke but as a political attack on the Poor Law system. Here he gibes (75) at the sudden interest in slum housing aroused by the *Bitter Cry* and his own *How the Poor Live*. Similar sentiments were expressed by *Punch*. The Conservative *Quarterly Review* (76) and two prominent Hull businessmen (77), both named Smith, blame poor housing in large part on the poor themselves, while the socialists J. A. Fallows (1864–1935) and Joseph Clayton (b 1868) point to working-class apathy as a reason for the persistence of slums (78 and 79). ("DV's" were District Visitors, religious or charitable social workers.)

75 "Dagonet" (George R. Sims) "Mustard and Cress" Column
In *The Referee* (18 November 1883), 7

Public indignation is a fickle sentiment. It is here to-day and gone to-morrow. It is aroused by the merest accident as a rule. How to arouse it with any degree of certainty, no man has yet discovered. To this very question which now engages every hand that can wield a pen, dozens of good men and true have for years devoted their untiring energies. Charles Dickens and Henry Mayhew worked at it; Mr. Sala and Mr. James Greenwood have worked at it for years; ever since I had a public journal to write in I, too, in my humble way, have worked at it. The *Daily News*, the *Daily Telegraph*, the *Standard*, the *Pall Mall Gazette*, the *Referee*, and dozens of other influential journals, have freely given their columns to a discussion of the evil; but we all piped in vain—the public refused to dance. Now all is changed. The public has started dancing at such a rate that the spectacle is a little confusing to the looker-on.

The most useful and much to-be praised crusade now going on has, of course, its comic side. Was there ever a great movement that had not? But that I am getting staid and sober as old age creeps over my pen, I should be tempted to exaggerate a little, and describe a recent visit of mine to the slums. This is the sort of thing I should have probably incorporated with my "Mustard and Cress" in the days when I was sowing my journalistic wild oats.

IN THE SLUMS. – (A DRAMA OF THE DAY.)
(By a Frivolous Flâneur.)

Scene 1. – An Awful Alley in the East.
(*Enter a Special Correspondent.*)

SPECIAL – H'm! It's very unpleasant here, but I must do my duty. Let me see. I'll go down into the cellar of this house, and see if it's true that the pigs sleep with the family.
(*Goes down into cellar; knocks up against somebody in the dark.*)
SOMEBODY – Hullo! Where are you coming to?
SPECIAL – Good gracious! I know that voice. It is – no, it can't be – yes, it is – the Marquis of Salisbury!
SALISBURY – Hullo, Jones, is that you! I'm just investigating a little. Awful place, isn't it?
SPECIAL – Awful! Let's get outside. (*They get outside.*)
SALISBURY – Come along. I'm going to sleep in a common lodging-house to-night, to see if it's all right. Will you come?
SPECIAL – Delighted! (*They go and sleep in two fourpenny beds at a common lodging-house.*)

Scene 2 – A Common Lodging-house. Night.

FIRST COMMON LODGER – Ahem! I say, my dear fellow next to me – I mean old pal – could you oblige me by not snoring so loud?
SALISBURY (*in next bed*) – Dear me, what a gentlemanly fellow!
SPECIAL – Very. Broken-down tradesman perhaps.
SECOND COMMON LODGER (*getting up and striking a light*) – I wonder what the time is? My watch is under my pillow.
SALISBURY – Why, that fellow's got a watch! He must be a thief. (*Light burns. Salisbury, Special, and Two Common Lodgers start up and look at each other.*)
ALL – Good gracious!
SALISBURY – Why, Dilke!
DILKE – Why, Salisbury!
SPECIAL – Why, Lord Carnarvon!
SALISBURY – And the Duke of Peckham as I'm alive!
THIRD COMMON LODGER (*aroused by noise*) – I say – I say. How am I to get to sleep if –
SALISBURY – Why, Canterbury!

ARCHBISHOP – Well, upon my word! Who'd have thought of seeing you here?

SALISBURY – What are you doing here, and in a fourpenny bed too?

ARCHBISHOP – I'm investigating.

ALL – So are we.

SALISBURY – I say, did you cook a herring for supper in the kitchen?

ARCHBISHOP – No, I tried. I burnt mine to a cinder.

FOURTH COMMON LODGER – Look here, if this noise goes on I'll call the deputy!

ALL – That voice! Why, Mr. Gladstone!

GLADSTONE – Good gracious! Those outcasts know me.

ARCHBISHOP – Outcasts, indeed!

GLADSTONE (*sitting up and rubbing his eyes*) – What, Canterbury and Salisbury! Well, I never!

SALISBURY – Dilke's in the next bed to me.
(*Enter Colonel Henderson, conducting M. De Lesseps, who wishes to see a common lodging-house.*)

COLONEL HENDERSON – Here, mon cher monsieur, you see all the most degraded of our abject poor.

DE LESSEPS – Indeed! It is wonderful!

GLADSTONE – My dear De Lesseps, this is an unexpected pleasure.

DE LESSEPS (*starting*) – Eh? Mon Dieu! Sir Gladstones, et le Baron Dilkes, et Marquis Salisbury Esquire, et Canterbury Archbishops – mille tonnerres! mais qu'est ce que cela veut?

GLADSTONE – Ah! vous ne comprenez pas-er-me-nous sommes incognito.

FIFTH COMMON LODGER (*leaping out of bed*) – 'Ere – 'ow's a cove to sleep if you keep on a-jorin', you blokes! Blarm me, I'll make yer 'old yer row! Take that, yer bad-languaged collective term for pigs! (*Hits out right and left at the Distinguished Strangers. Free fight of the Common Lodgers, and ignominious expulsion of the Prime Minister, Salisbury, Dilke, Henderson, De Lesseps, and Co.*)

FRENCH JOURNALIST (*who has taken a bed in order to study low life in London, making a note for his newspaper*) – The common lodging-houses of the East-end are the nightly haunt of distinguished statesmen and dignitaries of the Church. So bad are the times in the Isle of John Bull that the Marquis of Salisbury and the Archbishop of Canterbury cook a bloater over the fire of a thieves' kitchen, and pay fourpence a night for their beds. (*Enter a Common Lodger, who has crept under a bed.*)

COMMON LODGER – I say – er – is there anybody here who wants to earn a pound?

THIEF – (*waking up*), Eh, earn a quid! – what do you want?

COMMON LODGER – O, if you please, I'm the Lord Mayor of London, and I came here to investigate for myself, and I'm frightened. If you see me out of this place, and direct me to the Mansion House, you may take all I've got.

THIEF – All right! You come along o' me. (*Takes him outside, takes all he's got, and leaves him wandering up and down the Mint, and inquiring of the " 'appy dossers" where the nearest cab stand is.*)

76 [Lewis Dibdin]   Dwellings of the Poor
Quarterly Review (January 1884), 146

The experiment of putting the poor in better dwellings can only be successful in proportion to their fitness for better dwellings. Here is a real difficulty. The habits and tastes and desires of the people are to a great extent hostile to improvement. Take, for instance, overcrowding. Generations of overcrowding have affected, not only the conduct, but the instincts of the poorest class. Their code of decency is different from ours. Not long ago a medical officer was trying to persuade an Irishwoman that it was, at any rate, undesirable that she and her husband, their grown-up sons and daughters, and divers collateral relations, should all sleep in the same room, when she turned on him full of wrath at what she deemed a prurient insinuation—"Oh, you're a bad man! Don't we all belong to one family?" If a distaste for squalor could by any human contrivance be created in the hearts of some hundreds of thousands of Her Majesty's lieges, who now greatly prefer dirt to cleanliness, the houses of the London poor would mend themselves without any aid from outside. At present the most disheartening feature in the whole matter is, the dull callous indifference to misery of those on whose behalf so much effort is made. In a part of London which shall be nameless, there stands a block of artizans' tenements, containing 150 inhabitants. It is within fifty yards of the district sanitary office. A few weeks ago the Inspector of Nuisances found every privy in this building (there were fourteen) stopped, and of course emitting a disgusting effluvium. The nuisance was evidently of several days' standing, but not one of the 150 tenants had cared enough about it to inform the authorities close at hand.

77 Homes of the People
(Hull, 1884), 19, 35–6

They must try to elevate the social habits of the people. As an old employer, and one who had had considerable experience of the ways and habits of workpeople of Hull, now extending over 30 years, his experience told him that if they put pigs into a palace they would make a pigstye. The only way they could fairly elevate the people of Hull and elsewhere, to exterminate the misery, squalor, and vice, was to teach them temperance, thrift, and providence. What could they expect, in a country where £135,000,000 were spent in drink in one year, more than double what was spent in bread and flour? When an accident happened in their works and they followed the poor victim home, what did they find? An absence of furniture, absence of comfort, and there was nothing to elevate. Where had the man's money gone, hardly earned, week by week, year by year? Why, into the hundreds and thousands of public-houses foisted upon the country. . . .

We have the lower and the lowest members of society to deal with—the criminals, the rowdies, the loafers, the incompetent,

the thieves, and the lowest form of prostitute. I am afraid that
it is only the anthropologist who can quite appreciate many of
the varieties of the residuum of mankind. St. Francis has it that
the animals are our poorer brethren. Many tenants and lodgers
would compare most unfavourably, in their habits of life, in
their filth, and want of natural affection, with members of the
animal creation, as popularly understood. Tennyson recognises
this class when he says—

> "Move upward, working out the beast,
> And let the ape and tiger die."

Eastern Europe likens them to ownerless dogs, who are the
scavengers of their towns, and live on its garbage. Western
Europe recognises them under a similar appellation. They are
referred to in the injunction "not to throw your pearls before
swine". To call these the poor is unscientific—to call them the
filthy would be correct. They are in many cases brutal in
nature—semi-savages.

78 J. A. Fallows The Housing of the Poor
(Birmingham, 1899), 13

It is well known that the bulk of the working classes are *ready
to submit to any grievance*, except, perhaps, the prohibition of
betting and drinking, at the hands of a Puritan dictator. "The
demoralisation of the poor is such that they do not resent their
demoralisation," says Rev. Robins. Reformers want to make the
people discontented, better educated, and therefore demanding
a higher standard of life. "Sympathetic coddling will do the
people no good; make them dissatisfied with their conditions,
make them agitate for decent homes." (Julia Dawson.) "The
big cure was to make people dissatisfied with their surroundings." (J. T. Middlemore, M.P.) The Sheriff of Glasgow said
to an agent, in May of this year, who pleaded that most of his
tenants made no objection to paying high rents, "Oh, Mr.
McArthur, the patience of that class of people is wonderfully
pathetic, and the hardness and cruelty of many people of your

class is very shameful." Landlords take advantage of the doles which the poor receive from D.V.'s and other charitable people. The rich people of Edgbaston need have no fear of revolution of any sort; no such idea ever occurs to the brains of the majority of the heavy Saxons of the Midlands. All classes are to blame. Society tolerates noble land-owners and jerry builders; it also encourages the small butcher and the thrifty artisan to join a Building Society, or to become possessor of his own house, *i.e.*, to sublet it to poorer workers, as he cannot carry it away on his back, like a snail, if circumstances force him to change his abode.

79 Joseph Clayton   Housing of the Poor
In Albert T. Marles (ed). *Hypnotic Leeds* (1894), 15–16

The typical workman's house in Leeds has one living room, adorned with sink and taps for washing purposes, two bedrooms, and an attic in which possibly is a bath. The bath is the one redeeming point, and the corporation should insist on it being built in every house.

The sinks and taps on the other hand are depressing in a sitting-room, and the smell of the atmosphere of the weekly wash not conducive to health of mind or body. If we prefer to dry our clothes across the street and not indoors we may gratify our neighbours' curiosity as to the condition and quality of our underclothing, but the smoke of Leeds resents our brandishing clean clothes in the open air and showers down smuts. Of the necessary sanitary arrangements of every dwelling-house—it is difficult to speak calmly in Leeds. Our ashpits which adorn the street are the resting place for decayed vegetable matter, and domestic refuse generally; the stench from them is probably a sweet smelling savour to the arch-fiend, but it is poison to the children who play around them.

The worst of it is these houses with their ashpits, etc., are still being built—in the face of all our sanitary knowledge,—and no one protests. . . .

Only a few agitators and dreamy enthusiasts have declaimed on the subjects.

The weary victims of slumland soon succumb and feel that after all a cellar is better than the street or the workhouse.

Man either makes or is made by his surroundings. The daily environment of filth, disease, and impurity soon tells on those within it, and chokes them morally and physically.

Hence slums afford much occupation (with salary), for clergymen, doctors, policemen, and magistrates who don't live in them. Notoriously too they are a paying investment for the landlord.

Perhaps that is why it is so difficult for all these well-housed people to agitate on the question. Demos lies drugged by poisonous fumes; when he is risen the time for agitation will be over. The back-to-back house, which distinguishes Leeds from other commercial centres, is more respectable than slums, and is considered a desirable residence for workpeople. It lacks ventilation it is true, and if you knock a nail in the wall there is the chance of sending the brick through into your neighbour's apartment; but then it is warm in the winter, and if you have been working all day in a stuffy mill or factory you don't notice the bad air at home.

The System

Thoroughgoing social reformers went behind the housing problem itself to blame the economic and social order for bad housing. *Justice*, the journal of the Marxist Social-Democratic Federation, lays the blame at the door of capitalism (80), while George Bernard Shaw (1856–1950), like *Justice* drawing his ammunition from the Royal Commission on Housing, points out that both the landlord Sartorius and the respectable Dr Trench (who symbolises the wilfully ignorant middle classes) batten on the existing system (81). Sartorius, who has just dismissed his agent, Lickcheese, speaks the words which lay at the centre of Shaw's philosophy: "When people are very poor, you *cannot* help them. . . ." Shaw enunciated his solution in *Major Barbara* (1905)—to make poverty a crime and to outlaw it. B.F.C. Costelloe (1855–99) was a Progressive member of the London County Council from 1889 until 1899, who knew well that whichever way the LCC turned, the housing problem seemed only to deteriorate (82).

80 A Chronicle of Crime
Justice (16 May 1885), 4

The Report of the Royal Commission on the Housing of the Poor is at last issued. . . . In itself it is of very little value. It is worth noting however that though it contains nothing whatever new, all the statements that have been made time after time in Socialist publications are fully confirmed, and there is not a single suggestion worth anything at all which has not been made already in these columns. The Report itself is practically a deliberate registration of the infamy of the classes which the Royal Commissioners represent, and a verdict of wilful murder against our "rulers" who permit such a system to continue. Bad housing is due first of all to poverty. Why so it is. We wanted no Royal Commission to tell us that. The wages of the unskilled labourers amount to less than 12s. a week when in work, and of this one-fifth or one-fourth must be paid for rent. Altogether, as we have often urged, the working classes pay from one-fifth to one-third of their scanty earnings for house room. The overcrowding is increased by the removal of buildings and improvements for the benefit of the well-to-do. As a result, the workers have to pay higher and higher rents for worse accommodation. The worst dwellings are frequently owned by vestrymen who never think of administering existing laws to their own disadvantage, and there are not nearly enough sanitary inspectors in poor districts, though of course plenty in rich. In short there is not a word of denunciation of our present arrangements that has ever been printed which is not justified by this Report. The tone of the whole is hopeless to the last degree. The plunderers and profitmongers cannot help showing that they are barren in ideas, and the recommendations by the Commissioners as a whole. . . . amount to little or nothing.

The truth is that these people one and all have an uneasy consciousness that such a Report as this proclaims their own incompetence and is another step onwards to the inevitable Revolution. They trust to public opinion they say to carry out their pitiful proposals. Public Opinion! the public opinion of the class that owns the Press, the Platform, and Parliament, the public opinion of the rackrenting vestryman, the adulterating profitmonger, and the indifferent landlord! If the public opinion of the dominant class could be moved at all there was as much evidence of need for action twenty, thirty, forty years ago as there is to-day. And yet, practically, nothing has been done. Let the Commissioners face the facts for once if they dare, and boldly admit that the bottom is out of our present system of Society, "public opinion," and all. It is something, nevertheless, to have as many admissions as we have got here signed by the names of such very respectable people. When in future Social-Democrats are asked why they are Revolutionists and not pottering reformers they may safely refer for an answer to the pages of the Report of the Royal Commission on the Housing of the Poor.

81 George Bernard Shaw Widowers' Houses
(1892), Act II

SARTORIUS . . . As to my business, it is simply to provide homes suited to the small means of very poor people, who require roofs to shelter them just like other people. Do you suppose I can keep up those roofs for nothing?

TRENCH Yes: thats all very fine; but the point is, what sort of homes do you give them for their money? People must live somewhere, or else go to jail. Advantage is taken of that to make them pay for houses that are not fit for dogs. Why dont you build proper dwellings, and give fair value for the money you take?

SARTORIUS [*pitying his innocence*] My young friend: these poor people do not know how to live in proper dwellings: they would wreck them in a week. You doubt me: try it for yourself. You are welcome to replace all the missing banisters, handrails, cistern lids and dusthole tops at your own expense; and you will find them missing again in less than three days: burnt, sir, every stick of them. I do not blame the poor creatures: they need fires, and often have no other way of getting them. But I really cannot spend pound after pound in repairs for them to pull down, when I can barely get them to pay me four and sixpence a week for a room, which is the recognized fair London rent. No, gentlemen: when people are very poor, you *cannot* help them, no matter how much you may sympathize with them. It does them more harm than good in the long run. I prefer to save my money in order to provide additional houses for the homeless, and to lay by a little for Blanche. And now, Dr Trench, may I ask what *your* income is derived from?

TRENCH [*defiantly*] From interest: not from houses. My hands are clean as far as that goes. Interest on a mortgage.

SARTORIUS [*forcibly*] Yes: a mortgage on *my* property. When I, to use your own words, screw, and bully, and drive these people to pay what they have freely undertaken to pay me, I cannot touch one penny of the money they give me until I have first paid you your seven hundred a year out of it. What Lickcheese did for me, I do for you. He and I are alike intermediaries: *you* are the principal. It is because of the risks I run through the poverty of my tenants that you exact interest from me at the monstrous and exorbitant rate of seven per cent, forcing me to exact the uttermost farthing in my turn from the tenants. And yet, Dr Trench, you, who have never done a hand's turn of work in connection with the place, you have not hesitated to speak contemptuously of me because I have applied my industry and forethought to the management of *our* property, and am maintaining it by the same honorable means.

82 B.F.C. Costelloe   The Housing Problem
Transactions of the Manchester Statistical Society (1898–9), 52–4

By the effluxion of the old leases, by railway and other private clearances—not to mention public schemes—thousands and tens of thousands of old workers' homes are now being cleared. The public schemes themselves have only added to the difficulty, for we have unhoused far more than ever we have housed again; and of late the tendency has been to get leave in each new scheme to re-house only half the number cleared. A few weeks ago the London County Council heroically resolved to change all that.

. . . To put it shortly . . . public clearances have made less than no impression since the census of 1891 on the general want of housing. It is, indeed, agreed that the deficit of sleeping room for the poor workers is worse now than it was then. New policy belongs to the future, and has its own conundrums. It may easily be destroyed by an electoral reverse, or obstructed, or it may be tried and fail. The master fact is that the courts and streets where these poor folks lived are being destroyed, and soon will be replaced by new buildings, and put to commercial uses, which are indefinitely more remunerative than housing the people.

. . . Land near the Bank is said to be running up now towards a million an acre. Even a mile or two away the commercial value is so great that the residential population is steadily and rapidly vanishing. The area, not merely of the City, but of the Strand, of St. Olave's in the South, of Finsbury, and now even of Whitechapel and Wapping, is visibly passing to non-residential uses. And one result of this is that the rent in the east of London for slum tenements and shops in the small streets have suddenly leapt up of late, sometimes by 70 to 80 per cent. The house-knacker may not yet be able to clear and re-build, but he practically tells his tenants that if they choose to sleep there they must pay a business price. He knows that it is disastrous for them to leave, and that most of them will pay it—

and in all probability will try to mitigate the bitter pressure by gross and indecent overcrowding with increased numbers of lodgers, already far too numerous.

We find ourselves, then, at this pass. A multitude of poor workers' families must live near the centre; and the land near the centre has attained a value the equivalent of which they cannot conceivably pay, and it goes on increasing with fatal certainty. Many workers are probably now living in places which are economically worth £100 a year per room, if they could be put to their most profitable use. To that they will surely return when the leases end—perhaps sooner—for there is no legal check on private "improvements," and men like Lord Cadogan have already evicted thousands with hardly a protest. Even the legal check on public works is evaded. It rules that any scheme which displaces twenty families of the working class must provide a corresponding means of re-housing. But the great railways, and even the School Board itself, habitually arrange their plans so as to take only nineteen familes at a time, whenever they can plan a year or two in advance. The people go somewhere, and no one much cares where. In the Chelsea case they could find vacant and fairly cheap ground at Battersea, a mile or two away, and even then it was bad enough. But if Whitechapel, and Stepney, and Limehouse, and Mile End, and Bethnal Green, and Shoreditch, and Spitalfields are all depopulated—as they may well be—where will these myriads go?

This problem, I think, no one has seriously faced. To say that it should be left to settle itself seems to me to be one of those inhuman counsels which are the seed of revolutionary discontent, and bring on in the end more violent remedies than even the extremists would wish. To say that the community should buy up slum areas, and re-erect on them an adequate number of workmen's dwellings, under present conditions of cost, is almost appalling. The Metropolitan Board of Works cleared 22 acres, at a net loss of over a million and a half. Other towns, such as Glasgow and Birmingham, have turned these operations into speculations almost remunerative; but in London, with such districts as those I speak of, it is absurd to propose it. We must be prepared, if we go in for municipal housing of this kind, to face the fact that we will be sacrificing vast portions of the possible economic value of sites in the very centre of the world, and will be providing homes for certain needful servants of the community at wholly artificial rents. It will be said that to do this is to "pay rent out of the rates" for a favoured class. To that the London County Council will certainly not allow itself to be driven except in the last resort. But I ask myself, Can the London County Council, or Parliament, or anybody else, avoid this necessity in the long run, if we are really in earnest about the housing of the casual poor of London?

THE GOVERNMENT AND LOCAL AUTHORITIES:
DISCUSSION AND ACHIEVEMENT

Private Initiative versus Public Enterprise

Preceding documents will have made clear that the role of the state in improving housing conditions was bitterly disputed during the later nineteenth century. Even those like Joseph Chamberlain who were keenest to attack abuses were often reluctant to countenance state or local authority-financed housing. Dr Child (1832–96), the Medical Officer of Health for Oxfordshire, was prepared to move further (83). He advocated local authority building of houses at a subsidised rent and went over to the attack in doing so. It is significant that he was a medical man, not a radical politician. Lord Shaftesbury (84) and the *Westminster Review* (85) both opposed state aid, the *Review* adding some uncomprehending words about the "lower orders" while so doing. (For the work of Octavia Hill, praised by the *Westminster Review*, see Document 107.) Finally, in the debate which resulted in the appointment of the Royal Commission on Housing, Lord Salisbury justified his support for social reform (86), despite the rebukes of the extreme laissez-faire body called the Liberty and Property Defence League. For a further reference to the pioneering researches on overcrowding of T. Marchant Williams, mentioned by Salisbury, see p 253.

83 Dr G. W. Child   How Best to Overcome the Difficulties of Overcrowding among the Necessitous Classes
Transactions of the National Association for the Promotion of Social Science (1878), 502–5

I am, of course, aware that there will be no lack of objections to such a scheme as this. I am prepared to hear any amount of exclamations, such as "Wholesale pauperization!" "Rates in aid of wages!" "Communism in disguise!" "Contrary to the plainest principles of political economy!" *et hoc genus omne.* To which I have at once to reply that all such objections are obvious, and that some of them are weighty; but that I should not be disposed to advocate so unpalatable a remedy if I were not very thoroughly convinced that the disease to be treated is a dangerous if not a fatal one, and that the remedies hitherto applied have been palliatives of the most inefficient character. On the latter subject I have already spoken; and here I will merely add that the Artisans and Labourers' Dwellings Act, the proposed extension of which to small towns and rural districts is the one remedy hitherto proposed which I have not noticed, is included by implication; for this Act, so far as I understand it, can only come into operation where builders can be found who can see their way to making a profit out of building decent habitations for the poor. Whether this can yet be done on any large scale in towns, it is probably too soon to determine finally: but that it can*not* be done in rural districts is a proposition which admits of no dispute. Upon the other point just raised a few more words must yet be spoken. Pauperism is a word which is heard by an English audience with a kind of shudder, and not unreasonably, since it stands as the greatest curse of modern English society;

and for the purpose of avoiding the danger of establishing a new
form of permanent pauperism I should be glad to see any legislation which may take place on this subject limited in its action
to a certain definite period of years. But I cannot help remarking that the dread of pauperism which is almost conventional
among us appears to be attached much more closely to the
sound of the word than to the actual presence of the thing;
for when what is called public opinion has been sufficiently
worked up on any particular subject we find that Parliament is
not only willing to "pauperize" to an indefinite extent, but
will even go out of its way to declare that for the particular
purpose in hand pauperism shall not be pauperism! I am
referring, of course, to the Elementary Education Act, in which
exactly this course has been pursued; and certainly it does not
seem easy to show a reason in the nature of the case why a man
should be held to be pauperized by receiving State aid in order
to house his children decently, when he is not held to be so
pauperized by receiving the same aid in order to educate them.
I would rather, for my own part, see the fact of pauperization
honestly admitted in both cases; but if that ugly word is hence-
forth to represent, not a fact, but only a convention, I think
there is as good reason for declining to apply it in the former
case as in the latter.

. . . It has been shown over and over again (1) that the overcrowding of our population and the condition of their dwellings
is such as to be at once a disgrace to our boasted civilization, a
reproach to our profession of Christianity, and an ever-increasing source of political and social danger; (2) that the evil is
increasing rather than diminishing; and (3) that no remedy
short of intervention by the State is at all likely to remove the
evil. All this is well known and practically admitted. What is
less well known is, that of the legislation hitherto attempted one
part, the Sanitary Act, is generally inoperative, and where it is
put in force tends to aggravate the mischief; the other, the
Artisans and Labourers' Dwellings Act, is confessedly on its
trial, and is only partial in its action, and, as I have shown

reason to believe, will certainly prove inapplicable to rural districts.

Further, I have endeavoured to show that the dread of pauperizing people by giving them houses at an unremunerative rent, though an eminently rational one, may be met in the present case by the consideration that, of those portions of our rural population who live in decent houses at all, a large number pay an unremunerative rent, and thus are as much pauperized when they receive houses on these terms from private individuals as they would be if they received them on the same terms from the State—possibly even more so; and, finally, I have pointed out that an investigation of the innumerable local charities, themselves fruitful sources of pauperization, and requiring investigation on every account, might go far to afford a solution to the financial difficulties of the problem before us, without trenching further on the resources of the overburdened rate-payer. Lastly, I cannot forbear to ask whether, before we lend our support to a "spirited foreign policy," before we take up the part of a kind of ubiquitous knight-errant and ride abroad redressing human wrongs in Turkey, Bulgaria, Afghanistan, and the ends of the earth generally, we had not better remember that charity begins at home; and before we spend 40,000,000l. in two years for some Crimean war for which no human being is one penny the better, we might not reflect with advantage that the cost of two Crimean wars would, according to Lord Napier's estimate above quoted, more than suffice to house the population of the country, even if *all* the money had to be found by the Exchequer—a quite unnecessary hypothesis? The nation, as we know, soon ceased to feel the cost of the Crimean war as a substantial burden, and would soon recover also from the expenditure now suggested. In any case I cannot but believe that such an expenditure would better become a rational, a free, a civilized, and a Christian nation than to lavish the same sums upon gigantic and unremunerative armaments, upon those services which Mr. Bright has described as "a gigantic system of out-door relief for the members of the aristocracy."

84 Lord Shaftesbury   Common Sense and the Dwellings of the Poor: The Mischief of State Aid
Nineteenth Century (December 1883), 934–5, 937–8

The sudden manifestation of public feeling in regard to the domiciliary condition of large portions of the working classes in our cities and great towns, and specially in London, is one of the healthiest signs of modern times. It is strange that this feeling has lain so long dormant, for the disclosure of the evil was made more than forty years ago, and ever since that date, the efforts of individuals, companies and associations have been unremitting to proclaim the mischief, to devise remedies, and, in some instances, to apply them. . . .

Hitherto we have done too little; there is now a fear that in some respects we may do too much.

There is a loud cry, from many quarters, for the Government of the country to undertake this mighty question; and any one who sets himself against such an opinion is likely to incur much rebuke and condemnation. Be it so. But if the State is to be summoned not only to provide houses for the labouring classes, but also to supply such dwellings at nominal rents, it will, while doing something on behalf of their physical condition, utterly destroy their moral energies. It will, in fact, be an official proclamation that, without any efforts of their own, certain portions of the people shall enter into the enjoyment of many good things, altogether at the expense of others. The State is bound, in a case such as this, to give every facility by law and enabling statutes; but the work itself should be founded, and proceed, on voluntary effort, for which there is in the country an adequate amount of wealth, zeal, and intelligence. . . .

The whole affair is a question of money; and, though it may be called Utopian to entertain the hope of raising an adequate amount, it is nevertheless permissible to consider the form in which it might be asked for, and, if obtained, the mode of distribution.

Were a central committee formed in the city of London, consisting of gentlemen of power, wealth, and influence, who would undertake to organise such a movement, form local committees (for local committees there must be in the several districts), and issue an appeal, there would be in the present day—few can doubt it—a ready and ample response. These gentlemen would determine how far they could proceed without new legislation; though additional laws, if required at all, would be required rather for the completion, than for the commencement, of the work.

Meanwhile the powers already in existence should be called into operation. They are far greater than most people are aware of. "It would be a good thing"—the quotation is from a letter written by a most learned and able lawyer—"if the Local Government Board would issue a summary or handy-book, expressed in simple language of the laws relating to the building of houses, to nuisances in relation to health, and to the powers of local authorities. I am sure such a book would be more useful than much legislation." It would, indeed, be a very good thing if the Board would so do, and add moreover its injunctions for immediate attention to such counsel. . . .

Should private bounty and private zeal be insufficient for the great issue now sought, it might then be necessary for the Government to interpose, and use the money of the State for the improvement of the domiciliary condition of some portions of the labouring classes by placing them in new homes at eleemosynary rents; but such interposition must not take place until every effort has been made, every expedient exhausted, and indisputable proof given that, if the State does not do the work, it will never be done at all.

The mischief of it would be very serious, it would assume many menacing forms, and be of wide extent. It would, besides being a kind of legal pauperization, give a "heavy blow and great discouragement" to the spirit of healthy thrift now rising among the people.

85 The Dwellings of the Poor

Westminster Review (January 1884), 137–8, 149–50

Public attention has been thoroughly aroused on this subject, which is full of the gravest difficulties. Everybody is agreed that something must be done, and at once, but nobody knows precisely what should be done. Lord Salisbury says it is the duty of the State to intervene, but he does not tell us in what way. Many schemes have been laid before the public, which, though well-meant, would be most dangerous to the State, and would probably aggravate rather than cure the evil. We cannot pass an Act making it penal for landlords to receive the highest rents they can get. This would be in flat contradiction to the laws of supply and demand. And it is difficult to see how the poor can combine to reduce the high rents they pay for such miserable accommodation, because they must live somewhere, and there is no room for them elsewhere. Nor can we pass an Act compelling employers of labour to pay their men higher wages. That again would be disregarding every principle of political economy. And, moreover, it would be futile, for the prices of everything would immediately rise in proportion; and the higher wages would purchase just as much as the lower wages used to and no more. In the meantime, also, English trade would have been ruined by foreign competition. Again there are very strong and obvious objections to any scheme by which the State should become landlord on any large scale. Even supposing it to be right to tax the upper and middle classes still further for the support of the poor, it would be a question whether such a plan would really benefit the class for whose good it was devised. The poor wretches who had never been used to any decent habitation would soon be ejected for breaking the Government regulations which they could not understand, and their places would be taken by clean and tidy artisans. On the other hand, if the plan succeeded, this question would at once arise:—If it is the duty of the State to house the people, is it not also the duty of the State to feed and clothe them too. And thus those whom we seek to teach to help themselves would be hopelessly pauperized, and a premium set upon idleness and sloth. . . .

Each of us must learn to do the best for himself and for his children, and improve by his own energy and exertions his own character, condition, and surroundings. Any measure which would sap the self-reliance, the prudence, the thrift, or the industry of the British workman, or which would induce him to look to aid from the State instead of to his own efforts and resources would be a national disaster. The only direction in which, in my opinion, the State could interfere with advantage is perhaps in aiding the emigration of widows and orphans when the bread-winner has been removed. . . .

No doubt there is a glut at present in the labour market. But we must remember that trade has been slack for many years. And the labouring classes by their early marriages and large families so rapidly increase the population that wages *must* decline. When a working man asks "How can I keep a wife and six children on twenty-five shillings a week?" one is tempted to reply, "On twenty-five shillings a week there ought to be no wife, or certainly not the six children." In the middle and upper classes a young man does not marry till he sees some reasonable prospect of maintaining a wife and family. But it is far otherwise with the lower orders: they marry before they have saved a single sovereign. A dissenting minister at Bristol, not long ago, stated to his congregation that having occasion to visit the office of the Registrar of Births, Deaths, and Marriages he turned over the banns of marriage that were posted up, and found to his surprise that half the intending brides were but seventeen years of age, and half the intending bridegrooms were under twenty! Does not this account for much poverty, for much infantile disease, and for much overcrowding?

And there is an especial reason why the State should not assume the position of universal landlord of the poor. The only chance of reforming them, of making them ashamed of their filthy and unhealthy habits, is by the direct personal influence of educated visitors. The only persons who have a right to enter periodically the dwellings of the poor, and who when there can speak with any authority, are the Sanitary Inspector and the landlord's rent-collector. The former is the tenants' natural enemy; he is the man who burnt their only bed after the baby had died on it of scarlet-fever. But the latter may be, and under Miss Hill's system is, their best and kindest friend. It is he, or she, that teaches them to take a pride in being clean and neat themselves, and in keeping the room clean and neat as well. The happiest thing that can happen to the outcasts of London is that they should come under the care of a truly philanthropic landlord.

86 Lord Salisbury   Speech in House of Lords
Parliamentary Debates, Third Series (Lords), Vol CCLXXXIV (22 February 1884), Cols 1679–80, 1688–90

The Marquess of SALISBURY, who rose to move an humble Address to Her Majesty, for the appointment of a Royal Commission to inquire into the housing of the working classes in populous places, said: My Lords. . . . The matters to which I have to draw your attention do not affect current politics; they do not concern the struggles of Parties, or the praise or blame of Ministries; and yet they touch more closely the springs of national well-being and prosperity than even the deep and grave questions with which Parliament has been recently occupied. My Lords, the matter which I have to bring before your Lordships, and upon which I have to ask your Lordships to address the Crown, is the question of the housing of the working classes. It is a question that has, of late, excited very much interest, and has elicited so large a mass of testimony, that I am relieved from the necessity of proving my case for the consideration of Parliament. I have received numberless pamphlets and writings during the past Recess on the subject; the attention of persons of every class, of every creed and school of politics, has been turned to this question of the housing of the poor; and I have met no one who does not admit that there is a great problem to be solved, and a great evil to be remedied. I know, however, that there are some who think that what has already been done, both in the way of inquiry and legislation, is sufficient to justify us in holding our hand, or, rather, sufficient to make it important that we should hold our hand, in order that we may not seem to interfere with the goodwill of those who have already taken this matter up. ... I see before me my noble Friend (the Earl of Wemyss), whom I think I can call the head of the Property and Liberty Defence Association. The sight of him reminds me that, for any proposals of this kind, I may have to defend myself against the charge of Socialism. Now, my Lords, I will at once say I do not favour any wild schemes of State interference. I am as earnest as any man in this House that, while we approach great public evils, and desire to remedy them, we should scrupulously observe that honesty which is the condition of continued and abiding prosperity for the industries of this country. But while I will maintain that doctrine as earnestly as my noble Friend, I yet would ask the House to avoid that kind of political cowardice which declines to consider and examine a problem, lest its urgency should afterwards seem to be a temptation to provide unlawful and illegitimate methods for its remedy. The evils that we have to deal with are very serious. After all, even my noble Friend may press as earnestly as he will upon us the necessity of leaving every Englishman to work out his own destiny, and not attempt to aid him at the expense of the State; but, on the other hand, he must always bear in mind there are no absolute truths or principles in politics. ... After all, whatever political arrangements we may adopt, whatever the political constitution of our State may be, the foundation of all its prosperity and welfare must be that the mass of the people shall be honest and manly, and shall have common sense. How are you to expect that these conditions will exist amongst people subjected to the frightful influences which the present overcrowding of our poor produce? I do not know if any of your Lordships have read the remarkable letter of Mr Williams in *The Times* of to-day, giving an account of the terrible over-crowding which the investigations of the School Board have found in various parts of London. The instances are numbered not by tens, but by hundreds, where there are six or seven of a family living in a single room. My Lords, these conditions are not conditions of a physical or material deterioration only; but they are conditions deleterious and ruinous to the moral progress and development of the race to which we belong. How can you hope that any of the home influences, which, after all, are the preserving and refining influences, which keep men good amidst the various temptations of life – how are you to hope that these influences are to flourish in such a state of things as this? We pay great attention to the education of the people; but how are we to hope that popular education will flourish, when men, after the education is over, are dismissed to their homes where they cannot undertake any study, and where anything like literary interest is impossible, owing to the great mental and physical depression of mind and body under which they exist? Constant efforts are made by our legislators to deal with the great plague of intemperance, which is the moral scourge of the present generation; but how are you to hope that men will be kept out of the public-house, when the home, which is the only alternative to the public-house, presents such horrible and loathsome features? My Lords, I hope Parliament will never transgress the laws of public honesty, but I equally hope that Parliament will not be deterred by fear of being tempted to transgress those laws, or, still more, by the fear of being accused of intending to transgress those laws, from fearlessly facing, and examining, and attempting to fathom these appalling problems, which involve the deepest moral, material, and spiritual interests of the vast mass of our fellow-countrymen. I beg to move the Resolution which stands in my name upon the Paper.

Moved, "That an humble Address be presented to Her Majesty to request that Her Majesty will be graciously pleased to appoint a Royal Commission to inquire into the housing of the working classes in populous places."—(*The Marquess of Salisbury*.)

The Nature of the Achievement

Victorian governments did something to encourage improved conditions, and local authorities had considerable powers if they chose to use them. Local acts affecting housing standards were passed in considerable numbers around the mid-century, and many bylaws also existed. Nonetheless, writing in 1866, Sir John Simon (1816–1904), the sanitary reformer and Medical Officer of the Privy Council, found that "neither against degrees of crowding which conduce immensely to the multiplication of disease, as well as to obvious moral evils, nor against the use of dwellings which are permanently unfit for human habitation, can local authorities in towns, except to a certain extent in some privileged places, exercise any effectual control." Rural areas were as bad. "And thus, speaking generally, it may be said that the evils are uncontrolled in England" (*Eighth Report of the Medical Officer of the Privy Council, PP*, Vol XXXIII, 1866, 12–13).

A new impetus came after the Public Health Act of 1875. Under its section 157, model bylaws were issued by the Local Government Board affecting such crucial subjects as streets, sewerage, space about buildings, water closets and privies. (See J. N. Tarn. *Five Per Cent Philanthropy: An Account of Housing in Urban Areas Between 1840 and 1914*, 1973, pp 75–6.) New areas of "bylaw housing" were now built. Blocks of "tunnel backs", separated by a passage from their neighbours and with their own backyards or gardens, began to replace back-to-backs. The hosts of local acts, however, were often ignored or laxly enforced. And new legislation did not affect standing buildings; Manchester forbade the building of new back-to-back houses under a local Act of 1844, but 40 years later the city still had 10,000 back-to-backs (Shena

Simon. *A Century of City Government: Manchester, 1838–1938,* 1938, 286–9, 297). The Act of 1877 quoted here (87) related to a number of towns; this part amended and strengthened the Kingston-upon-Hull Improvement Act of 1854 (the "Local Act"), so far as new houses were concerned. For the first time all new houses in Hull were to be provided with rear access, although the Act contained an escape clause.

While standards of administration and enforcement slowly improved in the final third of the century, local authorities, encouraged by the relatively favourable terms of the Housing Act of 1890, began to build their own houses. Arthur Hickmott (88) examines developments in the major towns, pointing out that London had set a lead to other authorities. The Boundary Street Estate (on the borders of Shoreditch and Bethnal Green) was the first large-scale London County Council estate, and certainly the most famous local authority housing enterprise in Victoria's reign. It was an area well known to social workers and writers, the "Jago" district of Arthur Morrison's *A Child of the Jago* (1896) and the location of a number of other books and studies. The district was actually called the "Nichol", from the name of its principal streets and, as Charles Booth (1840–1916), the pioneer social surveyor of London, suggests (89), it was a good place for large-scale destruction and rebuilding. The scheme cost 5,719 people their homes, and of these apparently only eleven were among the 5,380 new tenants of the Council. It was estimated that the cost of the scheme was about £300 per family. The standard of building and provision of amenities in the 23 blocks was high, but when one considers the cost, the very high rents (3s 6d to 14s 6d a week) and the displacement of the old tenants, one can easily understand the distress and discouragement felt by some reformers. (See C. J. Stewart, ed. *The Housing Question in London, 1855–1900* [nd; 1901], 190–213.) The LCC had to cope too with the criticism of those who claimed that council building discouraged the private builder and led to a smaller supply of dwellings than would otherwise have been the case. The Boundary Street flats, improved and modernised, are still standing.

Real progress was made in the 1890s, but what had been achieved when Victoria's reign ended hardly did more than scratch the surface of the housing problem. It is likely that in 1901 all the local authorities put together owned no more than 10,000 to 15,000 houses.

87 Local Government Board's Provisional Orders Confirmation Act
40 and 41 Vict, Ch CXXXII (1877), 25–6

II. Section 101 of the Local Act [for Hull] shall be altered and amended, so as to provide as follows; viz.:-

(a) No house or building referred to therein shall be occupied as a dwelling-house until the drainage thereof has been completed, and the house or building has been examined by the Surveyor or other Officer appointed by the Urban Sanitary Authority for that purpose, and has been certified by such Surveyor or other Officer as having been built in accordance with plans approved by them, and as being in every respect fit for human habitation. . . .

(e) Every house and building referred to in the said section and intended to be occupied as a dwelling-house shall be provided with such sufficient means of access as shall enable the contents of every privy, ashpit, or cesspool used in connexion therewith, to be removed from the premises without being carried through such house or building; and if such means of access cannot otherwise be provided, every such house or building shall have a backway thereto, which, when used in connexion with any three or more houses, shall be of a width of not less than two feet nine inches, and, when used in connexion with one or two houses only, shall be of a width of not less than two feet six inches, and every such backway shall be properly drained and paved prior to the houses in connexion with which it is used being occupied as dwelling-houses.

Provided that if in the opinion of the Urban Sanitary Authority it shall in any case not be reasonably practicable to provide such access as aforesaid, it shall be lawful for them in such case to dispense with the requirements of the foregoing provision.

III. Section 98 of the Local Act shall be altered so as to provide that in every case where the average height of the houses in any court, alley, square, or inclosure for houses to be hereafter built or constructed on vacant ground (not being the site of any court or square theretofore formed or built immediately previously to such construction) exceeds twenty feet, such court, alley, square, or inclosure shall have an open area or be of a width, measuring from front to front, of not less than the average height of such houses, unless such height is more than thirty feet, in which case the width of the open area shall be least thirty feet, and that every court, alley, square, and inclosure referred to therein shall be properly drained and paved prior to the houses fronting thereto being occupied as dwelling-houses, and that no such court, alley, square, or inclosure shall at any time be used as a carriageway, except with the consent in writing of the said Urban Sanitary Authority first had and obtained.

88 [Arthur Hickmott] Houses for the People

Fabian Society Tract 76 (1897; 3rd ed, 1900), 6, 8, 9, 11–13

LONDON

The Metropolis has done far more in the matter of housing than any other city—*its total expenditure under the various Housing Acts amounts, indeed, to nearly three millions, or as much as that of all the rest of the United Kingdom put together*—but it came into the field late. Not until 1876 did the Metropolitan Board of Works take action, and then only on the lines of clearing away slums at great expense, without itself re-housing; and selling the cleared land at a very low rate to various dwellings companies and the Peabody Trustees. Between 1876 and 1888, twenty-two schemes were carried out, averaging one each year, applying to 59 acres, at a net loss to the public of £1,318,935. As a result the companies erected, and now possess as their own freehold, 263 blocks of dwellings, accommodating some 27,000 persons.

When the London County Council was established, a change of policy took place. Instead of parting with the cleared land, the Council decided to retain it in public ownership, and itself erect workmen's dwellings upon it, sometimes by its own Works Department and sometimes by contractors. Between 1889 and 1900 twenty separate schemes have been undertaken by the Council itself (besides three other groups of dwellings erected under the Thames Tunnel Acts); and, in addition, the Council has contributed part (usually half) of the cost of twelve other schemes undertaken by the Vestries and District Boards. The capital outlay to the end of 1900 has already exceeded one-and-a-half millions, and the schemes in hand will involve a further million for completion. The dwellings provided are of all kinds, as required by local conditions, including great blocks of tenements in Central London, each tenement including from one to five rooms; in the suburbs detached or semi-detached cottages with gardens; and one common lodging house. The aim of the Council has been, not so much to reduce rents (which, it is argued, would in the long run merely benefit the employer by reducing London rates of wages to the provincial standards) as to raise the standard of working class dwellings by supplying a better article for the same money. Thus, the Council's rooms are loftier and better ventilated, its stairways and passages are wider and lighter, and its sanitary and other conveniences are healthier and more comfortable than are usually provided, but the rents are always fixed so as not to exceed per room those current in the locality. Hence no profit is made. On the whole of the housing operations, taking one year with another, the rents received about balance the actual outgoings. . . .

BIRMINGHAM

Ryder Street.—In order to rehouse the people displaced by the improvement scheme of some years earlier, the Council in the years 1890 to 1892 erected 103 dwellings of the cottage type, accommodating about 500 persons, let at 5s. to 6s. 3d. per week. They are five-roomed dwellings, substantially built, and cost about £175 each. The buildings have back doors opening on an enclosed brick-paved yard, 36 feet across. The houses at 5s. 6d. have on the ground floor a living room 13 feet square, and a kitchen 12 feet by 9 feet, fitted with an iron sink and a small copper. There is also a pantry and a coal cupboard. On the first floor there are two bedrooms, and above them, a spacious well-lighted attic. Good grates and ovens are provided in every house, and iron is largely used for mantelpieces and other fittings. Each house has a penny-in-the-slot gas meter, and a flushed w.c. The dwellings are never vacant. After paying interest, sinking-fund charges, various rates, etc., the net surplus is equal to an average annual ground-rent of 11d. per square yard per annum, an amount above the estimated market value of the land. . . .

GLASGOW

In 1866 Glasgow obtained special powers to deal with large crowded and unhealthy areas by pulling down insanitary property and erecting dwellings for the poorer working classes. At first it cleared away slums, but did not itself build. In 1889 a change of policy took place, and municipal housing was undertaken. The following gives the size and number of dwellings erected and completed to October, 1900:—

One-apartment houses	373
Two ,, ,, ...	853
Three ,, ,, ...	138
Houses above three apartments	11
	1,375

Much of the land upon which these tenements stand cost from £1 10s. to £6 10s. per square foot. Of the whole number of these houses there are 467 distinctively suitable for the poorest classes, with single-apartment houses at an average rent of £5 and two-apartment houses at an average rent of about £8 5s. Applicants whose wages do not exceed 26s. have preference for the double-roomed and those whose earnings do not exceed 22s. for the single-roomed houses. The houses have many useful fittings, are under good regulations, and are kept sweet and clean, and let well. Some of the two-roomed houses consist of a kitchen, 15 feet by 13 feet (with a bed recess 4 feet 4 inches by 6 feet), and a sitting room of about the same size. Each bed recess is fitted with a wire spring-mattress. In the single-roomed dwellings the bed recess is shut off by a partition. Every house has a water-closet, and there is a wash-house to each block of tenements. These municipal dwellings, despite the high price paid for the land, pay interest on the cost at the rate of 4½ per cent per annum.

Municipal enterprise in Glasgow seems to have succeeded best of all with common lodging houses. In all, seven lodging houses have been erected, containing 2,414 beds let at nightly charges of 3d., 3½d., 4d., and 4½d. per individual. In the year 1899 867,338 lodgers were accommodated, of whom 89,456 were women. Allowing for depreciation the net profit was about £4,400. . . .

LIVERPOOL

The Corporation have built 493 tenements on the block principle at a cost of about £98,000. The blocks are handsome, and the rooms of good size. The tenements are three, two, and one-roomed, and let at weekly rents of from 2s. 6d. to 5s. 6d. The dwellings (which pay about 3 per cent. per annum on the outlay) were built on land, the site of some slums, that cost 23s. per square yard.

The Corporation have recently built 88 tenements of three and two rooms, but chiefly two rooms. Each is provided with

pantry, scullery and w.c., and most with a back yard. They are
built in flats, three storeys high, and let at 2s. 3d. to 4s. 6d. a
week, or about 1s. per room, and the average per tenement is
2s. 10d. . . .

The Council resolved, in order that houses for the very
poorest, let at 1s. per room, should pay, to build *themselves*, and
this was done successfully. The designs were made by their own
officials, the work was done in the cheapest and solidest style.
The building surveyor engaged the foremen and operatives.
No plaster is used; the inside walls are faced brick same as the
outside, but they are color-washed. Between the floors everything is filled up with cement, to which the floor-boards are
nailed. The absence of plaster and wall papers will be a great
sanitary improvement. . . .

MANCHESTER

Houses are provided by the Improvements and Buildings
Committee and the Sanitary Committee.

(*a*) The former under one scheme have erected 60 cottages
in the Miles Platting district, which are let at 5s. 6d. per week.
Under two other schemes 22 cottages have been built in Miles
Platting, and 40 more are nearly completed. The accommodation of these is as follows:—

On the ground floor, a living room not less than 12 ft. ×
10 ft. 3 in., and 9 ft. high; a kitchen not less than 12 ft. × 10 ft.
6 in., and 9 ft. high; a scullery not less than 9 ft. 6 in. × 7 ft.
6 in., and 8 ft. high; a water-closet, a fuel-store, a dust-bin,
and a pantry so constructed and placed as to admit of the
interior being at all times kept cool and well ventilated.

On the first floor, three bedrooms, of which one shall be not
less than 13 ft. × 12 ft., and 9 ft. high; another not less than
12 ft. × 8 ft., and 9 ft. high; and the other not less than 9 ft.
6 in. × 7 ft. 6 in., and 9 ft. high.

(*b*) The Sanitary Committee have erected a block of dwellings containing 16 shops, 237 double tenements, and 48 single
tenements, in the Oldham Road district; and a second block

of 130 double tenements and 36 three-roomed tenements in Pollard Street, Ancoats. These are now fully occupied. Four other blocks have since been built and are all occupied. Block No. 1 contains 13 shops with five-roomed dwellings, 16 single tenements, 32 double tenements, 16 three-roomed tenements, and 18 five-roomed cottages. No. 2 in the Chester Street district the block contains 36 double tenements and 36 three-roomed tenements. The block in Pott Street contains 36 double tenements, 39 three-roomed tenements, and three four-roomed tenements. A lodging house to accommodate 363 men has been erected in Harrison Street, but has not been yet very largely used.

The Council has purchased 237 acres in the Blackley district, which is to be used for cottages. . . .

SHEFFIELD

On 9th May, 1894, the Council obtained a Provisional Order for an improvement scheme under Part I of the 1890 Act. It is proposed to expend a net sum of £59,672 upon the scheme. No operations were entered upon for some time, but since 1896 active steps have been taken to carry out the scheme.

In July, 1898, the Council resolved to adopt Part III of the Act.

In reply to enquiries, Councillor Charles Hobson confirms the above, and writes:—

"Our operations run in the following direction:

"1. We have bought 100 acres of land, at prices ranging from £100 to £150 per acre, on the fringe of the borough.

"2. We are erecting on the condemned area a number of tenements, suitable for poor people, to cost £30,000. This work is done partly by our own workmen, and other portions, such as woodwork, plumbing, etc., is let to tradesmen, but the whole is done under our own clerk of works.

"3. We are also building 20 houses on another site. These are nearing completion. We have borrowed a loan of £5,000 from the tramways committee at 3 per cent for 30 years out of their profits.

"4. We contemplate erecting lodging houses on the area named at an early date. The city surveyor is instructed to get out plans for same.

"5. We have just got powers to compulsorily purchase other lands required to complete an estate for workmen's dwellings, etc."

89 Charles Booth   Life and Labour of the People in London
3rd series, *Religious Influences*, Vol 2 (1902), 67–8, 71–2

There is here no quarter quite so low as Great Pearl Street or Dorset Street, with the adjacent courts, in Whitechapel, but, on the other hand, for brutality within the circle of family life, perhaps nothing in all London quite equalled the old Nichol Street neighbourhood. . . . It must be admitted that the place deserved destruction. A district of almost solid poverty and low life, in which the houses were as broken down and deplorable as their unfortunate inhabitants; it seemed to offer a very good opportunity for rebuilding on some entirely new plan, such as might provide light and air, and possibilities of welfare and health for all. The area, some thirteen acres, was "scheduled" by the County Council; a scheme was drawn up; powers were obtained from Parliament, the money borrowed, and the work put in hand. The result was a disturbance of the population comparable, on a smaller scale, to that produced in Whitechapel by the inroad and spread of the Jews, but with the marked difference that, while those who preceded the Jews have gone and left no trace, those who have been displaced in the Boundary Street area by the London County Council scheme of reconstruction still, for the most part, remain in the neighbourhood.

As, street by street, the inhabitants were turned out, they invariably sought new homes as near as possible to the old.

Accommodation was provided in the new buildings, which from time to time were opened as the demolition proceeded; and in designing these buildings trouble was taken to suit them to the special needs of the displaced people, room being provided for costers' barrows and workshops for cabinet-makers and others; while the rents were put as low as would cover working charges, and meet the interest and sinking fund on the money borrowed. But all to no purpose. The various expenses incurred in effecting the clearance had been enormous, and it may be that too much was yielded to the desire to build dwellings that should at once be a credit to the London County Council and an example to others. At any rate, the cost was too great, the rents too high, and, in addition, the regulations to be observed under the new conditions, demanded more orderliness of behaviour than suited the old residents. The result is that the new buildings are occupied by a different class, largely Jews, and that the inhabitants of the demolished dwellings have overrun the neighbouring poor streets, or have sought new homes further and further afield, as section after section was turned adrift.

Everywhere these people are recognised as coming from the "Nichol," and everywhere they have brought poverty, dirt and disorder with them, and an increase of crowding, the rooms previously occupied by one family having had to serve for two. Doubtless most of those whose places they have taken have moved further out to the North or East, but not a few have come to the new buildings, and may perhaps still maintain some slight connection with the parishes they have left, just as those of the inhabitants of the "Nichol," who still live near, are said to do in some cases with their old school and mission centres. Thus, to some extent, a curious shuffling of the population has been effected.

If we try to measure the results, the destruction of the old streets and buildings stands as so much to the good, and so does the dispersion of the inhabitants. The failure to re-house these people in the new buildings might have been anticipated, but it must be remembered that the scheme was carried through in the earlier, more experimental, and, perhaps, more sanguine days of the Council. The intention was to build improved dwellings for a low class of people; the result has been to bring in an entirely different class. Those who cling to the original plan may think success could have been won if the ideal had been a little less high and the buildings less expensive; while those who abandon any notion of rehousing the displaced, may feel that the new buildings might have been better adapted to the general needs of the neighbourhood; but both alike demand that, by some means, the rents should be lower.

It is undeniable that the scheme was weighed down by expense; and probable that an aim less exalted and more practical would have been of greater advantage to the neighbourhood.

PROSPERITY AMONG THE WORKING CLASSES

Comfort

Not all members of the working class lived in poverty. Some lived in considerable prosperity, particularly in the north of England. Those working-class relatives of Beatrice Webb's in Bacup who went off for a week to Blackpool or on trips to London (*My Apprenticeship*, 1926; Penguin edition, 1938, Vol 1, 193) in 1886 were the other side of the coin to those to whom Wakes weeks were a form of unpaid unemployment. Samuel Bamford (1788–1872) a former Radical who had participated in the Peterloo fracas, turned in later life towards moderate Liberalism. Here he notes prosperity in three weaving villages not far from Manchester (90). The journalist and local historian W. A. Abram (1835–94) writes enthusiastically about artisans' living conditions in Lancashire in the late 1860s (91), and, at the end of the century, Paul de Rousiers (1857–1934), a French writer on social questions, also takes a distinctly optimistic line (92): passages like this one are to be found scattered throughout his book.

Joseph Brown, whose home is the subject of this extract, was a small employer in the metal trade, but he was a former workman whose "mode of living", de Rousiers notes, "differs little from that of the other well-to-do workmen I visited in England. He lives like a working man, and not in the style of the middle class" (p. 15). It can be argued that some of these writers set out to discover the prosperity which they reported; much the same can be said of those who investigated the slums.

90 Samuel Bamford   Walks in South Lancashire
(1844), 32–3, 253, 275–6

A member of the hands lived in houses belonging to Mr C., for which they paid from one shilling and sixpence, to two shillings and nine-pence per week, and their rent was settled every pay day. I made excuses to enter some of the houses, and found them uniformly neat and clean, one tenement was beautifully clean; the walls were as white as lime could make them; the good housewife, who was up to the elbows in suds, gave me liberty to see her chambers, and I found the walls and the beds on a par with the house below; they were almost spotless, and the air was as untainted as the wind. This was one of a row of houses; several others which I entered were almost in as good condition; they had generally flowers and green shrubs in the windows, and before the doors were small gardens with flowers and a few pot herbs. The tenements consisted of a front room, a kitchen and two chambers, and the front rooms were furnished with handsome fire-grates, ovens, and boilers, all as well burnished as black lead, a good brush, and a willing hand could make them. The rent of these dwellings was two shillings and nine-pence per week, clear of all rates.

. . . But there was no outward sign of distress here, nor any great demonstration of discontent. The woman, to be sure, wished things were better—thought they had not enough for their work, and I thought the same; but there was nothing like

squalor, or dirt, or shiftless thriftless despair about them or
their little cot. The walls and the floors were clean, the windows
whole and shining, the place was decorated with maps and
pictures of fierce battles, Lady Godivia riding through Coventry
and other antiquated and legendary subjects, but all seemed
cleanly and cheerful, and the one woman with her babe, and
the other with her wheel, seemed disposed to make most of the
homely enjoyment of their own hearths, upon which burned a
good coal fire.

. . . First, we will have a description of the residence of the
worthy working man. The door and front windows looked
eastward; the space inside was about seven yards by eight;
the fire-place on the left of the entrance, and a good oaken
chest of drawers, with prints and drawings in glazed frames,
were on the right; a good oaken couch chair, with specimens
of needlework, and other pictures, was fronting the window;
and several bright and neat seats were in various places round
the house. Over head was a bread-flake, but with a few oat-
cakes on it; some bundles of dried herbs, &c., but no bacon,
ham, or beef were seen. Opposite the door was a flight of stairs
to the chambers, and a passage leading to the cellar, and to a
small parlour, used as a bed-room; and on the other side of the
house was a small recess used as a kitchen. The floors, the walls,
and the furniture, were all thoroughly clean. The chambers
above, of two heights, were the same size as the house; and it
should be remarked, that flannel weavers require capacious,
open rooms, on account of the space necessary for their jennies,
their working mills, looms, and other implements of manufacture. At the head of the stairs, in the first chamber, was a
good bed in an old-fashioned black oaken bedstead. Near that
was a loom, at which the weaver sat, tying in his work. Beyond
the loom was another decent-looking bed in an old bedstead,
next that was a warping mill, taking up much room; then a
stove, with a fire burning,—and then another loom. The
looms each contained flannel work, of a fineness called thirty-
two reed—such as is used for linings, petticoats, and other

personal wear. The room was comfortably warm, and the arrangements were of that primitive and homely cast which reminded me of the free distribution of a Dutch interior; such is a characteristic of most of the working and sleeping chambers of the flannel weavers in the neighbourhood of Rochdale.

91 W. A. Abram   Social Condition and Political Prospects of the Lancashire Workmen
Fortnightly Review (October 1868), 429

The homes of the more thrifty of the workpeople are moderately comfortable. The dwellings of the operatives are mostly long rows of two-storied buildings, with a couple of rooms upon each floor, the rental of which varies according to size and situation, from half-a-crown to four shillings and sixpence per week, the landlord generally paying the rates. The furniture of the living room may consist of a dresser, an eight-day clock, kitchen sofa, and a couple of rocking-chairs at either side of the fire-place. The walls are usually adorned with two or three framed engravings or coloured lithographs. The better-paid workmen improve upon this a little. Their front apartment on the ground-floor is dubbed a parlour, and its furniture includes a small book-case if the man be studious, or if, as is not unfrequent, he has a taste for music, a piano. The exclusive possession of a house, though ever so small, is no slight advantage to the artisan, and places the operative in these districts in a superior position for securing domestic comfort to the workman of London or Glasgow, who is fain to lodge his family in a portion of a tenement, often in the attic, and to whom privacy is a thing unknown and unattainable. I believe there is no operative population in the world so well and cheaply housed as are the factory workers in a Lancashire manufacturing town of the second or third magnitude.

92 Paul de Rousiers   The Labour Question in Britain
(1895; English translation, 1896), 15–18, discussing Birmingham

While I was alone in the parlour I had time to look at it well. The room was nearly square, about 12 feet each way, and well lighted by a window looking on to the street. The floor was covered with carpets, and from the middle of the ceiling hung a chandelier with three burners. The wall opposite the door was occupied by a white marble mantelpiece with a cast-iron grate; over the fire was an overmantel of wood. A suite upholstered in horse-hair looked like good solid family furniture, and consisted of six chairs, a sofa, and a low chair. There were two tables, covered with cloths. One stood in front of the window, and held a china flower-pot in which a fern was dying, the other was covered with books and albums. A mahogany chiffonier with glass panels and shelves completed the furniture. Photographs were scattered about on the mantelpiece and tables, and there were two or three indifferent pictures on the walls.

.... We also went upstairs to the rooms on the floor above. They were a little narrow, but well-furnished and clean. The bedroom occupied by Mr and Mrs Brown contained a large wooden bed, a marble washstand, a chest of drawers, the top of which Mrs Brown had fitted up as a dressing-table and a cupboard. Two daughters slept in a room containing two beds. It was carefully kept, and the walls were adorned with a profusion of pictures and nicknacks. Two rooms had fireplaces. I explained to Brown that it was necessary for my purpose to know the value of the different articles of furniture, and he very kindly took no offence at my impertinent questions.

"As to furniture," he said, "you can get goods now at all prices. You will have no difficulty in Birmingham in finding a parlour suite consisting of six chairs, two arm-chairs, and a sofa, at 6 guineas. Of course it is poor stuff, but it is showy. It is furniture made of unseasoned wood by cabinetmakers in Whitechapel, and upholstered in Birmingham. Many young couples buy one when they set up housekeeping, and at the end of five years not a single chair is sound. Now, compare our old chairs in the parlour which have seen twenty-seven years' service. They cost 22 guineas when new, but our children rolled on them and climbed on them to play at 'family coach,' and they are still in good condition. In the sitting-room, where we have meals and where we spend most of our time, the furniture is a little rougher, but very solid too; each chair cost £1 5s. and the sofa 7 guineas."

"As a rule, my wife and I have always thought it was worth while to pay more and get a good article. The chiffonier opposite the window in the parlour cost 15 guineas, but see how well it opens. The overmantel cost 7 guineas; it is a luxury, of course, but it is a constant pleasure to have one's home nice. The marble chimney-piece cost 6 guineas; when I built the house the contractor had not allowed in his estimate for such an expensive one, but we made ourselves a present of it, as an extra, to beautify our parlour. By the way, I do not recommend the grate which is put in; it is an old pattern, but the low price—£2—is compensated for by a great waste of coal. I keep it because we do not always have a fire there, but in the sitting-room I have for the same total cost a marble mantel-piece at 4 guineas, and a grate at the same price, and I do not burn more than 2s. worth of coal a week with a fire going all day in winter,"—and Brown, who is very well up about every-thing made in Birmingham, discussed at some length the merits of his different grates. In his bedroom the fireplace was entirely of cast-iron, and worth about £2 10s. There was another, quite small and unpretentious, in his daughters' room, which cost only 8s. There are even some to be had, it would seem, at 6s. All this information was useful to enable me to determine with precision the exact material position of Joseph Brown; and of interest too, because it gives a general idea of the cost of setting up housekeeping in the working class. English industry has devoted much attention to the manufacture of cheap articles of every kind which are sold at a price within the reach of a very large class of customers. Sometimes the result has been that quality is sacrificed, as in the case of furniture; sometimes an article has been invented combining good value

THE HOMES OF THE WORKING CLASSES

with a low price, as in the case of the little fire-grates. It is no small matter for a working-class family to be able to afford, at a trifling cost, the comfort of a well-warmed room, which, in case of illness, will afford favourable conditions of temperature and health in this damp and bitter climate. These are trifles, but they put very appreciable advantages within the reach of all.

The visit to Mrs. Brown's kitchener was interesting from this point of view. It is a marvel of ingenuity, capable of cooking the family meal, of heating irons, of drying linen, of providing a constant supply of hot water, and all in a very small space and with a trifling expenditure of fuel. It was rather dear, £8 for the kitchener and £1 for fixing, but the saving of coal largely compensates for the outlay. It burns only about 2s worth of coal a week.

Home-ownership

Quite large numbers of working men owned their own houses, thanks to the operations of building societies. A number of Government committees and commissions enquired into the subject and were given figures of home-ownership which clearly surprised some of their members. James Taylor, a representative of Birmingham building societies, told the Royal Commission on Friendly and Benefit Building Societies in 1871 that 13,000 houses in Birmingham belonged to working men and that the average wage of his members was about 30s per week. Again, Thomas Fatkin of the Leeds Permanent Benefit Building Society told the Royal Commission on Housing in 1884 that his society alone had enabled about 7,000 working men to buy houses.

But as time passed and "terminating" societies were replaced by "permanent" ones, middle-class members and borrowers tended to dominate. In Document 93 the 1871–2 Commission discusses the evidence. (The Starr-Bowkett societies worked on the principle that every member was a borrower. The member subscribed to the society for 25–30 years. At the end of that period he had bought his house free of interest and his subscriptions to the society were refunded.) Thomas Wright (b 1839?), who wrote several books as "The Journeyman Engineer", points out (94) that many working-class house owners acquired not only a home but also a capitalist mentality. This was a feature of building societies clearly reassuring to Samuel Smiles (1812–1904), the apostle of self-help (95).

It is difficult to assess how widespread was working-class home-ownership. The subject has been little studied, but it is worth pointing out that Seebohm Rowntree discovered in 1899 that nearly 6 per cent of working-class families in York owned their own homes (*Poverty*, 166).

93 Royal Commission on Friendly and Benefit Building Societies   Second Report
PP, Vol XXVI (1872), 16–17

46. It is admitted by even an adverse witness that on the whole permanent societies have as yet been judiciously managed; that failures of building societies, which used to be very frequent in the epoch of terminating societies alone, are now rare. It is, however, alleged that the growth of them has altogether changed the character and altered the sphere of the building society movement; that it tends to throw this more and more under the direction and into the hands of the middle classes, and to secure to them its benefits. It is, indeed, startling to hear of single advances, not only of thousands, but of twenty and thirty thousand pounds being made by building societies, sometimes on the security of mills and factories; and it is roundly alleged by some witnesses, that when this is the case, there is no more money to spare for small borrowers, and that the working classes, by whom and for whose benefit the system was primarily devised, are discountenanced and kept away. It is maintained as positively to the contrary, that the smaller advances are always preferred to the larger ones, as being much more secure, by dividing the chances of loss over a wider field, and

that the larger ones do themselves benefit the working classes, by serving as means of investment for the capital which these classes deposit with the societies, and which might otherwise often remain idle. . . .

48. It appears, indeed, unquestionable, that whilst the smaller terminating societies remain very often still under the management of the working classes, or of persons very near to them in point of station, the larger permanent societies at least are almost invariably under the direction of the middle class. That this is beneficial to the working class themselves, from the business habits and greater practical experience, as well as the more reponsible position of the latter class, is maintained by more than one witness. As respects the composition of the societies, the evidence is conflicting. There seems no reason to doubt that in the smaller Lancashire towns, Oldham especially, and in the Starr-Bowkett and other gratuitous loan societies of the metropolis, the bulk of the members consist still of working men. These would be mainly terminating societies; but the number of genuine working men in the better class of permanent societies in Birmingham, in Lancashire and Yorkshire, seems evidently to be very considerable, such members being indifferently either borrowers or investors. In the "Leeds Permanent" about five-sixths of the members belong to the working class. From Liverpool we have had some remarkable evidence, that whilst the working men seldom borrow, yet they supply as investors the larger portion of the capital put out by the societies. In the metropolis, on the other hand, the working men seem generally to form only a minority in the permanent societies, as compared with the middle classes, although in one of the largest London societies (the Birkbeck) the majority of the borrowers are said to be of the working class. And however the proportion may vary, it is safe to say that the English middle class now enter into the building society movement in much larger numbers, take a much larger share in its direction, and derive much greater benefit from it, than they did 30 or 35 years ago.

94 Thomas Wright   Our New Masters
(1873), 101, 196

The aim of the great majority of the best members of the
working classes—the cleverest, most energetic, and persevering
men—is to raise themselves *out* of those classes. Numbers of
them succeed in this aim, become in a greater or lesser degree
capitalists, or get into positions in which their interests are
identified with those of capital rather than those of labour.
Still larger numbers—numbers so large that they form a considerable section of the working classes—though they do not
rise out of their class, become, in their endeavour to do so,
comparatively rich men—have money in banks, and shares in
co-operative and building societies, and are as watchful against
and strongly opposed to anything that is alleged will tend to
interfere with "the sacredness of private property" or lessen
dividends, as are any of the great capitalists.

. . . . There are thousands of well-to-do workmen, men who
own houses, have shares in building societies, and money in
banks; men also who, by reason of the "push" and energy
which have, as a rule, enabled them to accumulate money or
property, are among the most influential of their class and with
their class, and these men are keenly opposed to anything that
tends to trench upon the "sacredness" of individual property.

95 Samuel Smiles   Thrift
(1875), 107, 109

Land and Building Societies constitute another form of co-
operation. These are chiefly supported by the minor middle-
class men, but also to a considerable extent by the skilled and
thrifty working-class men. By their means portions of land are
bought, and dwelling-houses are built. By means of a building
society, a person who desires to possess a house enters the
society as a member, and instead of paying his rent to the

landlord, pays his subscriptions and interest to a committee of his friends; and in course of time, when his subscriptions are paid up, the house is purchased, and conveyed to him by the society. The building society is thus a savings bank, where money accumulates for a certain purpose. But even those who do not purchase a house, receive a dividend and bonus on their shares, which sometimes amounts to a considerable sum.

The accumulation of property has the effect which it always has upon thrifty men; it makes them steady, sober, and diligent. It weans them from revolutionary notions, and makes them conservative. When workmen, by their industry and frugality, have secured their own independence, they will cease to regard the sight of others' well-being as a wrong inflicted on themselves; and it will no longer be possible to make political capital out of their imaginary woes. . . .

There are also exceptional towns and villages in Lancashire where large sums of money have been saved by the operatives for buying or building comfortable cottage dwellings. Last year Padiham saved about fifteen thousand pounds for this purpose, although its population is only about 8,000. Burnley has also been very successful. The Building Society there has 6,600 investors, who saved last year £160,000 or an average of twenty-four pounds for each investor. The members consist principally of mill operatives, miners, mechanics, engineers, carpenters, stonemasons, and labourers. They also include women, both married and unmarried. Our informant states that "great numbers of the working classes have purchased houses in which to live. They have likewise bought houses as a means of invest-ment. The building society has assisted in hundreds of these cases, by advancing money on mortgage—such mortgages being repaid by easy instalments."

Building Societies are, on the whole, among the most excellent methods of illustrating the advantages of Thrift. They induce men to save money for the purpose of buying their own homes; in which, so long as they live, they possess the best of all securities.

THE HOMES OF THE RURAL LABOURERS

Description

In contrast to urban slums, the plight of rural labourers received less sudden and sensational publicity. But throughout the Victorian period a steady stream of evidence, from Government and private enquiries, showed that rural housing was as bad or worse than housing in towns, and improvements were less common. Rural housing seemed particularly shocking for two reasons: because England had traditionally been a rural country and immense wealth came from the land, and because the English village looked so attractive. The first biographer of Joseph Arch, the farm workers' leader, wrote in 1872 that the English village was "one of the homeliest and most picturesque scenes to be found in the world. . . . Having regard to picturesque effect, we may pronounce most English villages to be successes; but having regard to light, air, pure water, cleanliness, decency, and health, nine out of ten of them must be pronounced failures" (F. S. Attenborough. *Joseph Arch*, 1872, quoted in Arthur Clayden. *The Revolt of the Field*, 1874, 9). Where "closed" villages, owned by a single landlord, existed, labourers were often pushed out to swarm into "open" villages; thus the attractions of one parish might be bought at the price of overcrowding and misery nearby. And, as Dr Henry Julian Hunter pointed out in an official report of 1864 (contained in the *Seventh Report of the Medical Officer of the Privy Council, PP*, Vol. XXVI, 1865, 140–1), where benevolent landlords built "model cottages" they were so expensive as to discourage more necessary and more modest efforts.

The Government reports of 1843 and 1893–4 (96, 101) sound all too much alike, despite the passage of half a century. Thresh's report (101), indeed, was regarded as typical of many rural areas by the Senior Assistant Agricultural Commissioner to the Royal Commission on Labour (*PP*, Vol. XXXVII–ii, 1893–4, 102). One of the *Morning Chronicle's*

talented team, Alexander Mackay (1808–52), examines
"Labour and the Poor" in Buckinghamshire and neighbouring counties (97), and Foster's report on the Durham coal
districts (98) shows that miners' living conditions were probably even worse than those of farm labourers. Hippolyte
Taine, writing about village life not far from London, strikes
a more optimistic note (99). Here Taine was at one with
Richard Jefferies (1848–87), Wiltshire writer and poet, who
also tended to stress the bright side of rural housing. The book
(100) by Francis George Heath (1843–1913), preservation-
ist, naturalist and writer, was an enlarged version of one first
published in 1872 as *The "Romance" of Peasant Life in the West
of England*, and in a first revision as *The English Peasantry* in
1874. In the passage from the 1880 edition included here
Heath describes a visit made in 1873.

96 Special Assistant Poor Law Commissioners on the Employment of Women and Children in Agriculture Report by Alfred Austin (Dorset)
PP, Vol. XII (1843), 19–21

With regard to lodging, there is no difference between that of
the women who labour in the fields and the women of the same
class who do not. The want of sufficient accommodation seems
universal. Cottages generally have only two bedrooms (with
very rare exceptions); a great many have only one. The consequence is, that it is very often extremely difficult, if not impossible, to divide a family so that grown-up persons of different
sexes, brothers and sisters, fathers and daughters, do not sleep
in the same room. Three or four persons not unfrequently sleep
in the same bed. In a few instances I found that two families,
neighbours, arranged so that the females of both families slept
together in one cottage and the males in the other; but such an
arrangement is very rare, and in the generality of cottages I
believe that the only attempt that is or that can be made to
separate beds, with occupants of different sexes, and necessarily

placed close together from the smallness of the rooms, is an old shawl or some article of dress suspended as a curtain between them. . . .

It is impossible not to be struck, in visiting the dwellings of the agricultural labourers, with the general want of new cottages, notwithstanding the universal increase of population. Everywhere the cottages are old, and frequently in a state of decay, and are consequently ill adapted for their increased number of inmates of late years. The floor of the room in which the family live during the day is always of stone in these counties, and wet or damp through the winter months, being frequently lower than the soil outside. The situation of the cottage is often extremely bad, no attention having been paid at the time of its building to facilities for draining. Cottages are frequently erected on a dead level, so that water cannot escape; and sometimes on spots lower than the surrounding ground. In the village of Stourpain, in Dorsetshire, there is a row of several labourers' cottages, mostly joining each other, and fronting the street, in the middle of which is an open gutter. There are two or three narrow passages leading from the street, between the houses, to the back of them. Behind the cottages the ground rises rather abruptly; and about three yards up the elevation are placed the pigsties and privies of the cottages. There are also shallow excavations, the receptacles apparently of all the dirt of the families. The matter constantly escaping from the pigsties, privies, &c., is allowed to find its way through the passages between the cottages into the gutter in the street, so that the cottages are nearly surrounded by streams of filth. It was in these cottages that a malignant typhus broke out about two years ago, which afterwards spread through the village. . . . I hardly visited a cottage where there were any attempts at draining. The dirt of the family is thrown down before or behind the cottage; if there is any natural inclination in the ground from the cottage, it escapes; if not, it remains till evaporated. Most cottages have pigsties joining them; and these add to the external uncleanliness of the labourer's dwelling.

97 [Alexander Mackay]   Labour and the Poor; Rural Districts, Letter II: The Labourer's Home

Morning Chronicle (24 October 1849) 5, Bucks, Berks, Wilts and Oxford

The cabin is so rude and uncouth that it has less the appearance of having been built than of having been suddenly thrown up out of the ground. The length is not above 15 feet, its width between 10 and 12. The wall, which has sunk at different points, and seems bedewed with a cold sweat, is composed of a species of imperfect sandstone, which is fast crumbling to decay. It is so low that your very face is almost on a level with the heavy thatched roof which covers it, and which seems to be pressing it into the earth. The thatch is thickly encrusted with a bright green vegetation, which, together with the appearance of the trees and the mason-work around, well attests the prevailing humidity of the atmosphere. In front it presents to the eye a door with one window below, and another window—a smaller one—in the thatch above. The door is awry from the sinking of the wall; the glass in the window above is unbroken, but the lower one is here and there stuffed with rags, which keep out both the air and the sunshine. As you look at the crazy fabric, you marvel how it stands. It is so twisted and distorted, that it seems as if it never had been strong and compact, and as if, from the very first, it had been erected, not as a human abode, but as a humble monument to dilapidation. But let us enter.

You approach the door-way through the mud, over some loose stones, which rock under your feet in using them. You have to stoop for admission, and cautiously look around ere you fairly trust yourself within. There are but two rooms in the house—one below, and the other above. On leaving the bright light without, the room which you enter is so dark that for a time you can with difficulty discern the objects which it contains. Before you, is a large but cheerless fireplace—it is not every poor man that may be said to have a hearth—with a few smouldering embers of a small wood fire, over which still hangs a pot, recently used for some culinary purpose. At one corner stands a small ricketty table, whilst scattered about are three old chairs—one without a back—and a stool or two, which, with a very limited and imperfect washing apparatus, and a shelf or two for plates, tea-cups, &c., constitute the whole furniture of the apartment. What could be more cheerless or comfortless? and yet you could fancy you could put up with everything but the close earthy smell, which you endeavour in vain to escape by breathing short and quickly. . . .

. . . Let us take a glance at their sleeping accommodations.

These are above, and are gained by means of a few greasy and ricketty steps, which lead through a species of hatchway in the ceiling. Yes, there is but one room, and yet we counted nine in the family! And such a room! The small window in the roof admits just light enough to enable you to discern its character and dimensions. The rafters, which are all exposed, spring from the very floor, so that it is only in the very centre of the apartment that you have any chance of standing erect. The thatch oozes through the wood work which supports it, the whole being begrimed with smoke and dust, and replete with vermin. There are no cobwebs, for the spider only spreads his net where flies are likely to be caught. You look in vain for a bedstead; there is none in the room. But there are their beds, lying side by side on the floor almost in contact with each other, and occupying nearly the whole length of the apartment. The beds are large sacks, filled with the chaff of oats, which the labourer sometimes gets and at others purchases from his employer. The chaff of wheat and barley is used on the farm for other purposes. The bed next the hatchway is that of the father and mother, with whom sleeps the infant, born but a few months ago in this very room. In the other beds sleep the children, the boys and girls together. The eldest girl is in her twelfth year, the eldest boy having nearly completed his eleventh, and they are likely to remain for years yet in the circumstances in which we now find them. With the exception of the youngest children, the family retire to rest about the same hour, generally undressing below, and then ascending and crawling over each other to their respective resting places for the night. There are two blankets on the bed occupied by the parents, the others being covered with a very heterogeneous assemblage of materials. It not unfrequently happens that the clothes worn by the parents in the day time form the chief part of the covering of the children by night. Such is the dormitory in which, lying side by side, the nine whom we have just left below at their wretched meal will pass the night. The sole ventilation is through the small aperture occupied by what is termed, by courtesy, a window. In other words there is scarcely any ventilation at all. What a den in the hour of sickness or death! What a den, indeed, at any time! And yet when the sable goddess stretches forth her leaden sceptre over the soft downy couch in Mayfair, such are the circumstances in which, in our rural parishes, she leaves a portion of her slumbering domain.

Let it not be said that this picture is overdrawn, or that it is a concentration for effect into one point of defects, spread in reality over a large surface. As a type of the extreme of domiciliary wretchedness in the rural districts, it is underdrawn. The cottage in question has two rooms. Some have only one, with as great a number of inmates to occupy it. Some of them, again, have three or four rooms, with a family occupying each room; the families so circumstanced amounting each, in some cases, to nine or ten individuals. In some cottages, too, a lodger is accommodated, who occupies the same apartment as the family. Such, fortunately, is not the condition of all the labourers in the agricultural districts; but it is the condition of a very great number of Englishmen—not in the back woods of a remote settlement, but in the heart of Anglo-Saxon civilization, in the year of grace 1849. It behoves the

"———gentlemen of England,
Who live at home at ease."

to ponder seriously upon the condition of such of their fellow-subjects as are so wretchedly circumstanced. Such anomalies but ill accord with the civilization to which we lay claim. In its main outline our national fabric may be brilliant and imposing; but is it sound in all its component parts? Whilst improvement has brushed over the prominent points, burnishing them brightly, it has passed over many of the deep crevices which intervene, and in which the gangrene is being engendered which is silently eating into the very vitals of society.

98 Royal Commission on the State of Popular Education in England (Newcastle Commission), Vol II, Report of Assistant Commissioner A. F. Foster on Mining Districts of Durham
PP, Vol XXI–ii (1861), 321–2

The colliers usually live quite as isolated communities, all the houses of each village being held by the coal owner, and appropriated exclusively to his workpeople and the small shop-keepers who supply their immediate wants. A collier village presents for the most part a miserable and repulsive aspect. It consists of parallel rows of low houses, without pavement, drainage, or enclosure, either in front or rear. Each house contains one, two, or three, but seldom more apartments, and in some villages there are out-houses in the proportion of one to every half-dozen families; in others there are none. If a house has three rooms one is used as kitchen and sitting room; the father and mother, with the younger children, sleep in one bedroom; the grown-up sons, daughters, and lodgers occupy the other. A very low state of morals and manners might be inferred from such arrangements, in connexion with full feeding and excessive drinking; but the actual condition of the people in these respects may not be described. It has been said that it is of no use to educate the labouring classes till their dwellings are improved; it is equally true that it is useless attempting to improve their dwellings till they are in some measure prepared by education to appreciate the improvements. Till a comparatively recent period, every effort in this direction was viewed with jealousy, and met by the cry that it was an attempt "to enslave" the workmen, that is, to attach them to the spot, and abridge the easy freedom with which they quit one employment for another; or, in case of a combination against their masters, turn out of their dwellings and bivouac in the open country. Even since the fear of a "take-in" has in a great measure subsided, there remains the obstacle to domiciliary improvement arising from ignorance and evil habits. Only last year a philanthropic coal-owner built two more commodious houses for large families, and placed in one of them a household in which eleven had been accustomed to sleep in two rooms; it was presently found that the enclosed yard of the new dwelling was made available for rearing pigs, and their food was stored up in the apartment which the agent had designed for the girls to sleep in, apart from their grown-up brothers.

99 Hippolyte Taine   Notes on England
(1872; English translation, 1872), 155–7

Several cottages are very poor, being of clay covered with laths, a thatched roof, the rooms are too low and too narrow, the windows too small, the partitions too thin. Think, of a large family huddled in winter in two of these rooms, with clothes drying, the swaddling clothes of infants, and the chimney roaring; during the long days of rain and snow, they must live in an unwholesome air, amid their own vapour. Many of the mothers have a lean face, marked with pimples, a worn-out pinched air; they have too many children and too much toil. The occupant of one of these thatched huts is a day-labourer, married, the father of six children, who earns twelve shillings a week, being generally employed by the year or by the half year; a cottage like his costs from three to four pounds sterling yearly; his features are delicate, drawn, his physiognomy is sad and humble. I was introduced to all these people with consideration and courtesy; they were asked with apologies to permit a French gentleman to enter. They instantly consented with civility and a pleasant smile. I remarked that I have seen in

France many thatched huts much worse furnished; whereupon my companion replied that was some consolation. The poor day-labourer did not appear to be of that opinion.

However, his little house is clean; the blue patterned plates are ranged in good order above a dresser; the fireplace is of iron and is well constructed. I had previously seen other cottages elsewhere of this stamp; nearly always, at least in one room, an old carpet covers the floor; often there is a coloured paper, chairs of polished wood, small framed engravings, always a Bible, sometimes other volumes, religious books, new novels, the art of rearing rabbits, &c., in short, more useful objects than in our very poor thatched huts. In addition, the care taken is greater; there are no doors off their hinges, hanging shutters, broken panes, stagnant pools, scattered dunghills; the pavement of the soil is well swept, nothing lies about at random. Probably confusion and uncleanliness are more unhealthy in this climate than in ours, and man is bound to be orderly, prudent, regular as in Holland.

The village contains but four hundred souls; yet the little inn is decent, shining with cleanliness; one would sleep there readily, and one would be comfortable. We visit a carpenter, then a carter's; they are seated at table by themselves and take tea with butter. Their houses are of brick and covered with red tiles; one of them is flanked with a pretty large garden filled with vegetables, well cultivated, garnished with fine strawberries, with some bee-hives in a corner; both of them have a small flower-garden, roses, ivy, some creeping plants, and adornment. The rooms are rather low, but are not wanting in air; the small panes of glass connected by slight triangles of lead allow plenty of light to enter; one goes along a passage of bricks carefully washed to enter the outhouse; the retiring place, half open, is as well kept as in a middle-class house; on the first-floor are two bedrooms. Some books, the "Whole Duty of Man," one of Murray's guides, the family Bible, five or six volumes of history. Not a particle of dust on the windows, not a speck of mud on the floors, not a hole in the garments. Many other persons of the same condition pass along the streets, and their clothes are the same; it is true that to-day is Sunday. But, on the whole, my impression is that they are better provided and more careful than the peasants of France. The glory, the foolish vanity, and the superiority of ours consist in possessing land; they prefer being abstinent, stinting themselves, and having their acre in the sun; in order to acquire it they save out of their comfort. But this acquisition is a fund; in case of sickness or scarcity, they have a sure resource at hand. On the contrary, here every one tells me that a countryman is as much a spendthrift as a workman, as improvident, as exacting as far as comfort is concerned. Let an accident occur, and he instantly becomes a burden upon the parish.

100 Francis George Heath   Peasant Life in the West of England
(Minehead, Somerset, 1880), 196–8

Never have we witnessed so sad a sight as we saw in that miserable garret of a miserable hut. There was one bedstead, besides two other—we cannot say articles of furniture—things purporting to represent a table and a chair, on the bare floor. On the bedstead, in the darkest corner of the room, which might have been some twelve or thirteen feet long, by some eight or nine feet wide, and perhaps seven feet high, lay the poor old bedridden grandmother, her poor wrinkled face looking the picture of patient and uncomplaining misery. Nothing on the floor besides the wretched bedstead and the table and chair; no pictures, even of the rudest kind, on the walls. One tiny window, cut through the thick wall of the cottage, admitted a little light into this chamber, and there, with her head in the darkest corner, had lain *for years* this poor old creature, the helpless mother of an English peasant.

It is terrible to witness want and misery in the foul slums of a great city; but is assuredly much more terrible to find it in rose-bound cottages—embosomed in the most charming of country nooks, where the very richness of nature seems to rebuke the meanness of man.

.... We went, before descending the stairs, into the other of the two bedrooms. Words can hardly convey with sufficient effect an impression of the abject poverty which silently but eloquently told its piteous tale in that small room! A wretched, ragged-looking bed was before us. It filled up the greater part of the room. An old brown, worn, patched tester stretched over this bed, in which the father, mother, and the two youngest children slept. Looking at the ceiling over this tester we noticed dark stains in the plaster, and we said, "Does the rain come in there?" The rain had come in upon their bed, we were told, often and often in wet weather, but now the roof was repaired, although many vain requests had been preferred before this work was done. On the floor at the foot of the bedstead there was a non-descript heap of rags, amongst which the three elder children slept. Seven human beings in this tiny, ill-lighted room! As in the case of the adjoining chamber, there was only one small window. Several of the panes were out, and we expressed our surprise that the landlord had not ordered new ones to be put in. But the landlord never mended windows; that was the tenant's duty.

101 Royal Commission on Labour   Reports of Assistant Agricultural Commissioners: Dr John C. Thresh on Chelmsford and Maldon Rural Sanitary Districts
PP, Vol. XXXV, Part V (1893–4), 84–5

The character of the cottages themselves varies very considerably in the different villages. In some there are very few dilapidated houses, very few of the old lath and plaster cottages roofed with thatch, few without ample gardens. In others the cottages are crowded together and a large proportion of them are so old or so structurally defective that they are really unfit for human habitation. . . . In nearly every parish there are so-called houses which are so structurally defective that they can never be converted into comfortable healthy dwellings, and which are becoming so decayed from age and neglect that they are really unfit for habitation. In many such instances neglect rather than age has been the cause of the dilapidated condition. In cottages, as with men, neglect leads to premature decay. These old places are built of a timber frame-work, studded outside with laths, and daubed over with plaster, or with a mixture of clay and chopped straw. Many of them have not been lined with lath and plaster inside, and consequently are fearfully cold in winter. The walls may not be an inch in thickness, and where the laths are decayed the fingers can easily be pushed through. Every time also a piece of plaster falls off outside the interior is exposed. The floors downstairs usually are of brick, laid directly on the ground, and are almost invariably damp, often indeed reeking with moisture. The bricks also get broken, the floor becomes uneven, and the bare earth may be exposed. To obtain some slight degree of comfort bits of board are laid down and several thicknesses of sacking and mats are laid upon the floor. These have to be renewed periodically, as the damp causes them to rot and become useless.

The roof is of thatch, which, if kept in good repair forms a good covering, warm in winter and cool in summer, though doubtless in many instances it serves as a harbour for dirt, for vermin, for the condensed exhalations from the bodies of the occupants of the bedrooms, and where persons suffering from the various fevers are nursed therein, possibly also for the infectious material which propagates such diseases.

The bedrooms in such houses are almost invariably in the roof, and if there be more than one, the one is usually entered from the other. The windows are small, formed of small panes of glass let into a leaden framework. These windows are usually of the most rickety description, and often do not open, but this defect is atoned for by the ease with which the air can obtain access to the room around the side of the defective frame. The utmost care has to be taken when cleaning them to avoid pushing them out. In fact, in many cases I do not know how the housewife contrives to rub the panes without someone is pushing against them outside to prevent a catastrophe. Where a back window has been so pushed out the opening is usually found covered over with a piece of matting. The doors are of the rudest description. Probably when originally made there was some pretence to "fitting," but there is none now. To keep out the draught bits of listing or pieces of wood have been nailed along the edges or over the cracks, but the result is rarely satisfactory. The fireplace also, and usually there is only one in the whole house, is of the most primitive character. A few iron bars are set in the brickwork, and as if further to prevent any economy in fuel, the bricks at the back crack and crumble away and rarely get replaced. The chimney corners are large and the chimneys wide, admitting sometimes of freer ingress for the external air than of egress for the air inside and the smoke from the fire.

Complaints are made of the draughtiness of even the best of these cottages. Often in winter the candle or lamp is said to be blown out, and yet it is impossible to tell where the draught came from. The ceilings are usually not underdrawn, and when the bedroom floor is in holes one can see into the room below. To prevent this, or to avoid the foot of the bed going through when moved, pieces of wood or of old iron are nailed over the apertures. I came across an old man who tripped over one of these holes (or a piece of wood which had been nailed over it, I forget which), and broke his leg, an accident which I only wonder is not more common.

Very few of these cottages have more than two bedrooms, many of them have only one, and usually, from their being placed in the roof, it is only possible to stand upright in the middle. The living rooms are low, many only from 6 ft. to 6 ft. 6 in. in height, yet the floor space is usually larger than the majority of the more modern cottages.

Apparently at the time when they were erected such conveniences as ovens, coppers, or sinks, were considered luxuries which the poor man could very well dispense with, but it is difficult to conceive how the tenants get along without them. Sometimes a bakehouse with brick oven has been provided for a group of cottages, but these are now little used, or used only as storerooms for wood, &c., if, indeed, they are not too dilapidated even for such a purpose. In many cases an attempt has been made to render these dwellings more habitable by putting down a wooden floor to the living rooms and substituting modern sash windows for the old leaded ones. Without an occasional coat of paint these window frames rapidly decay, and in many cases they are now nearly in as bad condition as the ones then displaced. The floor boards are usually laid upon or within a few inches of the damp earth beneath, without ventilation under, and they speedily rot. To have raised them some inches above the level of the ground outside would have caused the rooms to be too low for an average adult to stand upright in, and to have removed some inches of the sodden earth and have laid a bed of concrete before putting in the floor would have entailed too great an expenditure, hence the present condition of things.

When these cottages were erected there were no sanitary authorities to prevent their being built anyhow and anywhere, and consequently we often find them in the most unlikely and most unsanitary positions, in old gravel or marl pits, on ground which is constantly waterlogged, and far from any source of water supply except as can be obtained from polluted ponds and ditches.

Discussion

How to improve the labourer's home was as intractable a problem in the country as in town. *Punch* tilts (102) at the sentimental "The Homes of England" (1827) of Felicia Hemans (1793–1835), misquoting her in so doing but giving a more realistic view of the English countryside. *Punch's* solution lay in philanthropic effort, such as the Prince of Wales had undertaken on his Sandringham estate. The remaining extracts demonstrate the intractable difficulties of an almost unworkable law and the virtual impossibility of building adequate rural cottages as a paying investment. George Haw discusses the problems of the sanitary reformer (103), while the journalist W. W. Crotch (1874–1947), writing of the villages of Kiveton Park and Wales near Sheffield (104), shows the pitfalls which faced the would-be housing reformer on a rural district council. Although the Housing Act of 1890 made it easier for urban local authorities to build houses, in rural areas the cumbersome legal process was only partly modified by the Housing Act of 1900. It was small wonder that almost nothing was done. Rider Haggard (1856–1925), the famous novelist, carried out a thorough and detailed study (105) of the English countryside in 1901–2, concluding that rural slums could only be mitigated by Government assistance to local authorities and private enterprise.

102 Princely Cottages
Punch (23 May 1874), 213

"The PRINCE OF WALES began, immediately after his marriage, by building the Alexandra Cottages, a row of twelve dwellings, built of Carr stone found on the estate, faced by white stone, and each entered through a pretty porch, with gardens in front and rear. For these a rent of £4 per year is paid by the tenant. The cost of the erection of each was £195. The Louise Cottages, built on the West Newton portion of the estate, are only inferior to the Alexandra Cottages in outward appearance; but they are also inferior in rent, and even their outside is attractive enough. They cost less than the Alexandra Cottages, the money laid out for the erection of each being only £140. For these the tenants pay a yearly rental of £3 10s. each. On the whole, the Sandringham Cottages produce only about one and a half per cent. on the capital invested."—*The Hour, May 12.*

"The Cottage-homes of England,
　　How beautiful they stand!"
(So once FELICIA HEMANS sang,)
　　Throughout the lovely land!
By many a shining river-side
　　These happy homes are seen,
And clustering round the commons wide,
　　And 'neath the woodlands green.

The Cottage-homes of England—
　　Alas, how strong they smell!
There's fever in the cesspool,
　　And sewage in the well.
With ruddy cheeks and flaxen curls,
　　Though their tots shout and play,
The health of those gay boys and girls,
　　Too soon will pass away.

The Cottage-homes of England!
　　Where each crammed sleeping-place
Foul air distils whose poison kills
　　Health, modesty and grace.
Who stables horse, or houseth kine,
　　As these poor peasants lie,
More thickly in their straw than swine
　　Are herded in a stye?

The Cottage-homes of England!—
　　But may they not be made
What Poetess FELICIA
　　In graceful verse portrayed?
With chambers where a purer air
　　The sleepers' lungs may bless,
And pretty porches, gardens fair?—
　　The PRINCE OF WALES says, "Yes."

The Cottage-homes of England,
   Whose aspect makes men wince,
May turn to happy dwellings yet,
   With landlords like the Prince:
Then quicker brain and readier arm,
   And more strength better spent,
May add an economic charm
   To less than two per cent.

The Cottage-homes of England!
   The toiler gay and blithe,
Who drinks his ale, and plies his flail,
   And swings his sweeping scythe,
His sons and daughters, braced anew
   With strength that nothing ails,
Will bless each Prince of landlords who
   Does like the PRINCE OF WALES.

103 [George Haw] No Room to Live
(1900), 156–7

If cottagers endure in silence the insanitary conditions I have described, if they put up with overcrowding, it is not because they like it. And in the case of the inspectors and officers of health themselves, if they do not take vigorous action it is not because, as a general rule, they are apathetic or neglectful.

They are helpless in face of the dominant fact of the scarcity of cottages. A considerable percentage of rural cottage property would be condemned as unfit for human habitation to-morrow if there were any other accommodation for the present occupants. Over and over again I have heard sanitary officers say, "That or that block of cottages ought to come down; but what would happen to the people if it were condemned?" It is the old cry of no room elsewhere. The choice is between the existing rotten hovel and the roadside or the workhouse. And it is for this reason that the cottagers themselves will not complain, will even represent to unknown inquirers that the condition of their houses is better than the facts warrant. Suggest to one of them that you should acquaint the authorities with the facts, and you will be implored to say nothing about it. "You would only get us turned out," they say. Hence the sanitary reformer in a village is often regarded as an enemy of the people.

I know of no more heart-breaking work than that of a conscientious sanitary officer in a rural district. At every turn he sees work that cries out to be done, sees the health and morals of the population destroyed by causes with which the law gives him power to deal; and finds that power reduced to a cypher by the fact that if he acts upon it he will be inflicting upon the people the still greater evil of absolute homelessness. All he can do for them is to get them turned out into the road. No wonder that he stays his hand, or that the tenants themselves put up with anything rather than invite what is almost certain eviction. To tell them that the law enables them to do this or that is merely to mock them. The assumption underlying the law is that the persons empowered to take certain action are in a position in other respects of freedom to take it; and that assumption is false.

104 W. W. Crotch   The Cottage Homes of England
(2nd ed, 1901), 64–7

I visited nearly every cottage in Kiveton Park—or Wales—and I can fearlessly say that I never saw a higher standard of industry and cleanliness in my life. But what a cramped life it was!—tiny living rooms, a cupboard for a scullery, and bedrooms totally and absolutely inadequate for the demands of the families.

The village was grossly overcrowded, and I marvelled that the standard of life, of health, and of morality could be so high as it was under conditions so positively and threateningly adverse. However, no one felt the iniquity of the situation more

than these splendid colliers themselves, and in course of time
they sent to the District Council as their representative, one of
the finest specimens of a workman the world could show. A man
entirely worthy; fired with love for his class, animated with the
highest ideals, passionately proud of the little culture he
possessed, a fluent speaker, a finer listener, held in almost
idolatrous esteem by the people who had watched him develop
from boyhood; incapable of an ungenerous word, undeniably one
of Nature's noblemen. It was he who was sent to represent his
people on the district authority. My friend gave himself to a
careful, plodding study of the Housing Act, and in the end he
won over by his gentleness, his courtesy, his winning persuasive-
ness, a hostile authority.

Application was thus made on behalf of Wales to the County
Council, praying that a certificate empowering them to build
cottages under Part III. of the Act, might be granted, and suggesting—probably as a sop to the objectors—that the entire cost
of the buildings, instead of being distributed over the whole
district, might be limited to the parish itself. The inevitable
Local Inquiry was held, and here the fatal blow was given the
project. The evidence of the need was overwhelming, but some
question of the probability of inducing the landowners of the
parish—hitherto unwilling—arose, and ultimately the Inquiry
was adjourned for *six months*, to enable members of the Rural
District Council and the local owners to meet and discuss means
for providing the badly needed accommodation. I hope the
term will not escape the reader. Six months to discuss the
matter, whilst every day and night to these cottagers was little
short of a tragedy. If everything possible were done to expedite
the progress of things, if no obstruction arose, if all authorities
had been agreed, the money been available, a plea of urgency
put in, it would then have been two years before the builder
could make a beginning. The Act requires that amount of
time as a minimum sacrifice to its insatiable lust for delay. In
spite of this fact, the Commission of Inquiry coolly prescribed
six months to make inquiries! Who can say that this was any-

thing more than an excuse for indolence, or a mask for inaction, if not a disguise for incapacity? Needless to remark, Wales in Kiveton Park has not got its municipal cottages to-day! Additional accommodation was, I believe, supplied by private enterprise; but that, I venture to suggest, is totally inadequate.

105 H. Rider Haggard   Rural England
Vol. II (1902), 527, 545, 547–8

The question of the better housing of the agricultural labourer is one which is purely financial. At the rents currently paid in Norfolk and Suffolk cottages cannot be built, kept in repair, and in such a condition as to meet modern requirements, to pay anything but a trifling return on the capital embarked. Owners of landed property, as a rule, provide excellent cottages and gardens for their labourers at half rents, because such cottages are necessary to attract the best of the men, and because they desire to see their neighbours comfortable and contented. But no capitalist, unless he is a landowner, will build cottages to pay him a precarious 2 to 2½ per cent. Why should he when he can invest his money to so much greater advantage in any other business concern? Cottage rents would have to be doubled at least to make them an attractive investment, and labourers' rents cannot be doubled unless they receive a large increase to their wage, which can only follow a substantial rise in the value of produce. For the country to demand that it shall have supplies of home-grown produce at the lowest possible price, and at the same time to expect that the men who help to create it, and whose living has to depend upon that price, shall have cottage accommodation superior to that which is generally provided on every well-managed estate is unreasonable. Unless the State provides the money—and what Government would venture to raise money for such an unremunerative investment?—it cannot be done. Owing to the very marked decrease in the rural population generally, the poorer class of cottage is rapidly disappearing in East Anglia.

. . . . In many instances, his cottage accommodation is very bad; indeed I have found wretched and insufficient dwellings to be a great factor in the hastening of the rural exodus; and he forgets that in the town it will probably be worse. . . . How, then, can these men be helped? By direct Government aid? I think not. Such aid pauperises and is foreign to our character and traditions. Indirect aid, which enables the individual to help himself, is another matter. I propose that it should take this form. First, the extension of the provisions of the Housing of the Working Classes Act of 1890, to enable public Bodies and land-owners to borrow money from the Treasury, to whatever extent they may wish, for the erection of both cottages and farm buildings sufficient for the purpose of small-holdings, at a more reasonable rate of interest than is at present charged by the Loan Commissioners. Such interest to be repayable over a term of sixty instead of forty years, as at present, and to include a provision for a sinking fund which would automatically ex-tinguish the debt at the termination of that period. As it is, the great majority of landowners are absolutely unable to afford to put up cottages and outbuildings, even when they so desire, without which, small-holdings can seldom be multiplied.

But it is undoubtedly to the interest of the nation that these should be multiplied, and still more so that the cottage accom-modation of the working classes in rural districts should be improved. Surely it would not be beyond the resources of financial experts to formulate a scheme under which the necessary funds might be forthcoming without actual loss to the Treasury, or, at the worst, at a loss so small that it should not be allowed to weigh against the advantage gained.

PHILANTHROPY

The Aims of Philanthropy
It is sometimes held to be surprising or reprehensible that

the wealthy adopted patronising attitudes towards the poor in Victorian England, that they feared and opposed the possibility of violent revolution and that they hoped through philanthropy to secure the trust and loyalty of the poor. Such attitudes were reasonable enough at a time when social classes were so distinct and when enormous contrasts in life style separated rich from poor. Two volumes edited by Viscount Ingestre, the future 19th Earl of Shrewsbury (1830–77), tried to show how philanthropists could help to improve the conditions of the poor. Included in the first volume were these lines (106) by Martin Tupper (1810–89), a popular versifier who found a response to the kind of sentiments quoted here.

Octavia Hill (1838–1912) was a social reformer of a more serious kind who believed that character as well as homes must be reformed (107). Her means of doing this was for rent collectors of gentle birth to supervise and improve the lives of the very poor, and for a small but steady profit to be made, so as not to pauperise the poor and to encourage the system to spread. "Miss Hill's system" received much praise, partly because slum life seemed to give some support to her assumptions, partly because the system involved little public expense and no revolutionary legislation. There is much more to be said on Octavia Hill's behalf than space allows; philanthropy is now so unfashionable that her pioneering social work in very different circumstances from our own is too often totally dismissed. However, it is certainly true that her efforts had no discernible effect on London's housing problem. Although philanthropic motives were already suspect by late Victorian times, the pamphlet (108) by the Rev. H. J. Wilkins (b. 1866), a Bristol clergyman, shows that appeals to assist the worthy poor continued throughout the reign.

106 Martin Tupper   The Homes of the Poor

In Viscount Ingestre (ed). *Meliora*, First Series (1852), 286–7

The halls of the rich have been famous in song,
  Ever since flattery fawn'd upon wealth;
Feigning, to palaces only belong
  Honour and virtue, contentment and health:
But, the glad tidings from heaven to earth
  Tell of true wealth in Humility's store;
Jewels of purity, patience, and worth,
  Blest above gold, in the homes of the poor.

Yes, the well-favour'd in fortune and rank
  Wisely will covet such riches untold,
While the good Giver they heartily thank
  For the two talents of honour and gold;
Wisely such jewels of price will they seek,
  Cherishing good as the real Koh-i-noor,
And from the diligent, modest, and meek,
  Learn to be rich in the homes of the poor.

Yet are those homes overclouded with night;
  Poverty's sisters are Care and Disease;
And the hard wrestler in life's uphill fight
  Faints in the battle, and dies by degrees!
Then, let his neighbour stand forth in his strength,
  Like the Samaritan, swift to procure
Comfort and balm for his struggles at length,
  Pouring in peace on the homes of the poor.

Cleanliness, healthiness, water, and light,
  Rent within reason, and temperate rules,
Work and fair wages (Humanity's right),
  Libraries, hospitals, churches, and schools,—
Thus, let us help the good brother in need,
  Dropping a treasure at Industry's door,
Glad, by God's favour, to lighten indeed
  The burdens of life in the homes of the poor.

O! there is much to be done, and that soon;
   Classes are standing asunder, aloof;
Hasten, Benevolence, with the free boon.
   Falling as sunshine on Misery's roof!
Hasten, good stewards of a bountiful Lord,
   Greatly to imitate Him evermore,
Binding together, in blessed accord,
   The halls of the rich with the homes of the poor!

107 Octavia Hill Homes of the London Poor
(1875), 2, 7–8, 38–40, 60–1, 102–3

I ... most heartily hope that whatever is done in building
for the people may be done on a thoroughly sound commercial
principle. I do not think it would help them the least in the long
run to adopt any other principle; in fact, I believe it would be
highly injurious to them. ...

The people's homes are bad, partly because they are badly
built and arranged; they are tenfold worse because the tenants'
habits and lives are what they are. Transplant them to-morrow
to healthy and commodious homes, and they would pollute and
destroy them. There needs, and will need for some time, a
reformatory work which will demand that loving zeal of
individuals which cannot be had for money, and cannot be
legislated for by Parliament. The heart of the English nation
will supply it—individual, reverent, firm, and wise. It may and
should be organised, but cannot be created. ...

As soon as I entered into possession, each family had an
opportunity of doing better: those who would not pay, or who
led clearly immoral lives, were ejected. The rooms they vacated
were cleansed; the tenants who showed signs of improvement
moved into them, and thus, in turn, an opportunity was
obtained for having each room distempered and painted. The
drains were put in order, a large slate cistern was fixed, the
wash-house was cleared of its lumber, and thrown open on
stated days to each tenant in turn. The roof, the plaster, the

woodwork were repaired; the staircase-walls were distempered; new grates were fixed; the layers of paper and rag (black with age) were torn from the windows, and glass was put in; out of 192 panes, only 8 were unbroken. The yard and footpath were paved.

The rooms, as a rule, were re-let at the same prices at which they had been let before; but tenants with large families were counselled to take two rooms, and for these much less was charged than if let singly: this plan I continue to pursue. In-coming tenants are not allowed to take a decidedly insufficient quantity of room, and no sub-letting is permitted. The elder girls are employed three times a week in scrubbing the passages in the houses, for the cleaning of which the landlady is respon-sible. For this work they are paid, and by it they learn habits of cleanliness. It is, of course, within the authority of the landlady also to insist on cleanliness of wash-houses, yards, staircases, and staircase-windows; and even to remonstrate concerning the rooms themselves if they are habitually dirty.

The pecuniary result has been very satisfactory. Five per cent. interest has been paid on all the capital invested. . . .

You may say, perhaps, "This is very well as far as you and your small knot of tenants are concerned, but how does it help us to deal with the vast masses of poor in our great towns?" I reply, "Are not the great masses made up of many small knots? Are not the great towns divisible into small districts? Are there not people who would gladly come forward to undertake the systematic supervision of some house or houses, if they could get authority from the owner? And why should there not be some way of registering such supervision, so that, bit by bit, as more volunteers should come forward, the whole metropolis might be mapped out, all the blocks fitting in like little bits of mosaic to form one connected whole?"

. . . . If any society had come there and put those houses into a state of perfect repair at once, it would have been of little use, because its work would have been undone again by the bad habits and carelessness of the people. If improvements were made on a large scale, and the people remained untouched, all would soon return to its former condition. You cannot deal with the people and their houses separately. The principle on which the whole work rests is, that the inhabitants and their surroundings must be improved together. It has never yet failed to succeed.

108 H. J. Wilkins What Can I Do to Promote the Better Housing of the Poor in Bristol? An Appeal to the Citizens and Women of Bristol
(nd; 1893), 7–8 *Employers of Labour:*—

A word as to the duty of those of you, who are Employers of Labour. Why do you not take an interest in the housing of your work people? You surely ought to take as much interest in the Housing of your Employees as you do in the stabling of your horses.

Go and view at least the outside, if you cannot get permission to see the inside of the Avonside Tannery Cottages, St. Phillip's Marsh, erected by the Employer for his work people, and see if you also cannot do something. If only you merchants and employers would attend to the housing of your workers, what a difference it would make in their lives and their attitude towards you.

You, who are the wives of Employers, ought to do something. Urge your husbands to erect houses for his employees. Visit the poor people already occupying the houses owned by him, and see that they are comfortable, but do not pauperize them. If your husband will not erect cottages or make comfortable those he already possesses, tell him you will be obliged to sell that horse he has lately given you or some of that costly jewellery he has presented to you and have the work done; or that you cannot entertain or have certain dishes for dinner of which he is very fond till he has done his duty. If HE feels a little of the "discomforts" of life, it may help him.

You also, who are the wives of wealthy men who have simply

invested their money and so are only "*indirect employers*," have duties. You cannot "get rid of your responsibility by putting your conscience in commission". Insist upon the spending of £500 or £1,000 at least in buying 4 or 5 houses for your poorer brethren, even if you do not get more than 2½ per cent in return. Buy them in the poorest parts and make these houses "your district". Let them at a fair rent, which must always be paid and which an agent could collect and then visit the people once a fortnight as a rule but weekly in the winter, because of sickness and the need of a "woman's sympathy". Be firm, do not pauperize them and they will soon look forward to your visit with their cheering words and love without any expectation of "favours to come". How you could help to break down that gulf which threatens to grow wider and wider, and which separates you from your poorer brethren! Will you try?

Philanthropic Buildings: Principles and Designs

Although there were too few "model cottages" to solve the housing problem, large numbers of them were erected in many different parts of the country, especially in London. The earliest seem to have been built in 1844, and by the early 1880s over 50,000 people in London were living in "model dwellings" of various types. (David Owen. *English Philanthropy, 1660–1960*, 1964, 385.) Most of the philanthropic or semi-philanthropic societies attempted to make a small profit, so as to encourage the work to expand, but this was difficult to achieve. *The Builder*, edited between 1844 and 1883 by the socially conscious George Godwin (1813–88), author of several works on social conditions, gave much publicity to this type of building. Its article (109) about Glasgow homes designed by James Wylson (1811–70) for James Lumsden (1808–79), a Glasgow stationer and local figure, brings out the essential points of such dwellings. They tended to be built in blocks of flats; the fittings were virtually indestructible and irremovable; and the tenants belonged to the respectable working class, not the very poor. The latter could neither afford the rent nor, it was alleged and feared, adequately care for the property. Weekly rents of the early flats varied from 2s to 8s or so. These were not high figures, but they were too high for the very poor, whose numbers and poverty necessitated their crowding into the minimum amount of space. Only Octavia Hill's system was designed for the very poor. (It is worth noting that the Wylson flats, while small and spartan, provided water closets, a common feature of even the earliest philanthropic homes.)

Henry Roberts (1802–76), architect to one of the London philanthropic housing societies, wrote several works in support of their aims (110); his work and his writing were highly influential in this field. Roberts was also the architect of the cottages sponsored by Prince Albert (1819–61) and displayed in conjunction with the Great Exhibition. Subsequently they were moved to Kennington Park, where they may still be seen. Prince Albert was an enthusiastic housing reformer who declared in a speech of 1848: "Depend upon it, the interests of classes too often contrasted are identical" (*The Principal Speeches and Addresses of his Royal Highness the Prince Consort*, 1862, 88). John Birch had designed cottages for the poor in both town and country; those described here (111) were built in Essex for Samuel Courtauld & Co. They enjoyed water closets and a form of central heating, but their cost suggests that they could not be widely copied. Birch summed up many of the hopes placed in these schemes: "The workman . . . would become attached to his home and employers." Equally revealing was his anxiety to prevent the labourer from becoming "independent of his proper calling".

109 Lumsden's Model Workmen's Dwellings
The Builder (28 October 1848), 523–4

Enough details have been published respecting the generally-comfortless condition of the homes of the working classes, to render the subject a familiar one to those to whom it is most personally interesting, namely, landlords and tenants. Where there is not perfect privacy in a dwelling, proper self-respect, if it have existed, must give way; and if it have not existed, can never spring up: where the decencies of life cannot be observed, morality cannot but break down: where the structural arrangements are not calculated to promote and preserve cleanliness and order, any attempts at these will prove futile, the love and pride of home will ere long be discouraged, and recklessness and degradation in due course ensue. It becomes thus obvious, that to the well-disposed portion of the labouring community, a better order of dwellings, in which they could enjoy the maximum of comfort of which their sphere is capable, and where they could rear their families without fear of contamination, moral or physical, must be an inestimable boon, and be hailed with feelings of pleasure and hope; and that to landlords, well disposed towards improving the social condition of the humbler classes, the exercise of the best philanthropy is peculiarly theirs; and that if it be granted that these classes are susceptible of moral amelioration, there is every reasonable prospect of their efforts meeting with an encouraging return. It has been stated that mechanics' institutions are not used by those for whom they were specially intended: if it be considered how incompatible a disorderly house is with the beneficial prosecution of studies, it will be plain enough where the drawback lies, and where the primary step should have been taken. Give the working-man a sanctum in his own dwelling, and, so far from the tavern possessing superior charms in his eyes, it will sink in his estimation: he will become too proud to be seen there, and find, instinctively, something in his home which yields him a meed of honour more heart-satisfying than his pot-participators can afford. . . .

. . . . The building above referred to as being now under course of erection, is situated to the north of the Normal School, New City-road: it consists of four storeys, and contains in all thirty-one dwellings. The houses on each floor are ranged along a wide central passage, which communicates with the common staircase, and is lighted by a window at each end. The houses are arranged with the view to giving to their one main apartment the utmost value, by obviating as much as possible the necessity for performing any cleansing operations within it, and forming the bed-closets opening out of the same, so that there is no occasion for the occupants creating disorder by strewing their clothes about the room: for this purpose these closets, of which there are two in each house, as wide apart as possible, are made large enough to afford space for undressing and dressing in: each is closed with a door; but at the same time, in order that they may be ventilated, the side which is next the main apartment stands only about 7 feet high, so that the air of the house circulates freely through them. The bed bottoms are fixtures, and of rod-iron filled in with hooping, to prevent the propagation of insects, as well as the loss which is so great a grievance to the proprietors of small houses, from the use of the sparred bed-bottoms for firewood. Each dwelling has also a scullery opening out of the main apartment, and containing a dresser, sink, coal-box, and press; and likewise a small well-aired larder in the outside wall; a kitchen grate, with oven and boiler; an ash-box with cinder-sieve in the hearth, which is of cast-iron, and includes a fender,—the latter being cast with it; and, opening from the small entrance lobby, is a water-closet, with apparatus of simple and economic construction, with, in one corner of it, a trap covering a shoot into a dust-shaft, through which all dry rubbish is conveyed to a cellar in the basement. Water is to be laid on in the scullery; and a jet of gas, for certain hours, in the main apartment, as well as in the central or common passages and staircases. . . .

. . . . It is expected that these houses will be occupied by a superior grade of working people, as regards conduct, in whom employers may have such confidence as to become surety for their rents, and thus obviate the trouble of weekly payments, and the increase of rent unavoidably accompanying that mode of collection. The rent which is looked for as sufficient to meet the views of the well-intentioned and energetic founder of this establishment, is 6*l*. per annum—a small sum as compared with the advantages which it offers to the labouring man.

110 Henry Roberts   The Dwellings of the Labouring Classes
(1850), 16–17

The Metropolitan Association[1] [for Improving the Dwellings of the Industrious Classes] . . . is established on the sound, and, indeed, only principle upon which it can be reasonably expected that an extensive improvement in the dwellings of the labouring classes in towns should be effected—viz., that of an investment of capital, with the prospect that, under good management, a fair return of interest on the outlay will be obtained. More can scarcely be expected from a benevolent public than funds sufficient, with careful economy, to effect the important object contemplated by the Society for Improving the Condition of the Labouring Classes—viz., the erection and completion of one model of each description of building required to meet the varied circumstances of the labouring classes, and at the same time the demonstration that such buildings may, with proper management, be made to yield a fair return on the outlay. . . .

. . . In reference to new buildings for the labouring classes, the most rigid economy of arrangement, consistent with accommodation sufficiently spacious to be convenient and healthy, and the utmost attention to cheapness of construction,

[1] The claims of this Association on public support were most powerfully advocated in the eloquent address of the Earl of Carlisle at the opening of the lodging-house in Spicer-street. "Let it be proved," said his Lordship, "that the act of doing good, in however unpretending and common-place a manner, to large masses of the struggling and impoverished, would pay its own way, and ensure its fair profit, and it would follow that benevolence, instead of being only an ethereal influence in the breasts of a few, fitful and confined in its operations, would become a settled, sober habit of the many; widening as it went, occasioning its own rebound, and adding all the calculations of prudence to all the impulses of generosity."

consistent with durability[2] and comfort, are essential elements of a really good and suitable plan. The Architect should bear in mind that the rents which the working classes usually pay, though exorbitantly high for the wretched accommodation afforded them, will only just yield a fair return for the outlay on buildings constructed for their express use, and fitted up with all the conveniences which it is desirable they should possess. Any expenditure on unnecessary accommodation, which involves an increase of rent beyond that usually paid by the occupants of such a class of dwellings, appears to be at least hazardous, and may jeopardize the whole, or a portion of the interest to be fairly expected from the investment.

111 John Birch Country Architecture
(1874), 9, 30–1

I do not think it advisable to build more than four Cottages in one block, as the occupants are sure to disagree when a number are located together. The Cottages should be built in pairs or in blocks of three or four according to the size of the farm or estate, and placed on different sites within easy distance of the farm buildings or bailiff's house.

From an eighth to a quarter of an acre of land is usually given to an ordinary Labourer's Cottage, except, of course, where they are allowed to keep a cow. I do not think it well to add a cow-shed to a labourer's cottage, and give to it three or four acres of land, as it renders the labourer independent of his proper calling, and causes labour to be scarce. Of course there are exceptional cases where a few acres added to the houses in the village would materially improve the rental without being detrimental to obtaining labour, but discrimination should be used in selecting the tenants. . . .

Large employers of labour would be consulting their interest

[2] The interior fittings of such buildings should be as indestructible as possible; iron pipes should be used instead of lead, and the ironmongery generally ought to be of special strength and simplicity.

were they to erect as near as possible to their works or factories a sufficient number of healthy and convenient dwellings for their work-people, where cleanliness, health, and morality could be observed, such houses would inspire habits of self-respect, frugality, and independence; the workman would be enabled to bring up his family in a respectable manner, and would become attached to his home and employers.

Proper dwellings for the working classes is of the utmost importance to the welfare and prosperity of all large towns, since statistics prove it to be a fact that much of the vice, misery, and disease, is chiefly attributable to the over-crowded and wretched state of the places where these poor people exist. The report which lately appeared on the sanitary condition of the county of Northamptonshire shews that this county, like many others, contains a number of houses totally unfitted for habitation, in some cases the cubical space to each inmate being little more than 100 feet, having as many as six occupants living in dwellings containing only one living room and bed-room. . . .

Outbuildings comprising a scullery, coal-house, and W.C. . . . are built in the rear of the Cottages. Each living room contains a cubical space of about 1550 feet; each parlour about 1260 feet, and each of the three bedrooms an average of about 1250 feet. The dwellings have been erected with red bricks, having white brick dressings to doors, windows, angles, &c., the roofs are covered with ornamental tiles. The external walls have been constructed hollow. Provision has also been made for warming and ventilation, the cold air is conducted from the outside of the building by means of a flue to the back of the living room and parlour fireplaces, it is there warmed by contact with the fire-lump back of the stoves, and thence passes through flues to the bedrooms above. In each room, valves communicate with these flues, admitting the warmed air at pleasure; by this means some heat is utilized which would otherwise be wasted, and a constant circulation of air maintained.

The cost of these five pairs of cottages, including outbuildings, drainage, water supply, fences and paths, completed ready for occupation, amounted to £2,723.

Success or Failure?

How successful model dwellings were was bitterly disputed. Against the buildings were held their ugly appearance (resulting in such nicknames as "barracks", "warehouses", "human ant-heaps" and "packing-cases for humanity"), their allegedly high incidence of disease and mortality (for refutation of which in the case of the Peabody dwellings see Dr Arthur Newsholme in the *Journal of the Royal Statistical Society*, March 1891, 70–111) and their location in over-crowded districts whose inhabitants were evicted to make room for them. The very poor could not afford to pay the rent (or the higher rents caused by increased demand for accommodation in areas where model dwellings were erected), and they lacked the self-control needed for 'life in buildings'. It was very difficult for the philanthropic bodies to eject workers whose stable homes contributed to their earning higher wages. A London School Board inspector and writer, T. Marchant Williams (1845–1924), soberly observed the result in the Peabody dwellings, the most commonly discussed and criticised of the philanthropic bodies: "The Peabody trustees inform us that they have 201 policemen as tenants; these men are probably employed in keeping order in the overcrowded courts in which are huddled in filth and misery the people who have been driven out of their homes to make room for them" (*The Times*, 1 March 1884, 6).

In Documents 112 and 113 two American writers wax lyrical over model dwellings: Harriet Beecher Stowe (1811–96) escorted by Lord Shaftesbury, and Phebe Hanaford (1829–1921) quoting an account in the *Boston* (Massachusetts) *Journal*. The Streatham Street flats to which Mrs Stowe refers were designed by Henry Roberts (see Document 110) in 1849–50 and may still be seen near the Trades Union

Congress building in Great Russell Street, London. As she implies, the flats provided an unusually high standard of amenity and comfort. In the third document (114), George Arkell traces improvements in block dwellings, though he, like Octavia Hill, found much to criticise.

112 Harriet Beecher Stowe Sunny Memories of Foreign Lands
(1854), 182–4

We drove to the Streatham Street Lodging House for families. This building is, in the first place, fireproof; in the second, the separation in the parts belonging to different families is rendered complete and perfect by the use of hollow brick for the partitions, which entirely prevents, as I am told, the transmission of sound.

By means of the sleeping closet adjoining the living room, each dwelling affords three good sleeping apartments. The meat safe preserves provisions. The dust flue is so arranged that all the sweepings of the house, and all the refuse of the cookery, have only to be thrown down to disappear for ever; while the sink is supplied to an unlimited extent with hot and cold water. These galleries, into which every tenement opens, run round the inside of the hollow court which the building encloses, and afford an admirable play-place for the little children, out of the dangers and temptations of the street, and in view of their respective mothers.

"Now," said Lord Shaftesbury, as he was shewing me through these tenements, which were models of neatness and good keeping, "you must bear in mind that these are tenanted by the very people who once were living in the dirtiest and filthiest lodging-houses; people whom the world said it did no good to try to help; that they liked to be dirty better than clean, and would be dirty under any circumstances."

He added the following anecdote to shew the effect of poor lodgings in degrading the character. A fine young man, of

some considerable taste and talent, obtained his living by
designing patterns for wall paper. A long and expensive illness
so reduced his circumstances, that he was obliged to remove to
one of those low filthy lodging-houses already alluded to. From
that time he became an altered man; his wife said that he lost
all energy, all taste in designing, love of reading, and fondness
for his family; began to frequent drinking shops, and was
visibly on the road to ruin. Hearing of these lodging-houses, he
succeeded in renting a tenement in one of them, for the same
sum which he had paid for the miserable dwelling. Under the
influence of a neat, airy, pleasant domestic home, the man's
better nature again awoke, his health improved, he ceased to
crave ardent spirits, and his former ingenuity in his profession
returned.

"Now, this shews," said Lord Shaftesbury, "that hundreds
may have been ruined simply by living in miserable dwellings."
I looked into this young man's tenement; it was not only neat,
but ornamented with a great variety of engravings tastefully
disposed upon the wall. On my expressing my pleasure in this
circumstance, he added, "It is one of the pleasantest features
of the case to notice how soon they begin to ornament their
little dwellings; some have cages with singing birds, and some
pots of flowering plants; some, pictures and engravings."

"And are these buildings successful in a pecuniary point of
view?" I said. "Do they pay their own way?"

"Yes," he replied, "they do. I consider that these buildings, if
they have done nothing more, have established two points:
first, that the poor do not prefer dirt and disorder, where it is
possible for them to secure neatness and order; and second, that
buildings with very poor accommodation can be afforded at a
price which will support an establishment" . . .

When we returned to our carriage after this survey, I
remarked to Lord Shaftesbury that the combined influence of
these causes must have wrought a considerable change in the
city. He answered, with energy, "You can have no idea. Whole
streets and districts have been revolutionized by it. The people

who were formerly savage and ferocious, because they supposed themselves despised and abandoned, are now perfectly quiet and docile. I can assure you that Lady Shaftesbury has walked alone, with no attendant but a little child, through streets in London where, years ago, a well-dressed man could not have passed safely without an escort of the police."

I said to him that I saw nothing now, with all the improvements they were making throughout the kingdom, to prevent their working classes from becoming quite as prosperous as ours, except the want of a temperance reformation.

He assented with earnestness. He believed, he said, that the amount spent in liquors of various kinds, which do no good, but much injury, was enough to furnish every labourer's dwelling, not only with comforts, but with elegancies. "But then," he said, "one thing is to be considered: a reform of the dwellings will do a great deal towards promoting a temperance reformation. A man who lives in a close, unwholesome dwelling, deprived of the natural stimulus of fresh air and pure water, comes into a morbid and unhealthy state; he craves stimulants to support the sinking of his vital powers, caused by these unhealthy influences."

113 Phebe Hanaford   The Life of George Peabody
(1870; reprinted 1882), 137–9

At last, cabby showed me up a narrow and dark alley, which finally opened on a square, around which were ranged four fine five-story stone blocks, each exactly like the other. Here were no quarrelling or fighting children, no drunken women, no discouraged-looking men. There were flowers in the windows, and bright, happy faces looked out from among them; but the blocks had a prison-like appearance, nevertheless. There was not a blade of grass, or a twig, to be seen in the stone-paved yard; and the fog settled down into the area worse than outside. The outer doors were open; and I soon made the acquaintance of a brawny Englishwoman in the porter's lodge of one of the blocks. How many families were there in each building?

"Forty-two; and p'raps six in a family, sir."

So I began to question her on the internal arrangements of this London Sybaris; because you often hear it said that Mr. Peabody's money has been misused, and that the workmen pay too highly for their tenements.

"Me'n my husban' has been porter (*sic*) here for more'n two year; an' my man was here from the beginnin', sir. We likes it ever so much. We pays four shillin' a week for these two rooms; and most o' them generally pays the same. 'Tisn't dear, —oh, no! but it's about all most o' them can pay. Still"—

We looked into some of the rooms. It depended on the taste, more than the resources, of the individual tenant, how comfortable he made himself. There were neatly tiled floors, whitewashed walls. The rooms were small, but planned as economically, as to space, as a travelling-jacket. I noticed, especially, that each room was well lighted and ventilated. Some families had three rooms, so planned as to avoid any of the lamentable lack of decency which large families crowded into small tenements sometimes exhibit in London and New York and Boston. Each floor is divided into lettered sections, which are traversed by spacious corridors. Each tenement, or suite of rooms, has one door, numbered, opening on these corridors. There are iron traps in the halls in each story, into which the dirt and rubbish from each tenement is swept; so that there is no chance for an accumulation of filth. In the upper story of each building is a co-operative laundry, which the women also consider as their exchange, and where they get acquainted over their work.

"Most all on us knows every other one on us here," said the portress. Pity Mr. Peabody didn't specify that all the tenants under his fund should be taught grammar! There was gas in many of the rooms; but that was paid for as an extra. "Are these workmen, living here, of what you would call the better class?" I asked.

"I rather think not, sir," was the answer. "Most o' them does common sort o' work; 'n sometimes they hasn't any in the dull season: but they manages to stick by the square, in any case. Me'n my man does all the hirin' rooms; and we never has any disputes. All pays, allers."

Which rather proves that the workmen find it cheap and advantageous to live there; because collecting rents elsewhere, in the dens which are made to serve the poor as houses, is sometimes even dangerous. But you have only to put a man in a den to make him a beast.

So, in this square, here are one hundred and sixty-eight families, averaging six members each, renting comfortable rooms, in a clean, airy, and respectable quarter of the city, for about five dollars per month, per tenement. Their condition is much improved by the arrangements made for them; and any drunkenness or fighting in the building is never known. I saw, in many of the rooms, the men at home, evidently enjoying the society of their families, instead of swilling beer at the public-house. I should give my testimony in favour of the success of Mr. Peabody's money as a most practical beneficence.

114 George Arkell   Model Dwellings—(1) Statistics

In Charles Booth (ed). *Labour and Life of the People, Vol II, London Continued* (1891), 257–8

That improvements in construction and fitting should be made in these dwellings was to be expected, and the experience of the older Companies has been utilized by modern builders. These improvements may be grouped under three heads; viz. (1) better appearance; (2) better light; and (3) more and better internal fittings. . . .

(1) In appearance the best modern buildings are a great advance on the older dwellings. A plain exterior was formerly deemed quite good enough for "models," but many of the modern blocks possess a high degree of architectural merit. This is well seen by comparing Thanksgivings Buildings, near Gray's

Inn Road, with some of the Improved Industrial Dwellings Company's Blocks, near Oxford Street, or with Marlborough Buildings, South Kensington, or even with such blocks as Waldeck Buildings, or Holsworthy Square.

(2) As regards light, the difference is most marked in the construction of the staircases. In the best of the older buildings (and it is useless to compare any but the best of the different epochs), while the rooms are well lighted, the staircases and passages are frequently dark. They appear to have been neglected for the sake of the tenements. This defect attaches in a minor degree to some of the earlier Peabody dwellings, in which the staircases have no direct light. In what is known as the "new" style this fault is corrected, and the stairs are lighted by a window. In other buildings light is obtained either by a large window, or what is becoming more general, the staircases are open to the air, protected by an iron railing. In many cases they are lined with white glazed bricks, which make them light even on dull days.

(3) It is in the internal fittings (and with these are included washhouses, baths, &c.), that the greatest advances have been made. In the older dwellings there is usually a deficiency of cupboard room; the rooms are seldom papered, and the tenements appear cheerless and bare. In the best of the modern buildings, however, there are plenty of cupboards; the walls are papered and the woodwork grained; windows are fitted with venetian blinds; dressers and other conveniences are provided, and it is the exception to find a room without a fireplace, a frequent occurrence in the three-roomed tenements of the older buildings.

MODEL VILLAGES AND GARDEN CITIES

Employers' Villages

Out of philanthropic housing schemes developed larger projects, entire villages built by employers with the twin aims of controlling their employees and improving their dwellings. Léon Faucher (1803–54), the French economist and politician, visited two early ventures near Manchester—the Ashton community at Hyde, and the Turton and Egerton cottages of the Ashworths (115). Disraeli's fictional description of a model village in *Sybil* (116) probably influenced Titus Salt (1803–76), a leading Bradford woollen manufacturer, who in the early 1850s built Saltaire, the first independent community on a new site. As time passed, many other ventures took place: two of the largest were the Lever enterprise at Port Sunlight (begun 1888), near Birkenhead, and the Cadbury village at Bournville near Birmingham, conceived in 1879 but not begun until 1895. Bournville was novel in that not all the residents were employees of Cadbury's. As Document 117 suggests, the standard of cottages belonging to these villages was usually well in advance of the usual working-class dwellings, notably in the case of water supply and sanitation.

115 Léon Faucher   Manchester in 1844
(1844), 106–7, 112–13

The houses inhabited by the work-people, form long and large streets. Mr. Ashton has built three hundred of them, which he lets at three shillings, or three shillings and sixpence per week. Each house contains upon the ground floor, a sitting-room, a kitchen, and a backyard, and above, are two or three bed-rooms. The proprietor furnishes, at his own charge, water to the houses, keeps them in good repair, and pays the local rates. As the value of a ton of coal is only eight or nine shillings, fuel is almost gratuitous. At all hours of the day there is warm water and a fire in each house. Every where is to be observed a cleanliness which bespeaks order and comfort. The furniture is simple, but sufficient; in some houses a clock is to be seen; in others a sofa; and, in others again, a piano-forte. Books are plentiful, but I have seen few Bibles; and this seems to confirm that character for indifference in religious matters, for which the work-people of Mr. Ashton are celebrated.

. . . The manufactory at Turton lies in the bosom of a valley, between two wooded hills, the summits of which are crowned on the one side by the house of Mr. Henry Ashworth, and on the other side by the cottages of the work-people. The manufactory of Egerton, which is remarkable for an immense hydraulic wheel, sixty feet in diameter, (a dimension I have never seen equalled, except at Wesserling,) occupies the centre of a more open valley; and the houses of the work-people, as if to welcome the approaching visitor, are ranged on both sides of the road. But, for my part, I prefer the cottages at Turton, because of the little gardens attached to each house, where the inmates can cultivate shrubs and flowers. In other respects, both villages are constructed upon the same plan. Nothing can be more commodious than these cottages, in which the interior appearance invites to order and cleanliness. A cast iron oven, which serves to bake bread as well as other provisions, is attached to the fireplace of every kitchen; the pantry is spacious enough to contain all sorts of provisions, and the upper story often contains four bed-rooms. But the benevolent intention of the proprietor has, in this instance, been too much in advance of the habits of his work-people. They have not the sentiment of modesty sufficiently developed to separate their children of both sexes, during the night. There are never more than two chambers occupied, and it is even a mark of attention to decency if they draw a curtain, or put a partition between themselves and their children. . . .

It is delightful to see the order which prevails in these households, furnished as they are with their chests of drawers, filled with linen and clothes, the polished furniture, and clean earthenware, with abundance of books—religious and historical —such as the *Bible, Memoirs of St. Helena,* weekly periodicals, and especially the *Anti-Corn-Law Circular.* The rent of each house is not more than £10 per annum; it costs £120 to build, and thus yields seven or eight per cent per annum. The workpeople all seek after these houses, for there are no others in the neighbourhood at all to be compared with them. Messrs. Ashworth have bought an extensive plot of ground, and have thus gained the power to exclude public houses from their villages. They attach much importance to the morality of the work-people, and do not receive into their employ any notorious characters. Many of the families have been settled for eighteen years near their establishments, and Mr. Henry Ashworth affirms that he has observed, from year to year, an improvement in their manners and habits.

116 Benjamin Disraeli   Sybil
(1845), Book III, Chapter 8

When the workpeople of Mr. Trafford left his factory they were not forgotten. Deeply had he pondered on the influence of the employer on the health and content of his workpeople. He knew well that the domestic virtues are dependent on the existence of a home, and one of his first efforts had been to build a village where every family might be well lodged. Though he was the principal proprietor, and proud of that character, he nevertheless encouraged his workmen to purchase the fee: there were some who had saved sufficient money to effect this; proud of their house and their little garden, and of the horticulutural society, where its produce permitted them to be annual competitors. In every street there was a well: behind the factory were the public baths; the schools were under the direction of the perpetual curate of the church, which Mr. Trafford, though a Roman Catholic, had raised and endowed. In the midst of this village, surrounded by beautiful gardens, which gave an impulse to the horticulture of the community, was the house of Trafford himself, who comprehended his position too well to withdraw himself with vulgar exclusiveness from his real dependants, but recognised the baronial principle, reviving in a new form, and adapted to the softer manners and more ingenious circumstances of the times.

And what was the influence of such an employer and such a system of employment on the morals and manners of the employed? Great; infinitely beneficial. The connexion of a labourer with his place of work, whether agricultural or manufacturing, is itself a vast advantage. Proximity to the employer brings cleanliness and order, because it brings observation and encouragement. In the settlement of Trafford crime was positively unknown, and offences were very slight. There was not a single person in the village of a reprobate character. The men were well clad; the women had a blooming cheek; drunkenness was unknown; while the moral condition of the softer sex was proportionately elevated.

117 T. R. Marr   Housing Conditions in Manchester and Salford
(1904), 78–9

It may be well to take perhaps the best known among recent English schemes, that of Messrs. Lever Brothers, Limited, at Port Sunlight. This firm has housed a large number of its workpeople in a village close to their works. The enterprise is frankly unremunerative. The income from rents only covers the cost of maintenance and repairs and does not yield a dividend on the capital invested. The head of the firm describes the scheme as "prosperity sharing"—the best means he can find of sharing profits with his workpeople—and he has recently stated that the firm gets a return in the better health and consequent increased efficiency of the workers. The value of the scheme to those who are interested in the general question of housing lies in the fact that at Port Sunlight the housing conditions are almost ideal. The houses are well built and well planned. A large well-lighted living room with a smaller back kitchen or scullery is provided on the ground floor and there are three bedrooms upstairs. A bath-room has been provided in nearly every house. In every case there is a small garden-patch in front of the house, and at the back there is a good yard with the necessary offices. In different parts of the village there are allotments which are let at nominal rents. Besides the allotments there are numerous open spaces, the roads are wide and well planted with trees, and recreation grounds are provided where tennis, bowls, cricket and football may be played. In this way the surroundings of the houses are made pleasant, and the cheerfulness of the village is increased by the care which has been taken to secure variety of form and colour in the exteriors of the houses.

The experiment of Messrs. Lever Brothers is of great value, first, to those who sympathise with the aims of the Garden City Association in its proposal to take industries into the country and to establish new towns there on model lines; and, secondly, to all who are concerned with the housing of the people, since the village sets an ideal which is not altogether out of reach. . . .

The name of Bourneville will almost certainly occur to most readers at this stage. Bourneville differs from Port Sunlight in that residents are not necessarily in the employment of those who provided the houses. Mr. Cadbury, who began the scheme, has now handed it over to a Trust, which lets the houses to suitable people, and proposes to utilise the profits, as they accrue, in the first place, to build more houses of a similar kind at Bourneville, and, ultimately, to buy land and to establish similar estates in other parts of the country.

As at Port Sunlight, the internal arrangements at Bourneville and their surroundings are almost ideal. Mr. George Cadbury, the founder of the Trust, has a strong belief in the value of gardening as a civilising influence, and he has arranged that each house on the estate shall have one-sixth of an acre of land. This land is carefully laid out and part of the garden is planted with fruit trees. Mr. Cadbury says that he has found town dwellers who moved to Bourneville took to gardening as a duck takes to water. A feature of the Bourneville Trust of interest to town dwellers is that it aims at purchasing land outside the towns where it is comparatively cheap and at restricting the density of population on area to a reasonable number, about 30 per acre.

Garden Cities

A crucial difference between the employer's village and the Garden City was that the latter did not belong to one man or firm, so that there was no attempt to control the private lives of those residents who were employees, as existed implicitly in even the most benevolent employer's village. Nor were houses in effect tied cottages which one could lose with one's job. James Silk Buckingham (1786–1855) was an Owenite social reformer who was far ahead of his time, though the rigidity of his plans (118) shows him in a more typical Victorian light. Like many other housing reformers, he was an advocate of temperance. His "Victoria" had water closets, iron buildings and a large central electric light. Sir Benjamin Richardson (1828–96) was a medical man, sanitary reformer and prolific writer, whose plan for a "city of health" (119) included many sanitary and other improvements, including bathrooms and hot and cold water in all bedrooms. General Booth (1829–1912) of the Salvation Army put forward his scheme in 1890 (120). By this decade Garden Cities were coming to be widely advocated. The most detailed and practicable scheme was put forward by Ebenezer Howard (1850–1928) in *To-morrow: A Peaceful Path to Real Reform*. In 1902 his book was reprinted as *Garden Cities of To-morrow*, and the next year the first Garden City, Letchworth, was founded.

118 James Silk Buckingham   National Evils and Practical Remedies
(nd; 1849), 142–7, 191, 195

1. The Company to be entitled "THE MODEL-TOWN

v.h.—I*

ASSOCIATION," to be incorporated by Royal Charter, or Act of Parliament, so as to limit the responsibility of each individual to the Shares held by him in its stock.

2. Its object to be, the building an entirely new Town, to be called "VICTORIA," as recording the name of the virtuous and benevolent Sovereign in whose reign its foundation is hoped to be laid, and at the same time as giving birth to the achievement of a great moral "victory" over many of the evils that now afflict society, in its present disorganized state.

3. The Town to contain every improvement, in its position, plan, drainage, ventilation, architecture, supply of water, light, and every other elegance and convenience which the improved state of art and science will admit of being conferred on it, within the means of the available capital to be raised for that purpose. Its size to be about a mile square, and the number of its inhabitants not to exceed 10,000.

4. An extent of territory or farm-land around the Town, of about 10,000 acres, to be purchased or rented on the longest attainable lease, for the purpose of introducing every description of agriculture, pasture, and horticulture, for which its soil may be adapted, to be worked under the most improved methods at present known. . . .

8. The introduction into the Town, or any part of its Estate, of any intoxicating liquids, or substances, such as spirits, wine, beer, liquors, opium, or any other materials by which intoxication can be produced, to be strictly prohibited—on pain of seizure and destruction wherever found, and the expulsion from the Association of the parties proved guilty of introducing them, with the forfeiture of all their rights;—the experience of a thousand years, and many millions of witnesses, having proved that these are among the most prolific sources of crime, disease, and misery, the bane of all existing communities, in Britain at least, and the benefit of none. . . .

16. Individuals and families to pay to the Company a rental, to be regulated by a moderate interest on the actual cost of the premises occupied by them, as the Association will

provide the buildings: but the furnishing of the apartments or houses thus occupied to be at the expense and according to the taste of each occupant.

17. Every dwelling, even the smallest, to be furnished with a water-closet, and with a full supply of water, air, and light, as conducive, not merely to health, but to morality.

18. Public baths, in sufficient number and variety of cost to suit the different classes of society, to be placed at convenient distances in each quarter of the Town.

19. Each single workman to occupy at least one entire and separate room for himself, to be used exclusively by him as his sleeping apartment. Each married couple, without children, to occupy two rooms: and each family, in which there are children, to occupy at least three rooms for domestic purposes.

20. To prevent the loss and waste, as well as the discomfort, which arises from each individual or family cooking their own food, or washing their own linen, large establishments to be provided for each of these, in which everything may be done much better, by the benefit of skill, and much cheaper, by the benefit of union, than could be accomplished at home. These to include several refectories or restaurants, at which persons may join the table d'hôte, at given hours, for breakfast, dinner, or tea, at a comparatively trifling expence, and dine better than they could alone:—though, in case of sickness, or peculiar tastes preferring such isolation, meals, at a somewhat increased rate of cost, may be supplied at their own homes; and families not caring for the increased expence, might, if they preferred, live entirely within themselves. . . .

In the centre of the whole is an Octagonal Tower, of 100 feet diameter at the base, to be crowned with a spire of 300 feet elevation, and to contain an Electric Light for lighting the whole Town; a large illuminated clock; the bells for public worship, and other occasions; with apartments in each stage, and galleries leading from them around the Tower for the enjoyment of the air and view. . . .

It should be observed, that, as all the buildings would be

constructed of iron, both their fronts and sides would be equally handsome, and not present the discrepancy and deformity of modern towns generally, in which stone or stuccoed fronts are contrasted with the brick backs of the houses, and the roughness and meanness of the one made the more visible by comparison with the other.

119 Benjamin Richardson   Hygeia—A City of Health
(1876), 18–22

Our city, which may be named *Hygeia,* has the advantage of being a new foundation, but it is so built that existing cities might be largely modelled upon it.

The population of the city may be placed at 100,000, living in 20,000 houses, built on 4,000 acres of land,—an average of 25 persons to an acre. This may be considered a large population for the space occupied, but, since the effect of density on vitality tells only determinately when it reaches a certain extreme degree, as in Liverpool and Glasgow, the estimate may be ventured.

The safety of the population of the city is provided for against density by the character of the houses, which ensures an equal distribution of the population. Tall houses overshadowing the streets, and creating necessity for one entrance to several tenements, are nowhere permitted. In streets devoted to business, where the tradespeople require a place of mart or shop, the houses are four stories high, and in some of the western streets where the houses are separate, three and four storied buildings are erected; but on the whole it is found bad to exceed this range, and as each story is limited to 15 feet, no house is higher than 60 feet.

The substratum of the city is of two kinds. At its northern and highest part, there is clay; at its southern and southeastern, gravel. Whatever disadvantages might spring in other places from a retention of water on a clay soil, is here met by the plan that is universally followed, of building every house on arches of solid brickwork. So, where in other towns there are areas, and kitchens, and servants' offices, there are here subways through which the air flows, freely, and down the inclines of which all currents of water are carried away.

The acreage of our model city allows room for three wide main streets or boulevards, which run from east to west, and which are the main thoroughfares. Beneath each of these is a railway along which the heavy traffic of the city is carried on. The streets from north to south which cross the main thoroughfares at right angles, and the minor streets which run parallel, are all wide, and, owing to the lowness of the houses, are thoroughly ventilated, and in the day are filled with sunlight. They are planted on each side of the pathways with trees, and in many places with shrubs and evergreens. All the interspaces between the backs of houses are gardens. The churches, hospitals, theatres, banks, lecture-rooms, and other public buildings, as well as some private buildings such as warehouses and stables, stand alone, forming parts of streets, and occupying the position of several houses. They are surrounded with garden space, and add not only to the beauty but to the healthiness of the city. The large houses of the wealthy are situated in a similar manner.

The streets of the city are paved throughout with the same material. As yet wood pavement set in asphalte has been found the best. It is noiseless, cleanly, and durable. Tramways are nowhere permitted, the system of underground railways being found amply sufficient for all purposes. The side pavements, which are everywhere ten feet wide, are of white or light grey stone. They have a slight incline towards the streets, and the streets have an incline from their centres towards the margins of the pavements.

From the circumstance that the houses of our model city are based on subways, there is no difficulty whatever in cleansing the streets, no more difficulty than is experienced in Paris. That disgrace to our modern civilisation, the mud cart, is not known, and even the necessity for Mr. E. H. Bayley's roadway moveable tanks for mud sweepings,—so much wanted in London and other towns similarly built,—does not exist. The accumulation of mud and dirt in the streets is washed away every day through side openings into the subways, and is conveyed with the sewage, to a destination apart from the city. Thus the streets everywhere are dry and clean, free alike of holes and open drains. Gutter children are an impossibility in a place where there are no gutters for their innocent delectation. Instead of the gutter, the poorest child has the garden; for the foul sight and smell of unwholesome garbage, he has flowers and green sward.

It will be seen, from what has been already told, that in this our model city there are no underground cellars, kitchens, or other caves, which, worse than those ancient British caves that Nottingham still can show the antiquarian as the once fast-nesses of her savage children, are even now the loathsome residences of many millions of our domestic and industrial classes. There is not permitted to be one room underground.

120 William Booth   In Darkest England and the Way Out
(nd; 1890), 211–12

The Village should not be more than twelve miles from town; should be in a dry and healthy situation, and on a line of railway. It is not absolutely necessary that it should be near a station, seeing that the company would, for their own interests, immediately erect one.

The Cottages should be built of the best material and workmanship. This would be effected most satisfactorily by securing a contract for the labour only, the projectors of the Scheme purchasing the materials and supplying them direct from the manufacturers to the builders. The cottages would consist of three or four rooms, with a scullery, and out-building in the garden. The cottages should be built in terraces, each having a good garden attached.

Arrangements should be made for the erection of from one thousand to two thousand houses at the onset.

In the Village a Co-operative Goods Store should be established, supplying everything that was really necessary for the villagers at the most economic prices.

The sale of intoxicating drink should be strictly forbidden on the Estate, and, if possible, the landowner from whom the land is obtained should be tied off from allowing any licences to be held on any other portion of the adjoining land.

It is thought that the Railway Company, in consideration of the inconvenience and suffering they have inflicted on the poor, and in their own interests, might be induced to make the following advantageous arrangements:—

(1) The conveyance of each member actually living in the village to and from London at the rate of sixpence per week. Each pass should have on it the portait of the owner, and be fastened to some article of the dress, and be available only by Workmen's Trains running early and late and during certain hours of the day, when the trains are almost empty.

(2) The conveyance of goods and parcels should be at half the ordinary rates. . . .

Lastly, the rent of a four-roomed cottage must not exceed 3*s*. per week.

Suggestions for Further Reading

No single work has attempted to cover comprehensively the vast field of Victorian homes. However, an excellent introduction can be found, together with a good list of references, in Vanessa Parker's Historical Association pamphlet *The English House in the Nineteenth Century* (1970). There are numerous general accounts of Victorian homes and households, all of which treat working-class homes briefly if at all. Among the best are Robert Harling. *Home: A Victorian Vignette* (1938); Ralph Dutton. *The Victorian Home* (1954); Marion Lochhead. *The Victorian Household* (1964); and Elizabeth Burton. *The Early Victorians at Home, 1837–1861* (1972). Two good books of illustrations which include the Victorian period are R. Furneaux Jordan. *A Picture History of the English House* (1959) and M. W. Barley. *The House and Home* (1963).

Nobody interested in Victorian homes can ignore the voluminous and scholarly work of Nikolaus Pevsner. The monumental *The Buildings of England* series (46 volumes, Harmondsworth, 1951–74), which he has written or, less often, co-authored or edited, contains much material on the homes of all social classes. The fascinating *Pioneers of Modern Design from William Morris to Walter Gropius* (Harmondsworth, 1960, first published in 1936 as *Pioneers of the Modern Movement*) was itself a pioneering work, dealing with new trends in architecture and design between 1851 and 1914. Other relevant works by Pevsner include *High Victorian Design* (1951); "Architecture and Applied Arts" in Jean Cassou, Émile Langui and Nikolaus Pevsner. *The Sources of Modern Art* (1962; the Pevsner section reprinted 1968 as *The Sources of Modern Architecture and Design*); two volumes of reprinted pieces entitled *Studies in Art, Architecture and Design* (1968), containing an invaluable article on "Early Working Class Housing"; and *Some Architectural Writers of the Nineteenth Century* (Oxford, 1972).

Less important only than Pevsner as writers on Victorian architecture and design are Girouard, Gloag, Hitchcock and Summerson. Mark Girouard's principal work is *The Victorian Country House* (Oxford, 1971), a scholarly and absorbing study which is not only definitive on its subject but includes helpful sections dealing with architectural and technical change; its footnotes indicate many other sources for further reading. John Gloag has written prolifically and entertainingly on architecture and design; his most useful books on the present subject are *Victorian Comfort* (1961), *Victorian Taste* (1962) and *Mr. Loudon's England* (Newcastle upon Tyne, 1970). Henry-Russell Hitchcock's *Early Victorian Architecture* in Britain (2 vols, 1954) is a masterly and comprehensive study, dealing with the homes of all social classes among many other subjects. Hitchcock's *Architecture: Nineteenth and Twentieth Centuries* (Harmondsworth, 1958) is not exclusively devoted to Britain, but contains valuable material on it. John Summerson's collection of little gems includes *The Architectural Association, 1847–1947* (1947), *Heavenly Mansions* (1949), *Concerning Architecture* (ed, 1968), *Victorian Architecture* (New York, 1970), a lucid and fascinating chapter "London the Artifact" in H. J. Dyos and Michael Wolff (eds). *The Victorian City* (2 vols, 1973) and the well illustrated lecture *The London Building World of the Eighteen-Sixties* (1973).

Many other works on architectural style and design bear on Victorian homes, including a large number published in recent years. Some of the most authoritative and interesting are Kenneth Clark. *The Gothic Revival* (1928, new edition 1950); John Steegman. *Consort of Taste 1830–1870* (1950, new edition 1970 entitled *Victorian Taste*); John Betjeman. *First and Last*

Loves (1952); H. S. Goodhart-Rendel. *English Architecture since the Regency* (1953); T. S. R. Boase. *English Art 1800–1870* (Oxford, 1959); Peter Ferriday (ed). *Victorian Architecture* (1963); Robert Furneaux Jordan. *Victorian Architecture* (Harmondsworth, 1966); S. Tschudi Madsen. *Art Nouveau* (1967); Elizabeth Aslin. *The Aesthetic Movement* (1969); Robert Macleod. *Style and Society: Architectural Ideology in Britain, 1835–1914* (1971); two biographies of architects both published in 1971, the short but stimulating *Pugin* by Phoebe Stanton and the massive *William Butterfield* by Paul Thompson; the first part of Fiona MacCarthy's *All Things Bright and Beautiful: Design in Britain 1830 to Today* (1972); Stephen Muthesius. *The High Victorian Movement in Architecture, 1850–1870* (1972); and Robin Spencer. *The Aesthetic Movement* (1972). Attention should also be drawn to the series of books on Victorian architecture being planned by the Victorian Society under the general editorship of Nikolaus Pevsner; the first two titles are due late in 1974.

For the working interior of the homes of the better-off classes; heating, lighting, cooking (the last of which, regrettably, I have not been able to treat in this book); and sanitation see Siegfried Giedion. *Mechanisation Takes Command* (New York, 1948); Lawrence Wright's entertaining *Clean and Decent* (1960) and *Home Fires Burning* (1964); Alison Ravetz. "The Victorian Coal Kitchen and its Reformers", *Victorian Studies*, XI (1968); and Roy Palmer. *The Water Closet* (Newton Abbot, 1973). The fourth and fifth volumes of *A History of Technology* (Oxford, 1958), edited by Charles Singer, E. J. Holmyard, A. R. Hall and Trevor I. Williams, also contain useful material.

An important subject which has only recently begun to receive detailed attention is the growth of towns, urban planning and speculative building. London has been far and away the best served, and here the name of H. J. Dyos looms large. His *Victorian Suburb: A Study of the Growth of Camberwell* (Leicester 1961), is a pioneering and influential work; so too is a scholarly study "The Speculative Builders and Developers of Victorian London", *Victorian Studies*, XI (1968). See also his article written jointly with D. A. Reeder in Dyos and Wolff, op cit, "Slums and Suburbs". Reeder's other articles include: "The Politics of Urban Leaseholds in Late Victorian England", *International Review of Social History*, VI (1961) and "A Theatre of Suburbs: Some Patterns of Development in West London, 1801–1911", in H. J. Dyos (ed). *The Study of Urban History* (1968). Among the other useful articles in the same book Francis Jones's 'The Aesthetic of the Nineteenth-Century Industrial Town" stands out. F. M. L. Thompson has made a splendid contribution to understanding the growth of a London suburb in *Hampstead: Building a Borough, 1650–1964* (1974), and for the general growth of London, Francis Sheppard's *London 1808–1870: The Infernal Wen* (1971) should be read in conjunction with the later volumes of the *Survey of London* under his editorship. L. C. B. Seaman. *Life in Victorian London* (1973), is a much slighter book which, however, should not be ignored.

A writer in the same field is Donald Olsen, whose *Town Planning in London: The Eighteenth and Nineteenth Centuries* (New Haven, 1964) should be supplemented by his contribution to the Dyos-Wolff volumes, "House upon House: Estate Development in London and Sheffield". William Ashworth's article, "Types of Social and Economic Development in Suburban Essex", in Centre for Urban Studies (ed). *London, Aspects of Change* (1964), should be consulted as well as his stimulating *The Genesis of Modern British Town Planning* (1954). Though now 20 years old, this book remains the most comprehensive introduction to its subject, dealing not only with town planning but also with employers' villages and Garden Cities. Among recent works dealing with the Garden City movement and its background the most authoritative is Walter Creese. *The Search for Environment* (New Haven, 1966); see also Colin and Rose Bell. *City Fathers* (1969) and Gerald Burke. *Towns in the Making* (1971). As a postscript readers can profitably consult Nicholas Taylor's discussion of Victorian planning in his provocative and entertaining attack on modern planning, *The Village in the City* (1973).

A number of recent books have attempted the difficult task of dealing with the whole range of Victorian urban working-class homes. An extremely useful one is Stanley Chapman (ed). *The History of Working-class Housing* (Newton Abbot, 1971), which contains articles on London (A. S. Wohl), Glasgow (John Butt), Leeds (M. W. Beresford), Nottingham (Stanley Chapman), Liverpool (James Treble), Birmingham (Stanley Chapman and J. N. Bartlett), South-east Lancashire and the adjacent Pennines (W. J. Smith), and Ebbw Vale (F. J. Ball). Two outstanding studies by John Nelson Tarn, profusely illustrated, explain many aspects of the evolution of the working class home. These are *Working-class Housing in 19th-century Britain* (1971) and the more comprehensive *Five Per Cent Philanthropy: An Account of Housing in Urban Areas Between 1840 and 1914* (Cambridge, 1973). Tarn is strongest on architecture, philanthropy, local government and the law, and his geographical emphasis is on London. Enid Gauldie. *Cruel Habitations: a History of Working-class Housing 1780–1918* (1974) is the latest work in this field. It is the best introduction to its study; a detailed, wide-ranging work.

Three older, essential works are Ernest Dewsnup. *The Housing Problem in England* (Manchester, 1907), which is particularly strong on the history of Victorian housing legislation; John J. Clarke. *The Housing Problem* (1920); and Harry Barnes. *The Slum: Its Story and Solution* (1931). W. M. Frazer. *A History of English Public Health, 1834–1939* (1950) and Asa Briggs *Victorian Cities* (1963), while not devoted exclusively to housing contain much interesting and relevant material.

Working-class housing can best be studied in its local context. Here again London is particularly well documented. C. J. Stewart (ed). *The Housing Question in London, 1855–1900* (nd; 1901) is an important early work. The two modern writers who have contributed most to this subject are H. J. Dyos and Anthony S. Wohl. Among Dyos's articles are a masterly study, "The Slums of Victorian London", *Victorian Studies*, XI (1967), which has a comprehensive bibliography; "Urban Transformation: A Note on the Objects of Street Improvement in Regency and Early Victorian London", *International Review of Social History*, II (1957); "Workmen's Fares in South London, 1860–1914", *Journal of Transport History*, I (1953–4); and three more in the same *Journal* dealing with demolition and the railways: "Railways and Housing in Victorian London" (two parts), II (1955–6) and "Some Social Costs of Railway Building in London", III (1957–8). Wohl has made contributions to the Chapman and Dyos–Wolff volumes (respectively "The Housing of the Working Classes in London, 1815–1914" and "Unfit for Human Habitation"). In addition he has written "The Bitter Cry of Outcast London", *International Review of Social History*, XIII (1968), and has edited and introduced a reprint of Andrew Mearns' pamphlet *The Bitter Cry of Outcast London* and other papers (Leicester, 1970). See also R. V. Steffel. "The Evolution of a Slum Control Policy in the East End, 1889–1907", *East London Papers*, 13 (1970).

Other areas are covered in more or less detail by specialist local studies of various types. A controversy over Friedrich Engels' account of Manchester in *The Condition of the Working-class in England in 1844* (1845) has shed both heat and light on social conditions, whose ramifications spread far beyond Manchester itself. The protagonists are W. O. Henderson and W. H. Chaloner on the one hand, and E. J. Hobsbawm on the other, in editions of Engels' book published in 1958 (Oxford) and 1969. Hobsbawm reviewed the Henderson–Chaloner edition, which was a new translation, in "History and 'The Dark Satanic Mills' " (1958, reprinted in *Labouring Men*, 1964), and Henderson and Chaloner returned to the attack in "Friedrich Engels and the England of the 'Hungry Forties' ", in Institute of Economic Affairs (ed). *The Long Debate on Poverty* (1972). An interesting complementary contribution to the discussion can be found in Steven Marcus. "Reading the Illegible" in Dyos and Wolff, op cit.

Two of the best town histories containing material on working-class housing are Shena Simon. *A Century of City*

Government: Manchester, 1838–1938 (1938) and Conrad Gill and Asa Briggs. *History of Birmingham* (2 vols, 1952). For homes of all social classes, recent volumes of *The Victoria History of the Counties of England* should be consulted. The following are among local economic and social histories which deal with housing in varying detail: W. H. Chaloner. *The Social and Economic Development of Crewe, 1780–1923* (Manchester, 1950); Theodore Barker and J. R. Harris. *A Merseyside Town in the Industrial Revolution: St. Helens, 1750–1900* (Liverpool, 1954); John Prest. *The Industrial Revolution in Coventry* (1960); C. M. Allan, "The Genesis of British Urban Redevelopment with Special Reference to Glasgow", *Economic History Review*, 2nd series, XVIII (1965); Roy Church. *Economic and Social Change in a Midland Town: Victorian Nottingham, 1815–1900* (1966); M. W. Beresford. "Prosperity Street and Others" in M. W. Beresford and G. R. J. Jones (eds). *Leeds and its Region* (Leeds, 1967); J. N. Tarn. "Housing in Liverpool and Glasgow, The Growth of Civic Responsibility", *Town Planning Review*, 39 (1969); and Geoffrey Best's study of Scottish cities, "Another Part of the Island" in Dyos and Wolff, op cit. A labour historian's approach is seen in Sidney Pollard. *A History of Labour in Sheffield* (Liverpool, 1959), a sociologist's in Michael Anderson. *Family Structure in Nineteenth Century Lancashire* (Cambridge, 1971) and a geographer's in C. A. Forster. *Court Housing in Kingston upon Hull* (Hull, 1972).

The growth of building societies may be studied in Harold Bellman. *Bricks and Mortals* (nd; 1949), Seymour Price. *Building Societies, Their Origin and History* (1958), and E. J. Cleary. *The Building Society Movement* (1965). G. E. Fussell. *The English Rural Labourer* (1949) deals with Victorian homes among other topics, and two gems of late Victorian rural life are Flora Thompson's autobiographical *Lark Rise to Candleford* (1939, 1941, 1943; one volume ed, 1945) and M. K. Ashby. *Joseph Ashby of Tysoe, 1859–1919* (Cambridge, 1961).

David Owen. *English Philanthropy, 1660–1960* (Cambridge, Mass, 1964) deals lucidly with philanthropic housing agencies, the work of Octavia Hill and that of benevolent employers and their villages. J. N. Tarn has written a number of important articles on philanthropy, including "The Peabody Donation Fund: The Role of a Housing Society in the Nineteenth Century", *Victorian Studies*, X (1966) and "The Improved Industrial Dwellings Company", *Transactions of the London and Middlesex Archaeological Society*, XXII (1968). The sympathetic account of Octavia Hill's work given in A. F. Young and E. T. Ashton. *British Social Work in the Nineteenth Century* (1956) should be balanced by the hostile account in Gareth Stedman Jones. *Outcast London* (Oxford, 1971), which deals expertly and combatively with a number of other relevant subjects.

The above titles, while among the principal modern works, do not pretend to be an exhaustive list of the mass of available sources. Biographies and autobiographies of such diverse figures as Charles Booth, Edwin Chadwick, Octavia Hill, James Hole, William Morris, Seebohm Rowntree, Lord Salisbury, Lord Shaftesbury, Sir John Simon and Beatrice Webb should be consulted, together with the lives of leading Victorian architects and builders. For the economic background J. H. Clapham's classic *An Economic History of Modern Britain* (3 vols, Cambridge, 1926, 1932, 1938) remains the best starting point, together with S. G. Checkland's more recent and concise *The Rise of Industrial Society in England, 1815–1885* (1964) and specialist works like A. K. Cairncross. *Home and Foreign Investment, 1870–1913* (Cambridge, 1953), J. Parry Lewis. *Building Cycles and Britain's Growth* (1965) and Brinley Thomas. *Migration and Urban Development* (1972). Finally, a number of general social histories containing material on housing are recommended: Karl de Schweinitz. *England's Road to Social Security* (Philadelphia, 1943); Maurice Bruce. *The Coming of the Welfare State* (1961); Geoffrey Best. *Mid-Victorian Britain, 1851–1875* (1971); J. F. C. Harrison. *The Early Victorians, 1832–1851* (1971); and Derek Fraser. *The Evolution of the British Welfare State* (1973).

Acknowledgements

I am grateful to many people and institutions for the assistance which I have been given in compiling the material for this book. Above all I am indebted to the library of the University of Hull, its inter-library loan service and in particular its photography department, for the many hours of work which they cheerfully devoted to my needs. I am grateful also to the staffs of the other libraries where I have worked: the Local History and Reference Libraries of the Hull Public Libraries, the British Museum Reading Room and Newspaper Library and the Library of the Royal Institute of British Architects. I also acknowledge with gratitude the assistance given by A. R. Neate of the Greater London Record Office, Sir John Summerson, R. J. Watson of the United Reformed Church History Society, and the public libraries of Birmingham, Bradford, Bristol, Glasgow, Leeds and Newcastle upon Tyne, all of whom supplied essential material or answered queries.

John Saville, as with past enterprises, has given freely of time, advice and assistance, and the form and content of the book owe very much to him. I am also grateful to those people who have suggested useful sources: in particular Sheila Smith, and also Stephen Green, Tony Michell, Arthur Pollard and Patsy Stoneman.

The typing pool of the University of Hull and Mrs B. Brown and Mrs P. Wilkinson did a great deal of typing speedily and efficiently, which I acknowledge with gratitude.

The work involved in the book necessitated a good deal of travel, together with expenses for photography of the requisite documents. Money for this purpose was provided by the Trustees of the Nuffield Foundation through the Small Grants Scheme in the Social Sciences. Warm thanks are due to them.

Finally, the warmest thanks of all go to my wife Ann, who provided unstinting encouragement and support when they were most needed.

D. R.

INDEX